The China Mystique

# The China Mystique

*Pearl S. Buck, Anna May Wong, Mayling Soong,*
*and the Transformation of American Orientalism*

Karen J. Leong

UNIVERSITY OF CALIFORNIA PRESS
*Berkeley · Los Angeles · London*

University of California Press
Berkeley and Los Angeles, California

University of California Press, Ltd.
London, England

© 2005 by Karen J. Leong

Grateful acknowledgment is made for permission to republish in
chapter 3 material that appears in slightly different form as "The
Racialized Image of Anna May Wong," in *Major Problems in
Asian American History,* ed. Lon Kurashige and Alice Yang Mur-
ray (New York: Houghton Mifflin, 2003); and as "Anna May
Wong and the British Film Industry," *Quarterly Review of Film
and Video* 23, no. 1 (forthcoming). Archival material from the
Houghton Library of Harvard University, the Lilly Library of Indi-
ana University, the Princeton University Library, and the Wellesley
College Archives appears with permission of these institutions.

Library of Congress Cataloging-in-Publication Data

Leong, Karen J., 1968–.
    The China mystique : Pearl S. Buck, Anna May Wong, Mayling
Soong, and the transformation of American Orientalism / Karen J.
Leong.
        p.      cm.
    Includes bibliographical references and index.
    ISBN 0-520-24422-2 (cloth : alk. paper). —
ISBN 0-520-24423-0 (pbk. : alk. paper)
        1. United States—Relations—China.    2. China—Relations—
United States.    3. Buck, Pearl S. (Pearl Sydenstricker),
1892–1973.    4. Wong, Anna May, 1905–1961.    5. Chiang,
May-ling Soong, 1897–.    I. Title: Pearl S. Buck, Anna May Wong,
Mayling Soong, and the transformation of American Orientalism.
II. Title.

E183.8.C5L386    2005
305.48'8951073'0922—dc22                                    2004024699

Manufactured in the United States of America

13    12    11    10    09    08    07    06    05
10    9    8    7    6    5    4    3    2    1

Printed on Ecobook 50 containing a minimum 50% post-
consumer waste, processed chlorine free. The balance contains virgin pulp, including 25% Forest Stewardship Council Certified for
no old growth tree cutting, processed either TCF or ECF. The
sheet is acid-free and meets the minimum requirements of
ANSI/NISO Z39.48–1992 (R 1997) (Permanence of Paper).

*Dedicated with love*
*to my father, Raymond Leong,*
*and to my mother,*
*May Ying Fong Leong, 1938–1981*

# Contents

# Illustrations

# CHAPTER I

# Gendering American Orientalism

Throughout the history of the United States, images of China have pop-ulated the American imagination. Always in flux, these images can shift rapidly, as they did during the early decades of the twentieth century. During these years the United States experienced increasingly open de-bate regarding race relations and women's rights and confronted geopo-litical alignments and conflicts that contributed to the nation's gradual shift toward being an international power. Simultaneously, China de-veloped into a modern nation state and sought international legitimacy for its international role. As a result, beginning in the 1930s Americans began to imagine China differently, no longer as an alien and distant cul-ture and land, but as a demonstration of the promise held by American democracy and culture to transform other nations. At the height of World War II, this *China mystique*—a romanticized, progressive, and highly gendered image of China, the "new China"—would be cultivated by the governments of both nations and broadly held among the Amer-ican public.

While several scholars have observed a shift in American attitudes to-ward China during World War II, this study looks more closely at how American popular culture rationalized this shift by redefining China through the interlinking discourses of gender, race, and nation—dis-courses that have always informed orientalism within the United States. Within the specific context of the 1930s and 1940s, these discourses worked together to accommodate and define this different relationship between the United States and China. Thus the China mystique was an American ideology that incorporated notions of "modern women" and a more pluralistic U.S. national community in the production of a new China. The shifting values and meanings encompassed by the China mystique were articulated through the processes of diplomacy and international relations, individual and national identity formation, and productions of celebrity and popular culture. More than propaganda or public relations, the China mystique served the needs of an American public negotiating the United States' changing identity.

Three women embodied the China mystique for Americans during the 1930s and 1940s: Pearl S. Buck, Anna May Wong, and Mayling Soong. Being, respectively, the author of the best-selling novel *The Good Earth*, the only contemporary Chinese American actress to achieve international prominence, and the wife of the Chinese Nationalist leader Chiang Kai-shek, Buck, Wong, and Soong were by far the most prominent women associated with China during this time. As such, they substantially shaped and represented Americans' diverse imaginings of China and the Chinese from the 1920s through the 1940s. Even if their names or specific contributions were not made explicit, these women would become known, named authorities about what Americans perceived to be China: the China mystique.

Buck, Wong, and Soong shared a transnational relationship with both the United States and China; despite their different backgrounds, each woman's life was shaped by America's perceptions of China and the Chinese. Each woman encountered constraints and opportunities due to her gender and race but sought opportunities and ways to succeed both within and despite these constraints. At the same time, each took an active role in recasting earlier forms of orientalist representations of Asia and Asians in the United States and creating new ones as well.

Orientalism's incipient form derived from nineteenth-century European imperialist imaginings of Asia's cultures and peoples through the lens of European values, norms, and culture. *American orientalism* draws on orientalism more generally to affirm the political, social, and cultural superiority of the United States and European Americans relative to Asia and Asian Americans. One especially powerful discursive trope of orientalism is the exoticization and feminization of Asian nations and their cultures. As viewed through the lens of gendered and heteronormative relations of power, European *and* American orientalism justified power inequities resulting from colonization, territorialization, and imperialist destiny. Although American orientalism could be and was applied to any Asian culture generally, the United States' relations with China and Japan from the republican era through the 1940s shaped a particular form of American orientalism that in turn directly affected U.S. foreign policy toward Japan and China, immigration policy for Chinese and Japanese immigrants, legal decisions on the rights of Americans of Chinese and Japanese descent, and representations of "the Orient" in mass-produced, popular culture.

A particularly prominent expression of American orientalism was the American missionary enterprise. In the mid-nineteenth century, American evangelical Christianity inspired devout Protestants to become missionaries in the hopes of converting "heathen" souls. With its abundant population, China attracted a particularly large cohort of missionaries. Among these were Absalom and Carie Sydenstricker from the state of Virginia. After several years in China, in 1892 the couple and their son, Edgar, returned on furlough to Virginia, where Carie gave birth to a daughter named Pearl Comfort; the Sydenstrickers returned to China three months later. At the age of eighteen Buck came back to an unfamiliar homeland to attend college. After graduating, she returned to China and in 1917 married J. Lossing Buck. Buck would spend another fifteen years in China before moving to the United States to focus on her career as a writer.[1] The publication in 1931 of her novel *The Good Earth* established her public reputation as a China expert. From then on Buck would increasingly cultivate and enjoy a public persona as someone who understood the "real Chinese."

American missions to China were but one symptom of greater socioeconomic changes wrought by the demands of European and American nations on China to open its borders to a global market. Another was the migration of Chinese to the United States.[2] Anna May Wong was the daughter of self-identified Chinese Americans. Born in 1905 and raised in the heart of Los Angeles, Wong started her career as an extra in silent films while still attending high school. Her family was reportedly not thrilled with her decision to pursue acting, particularly given the exotic, sexualized roles available to her as a Chinese American woman. Although Wong had never seen her parents' homeland, she enjoyed limited success portraying highly orientalized roles such as the Mongol slave in Douglas Fairbanks' *Thief of Baghdad* and a part inspired by Madama Butterfly in the 1924 Technicolor production *Toll of the Sea*. These film appearances would eventually open the doors for greater roles, both in Europe and the United States. In the process Wong established her rep-

utation as a unique, Americanized Chinese personality on both sides of
the Atlantic. Wong shrewdly crafted a fluid image of herself as both
American and oriental, shifting this image repeatedly to increase her
public visibility and professional viability.

Yet another result of socioeconomic changes during the late nineteenth century was the rise of a nouveau-riche Chinese class that profited from conducting business with foreigners. Among these was Charles
Jones (Yao-ju) Soong, who prospered as a liaison between Chinese and
Americans. He and his wife, Kwei Tweng Nyi—both converted Christians—welcomed the birth of their fourth child and third daughter,
Mayling, in March 1897. Soong was born into the cosmopolitan culture
of Shanghai, a prominent treaty port opened to the European nations
and the United States. In the face of intensifying political uprisings in
China, the nine-year-old Soong accompanied her sisters to Georgia,
where she received private schooling while they attended Wesleyan College. She herself enrolled in Wellesley College nine years later. After graduating in 1917, Soong returned to Shanghai and reacquainted herself
with the Mandarin language and Chinese culture. Ten years later, she
married Chiang Kai-shek, a young general who in 1936 would become
the sole leader of the Chinese Nationalist (Kuomintang) Party. Over the
years she cultivated great popularity among Americans for her English-
language books and articles about the new China she came to symbolize
for many Americans.

In the chapters that follow, I devote a chapter to each woman's life.
Within each chapter I focus on how American perceptions of China and
the Chinese shaped their lives and on how each woman actively negotiated these perceptions. Their lives reflect and illuminate key sites of interaction and contestation between China and the United States, including the U.S. missionary enterprise to China; the politics of nationality
within China; and policies restricting Chinese immigration to the United
States. During the 1930s and 1940s, each woman enjoyed greater visibility within an increasingly global mass culture, with rising nationalism
throughout Asia, the emergence of the United States from the shadows
of imperialism to world power, and more assertive participation of
women in civic and consumer culture.

Each woman's transnational identification with both China and the
United States established her authority as a "China expert" for many in
the United States. This authority did not go uncontested by diplomats,
old China hands (businessmen and missionaries), government officials,
or even Chinese and Chinese Americans. Indeed, Soong and Buck often

questioned each other's legitimacy to "interpret China," and both dismissed Wong altogether.

By focusing on the roles that these women played in articulating the shift from American orientalism to the China mystique, I seek to analyze how gender shapes racial and national identity formations. Gender roles, for example, provided a key means to articulate the tension between idealism and imperialism exhibited by American ideology and China policy during the nineteenth century.[3] How did the China mystique mitigate similar tensions during wartime? Within each woman's individual story, I analyze the continuities between the China mystique and American orientalism as gendered discourses that employ feminized bodies of communication. Both discourses contributed to the articulation of a national ethos that defined Americans themselves, as well as their relations with other nations and cultures negotiating different effects of modernity. In addition to being gendered, the China mystique's transnational form of American orientalism influenced American nationalism during the 1930s and 1940s, when the relationship between the United States and China was dramatically, albeit temporarily, realigned.

Just as Buck, Wong, and Soong served as translators or bridges between cultures and nations, the China mystique also bridges the development of American orientalism and its newer, postwar forms to justify American empire as the United States increasingly involved itself throughout Asia and with the growth of the Asian American community. Granted, most studies about late twentieth-century American orientalism assume that orientalism is gendered and sexualized.[4] Yet few studies track the geopolitical and social changes that the United States encountered during the 1930s and 1940s, changes that resulted in the gendered embodiment of American orientalism I call the China mystique.[5]

In defining *orientalism,* Edward Said focused on Europeans' colonization of near Asian cultures and the aesthetic appropriation of "the East" as a manifestation of highly skewed power relations. Subsequent scholars have since demonstrated the ways in which orientalism was gendered and sexualized, and the articulation of multiple, simultaneous, and often contradictory orientalisms that are specific to individual nations.[6] In a critical survey of Hollywood's imperial films, Shohat and Stam extend this analysis to the ways in which the heteronormative gaze structures masculine/feminine, white/nonwhite relations onscreen as metaphors for national and racial hierarchies of power and inequity.[7] Still, studies on American orientalism are scarce. John Kuo-Twei Chen's fascinating work *New York Before Chinatown* identifies orientalist manifestations of American material and intellectual culture from the Nationalist period through nativism.[8] Mari Yoshihara sifts through the multiple ways in which Euro-American women produced and participated in material, literary, and aesthetic forms of American orientalism.[9]

What these studies have not explored, however, are the ways in which "orientalized subjects" engage orientalism. The dynamic inherent to orientalism sets a passive Asian object against an active European or American subject. With few exceptions, current scholarship perceives only Buck, a white American woman, as able to engage orientalist discourse and benefit from participating in a system that empowered Western women over Asian subjects.[10] Yet because they visibly engaged American orientalism, Wong and Soong also had limited power to shape the cultural discourse of U.S.-China relations.[11] Analyzing the distinct yet overlapping experiences of Buck, Wong, and Soong , I demonstrate the ways in which each woman embodied American orientalism and through her experiential knowledge communicated the China mystique.

The conclusion of this book compares the three women's social locations and explores the dynamic relationship between social location, personal identity, and institutional change. The collective experiences of Buck, Wong, and Soong during the thirties and forties show that popular culture and diplomatic relations both constitute significant sites for negotiating a national identity. Government as well as social and cultural institutions engaged the emerging China mystique and the long-standing tradition of American orientalism during the war. Simultaneously, the changing institutions of popular culture and government converged to allow for the articulation of the China mystique. Indeed, both governments of the United States and Nationalist China also emphasized the more benign aspects of American orientalism in their mutual wartime construction of the China mystique.

A note on my use of names in this book: as one of my insightful readers pointed out, authors often refer to women subjects (but not men) by their first names. In this study I refer to each woman by her full name or her last name as she was popularly known. Though this nomenclature is not chronological, I hope it is clear. Prominent Chinese women often kept their own surnames; hence I use Mayling Soong as a full name and refer to her as Soong or Madame Chiang (and refer to Soong's husband by his full name, Chiang Kai-shek, or as "the generalissimo"). Chinese personal names are in their original alphabetized form, with the pinyin in parentheses when I first discuss them in text below.

## AMERICAN ORIENTALISM

Orientalism in the United States had its roots in the attitudes and values of European immigrants who arrived in North America during the sixteenth and seventeenth centuries.[12] Europeans imagined civilizations to their east as more decadent, exotic, and immoral than their own. These attitudes were institutionalized into European empires during the eighteenth century and onward, as Britain, France, and other nations justified their global domination and quest for resources and labor as civilizing missions.

This orientalist discourse took root and thrived on the "virgin soil" of North America. The developing United States began incorporating distorted notions of "the Orient" and "Asiatics" within its social and political formations well before the arrival of Chinese immigrants in the nineteenth century.[13] During that century an orientalist aesthetic helped justify American nation-building beyond the borders of the United States, an ideology that crystallized in 1845 as Manifest Destiny. It claimed a divine mandate for the United States to dominate culturally, economically, and politically and captured the ambitions of many Euro-Americans. Manifest Destiny envisioned the conquest of the western frontier and from there projected its acquisitive gaze toward the Pacific Rim, imagining island civilizations and the Asian continent in need of moral direction and social progress. Building on European orientalism and its negative depictions of Asians, American orientalism took a form specific to and supportive of the United States' emerging role as a worldwide moral and economic force.

Orientalist perceptions were widespread throughout the United States, embedded in many levels of cultural expression and carried through a variety of channels.[14] Missionaries, diplomats, and business leaders, as well as the media, perpetuated this view of the Pacific Rim: if missionary and business interests marked the epitome of American accomplishment in both religious and economic matters, their Chinese, Japanese, and Pacific Island counterparts displayed a lack of religious and economic development and the need for conversion to Christianity and capitalism.[15]

As the United States expanded its sphere of influence into the Pacific Rim, motivated strongly by Manifest Destiny, American orientalism also expanded and shifted, reflecting the United States' increasing global influence as well as its increasing interactions with Asia and the Pacific

Rim. From the mid-nineteenth through the mid-twentieth century America enjoyed a time of industrialization, prosperity, and population growth. This Gilded Age ushered in the era of progressivism, as middle-class Euro-Americans sought to reform the American urban immigrant working class through temperance, education, and moral training. Not surprisingly, the era coincided with U.S. imperialism, as the nation expanded its influence over much of the western hemisphere. The historian Michael Hunt has suggested that U.S. foreign and domestic policy at the beginning of the twentieth century was based on "the process of nation building, . . . domestic social arrangements, . . . and ethnic and class division."[16] American orientalism likewise reflected American ideologies of gender, race, class, and nation. The convergence of American progressivism, Manifest Destiny, and prosperity thus depended in part on the existence of an American orientalism. Linking U.S. diplomacy to foreign policy, and U.S. domestic policy to popular culture, its pathological interpretation of Chinese people and culture justified uninvited American intervention to "protect" China and to convert it into something more Christian, modern, and American.

Manifest Destiny carried with it an explicit division of labor. The doctrine's rhetoric emphasized American masculinity and strength in the taming of the frontier. The cultural studies and literary scholar Amy Kaplan notes that an equally significant role was required of women—that of "manifest domesticity."[17] The feminization of China made it a site where Euro-American women could assert their individualism beyond the domestic sphere. Cultural imperialism relied on the feminine role of middle-class American women as the social housekeepers and civilizing forces. This manifest domesticity was nurtured as an impulse of progressive reformers among the urban centers and immigrant enclaves; it would find its full expression in missions abroad.

This intervention would come at a time when China was particularly vulnerable. At the turn of the nineteenth century, strong British demand for luxury goods like silks and teas from China resulted in a significant outflow of bullion from Great Britain to China. To balance this trade deficit, British merchants and shippers created a market selling opium to the Chinese. The resulting addiction, rise in crime, and decline in productivity led China's Qing government to threaten the end of the British opium trade. Great Britain protected its trade with military force, leading to the Opium War (1839–42) and the Anglo-Chinese War (1856–60), also known as the Second Opium War. With less advanced military technology and infrastructure, China lost both wars and paid heavily in territory, fines, and autonomy, forced to open its ports to foreigners and foreign influences.

As China's internal structure disintegrated, it was forced to accept the increasing presence of American businessmen and missionaries, and it signed the Open Door Treaty with the United States in 1860.[18] The Burlingame Treaty of 1868 facilitated free immigration between China and the United States, established trade agreements, and made possible the growth in American missions to China. This treaty allowed Chinese such as Anna May Wong's grandfather to immigrate to the United States, allowed Buck's parents to commence a mission in China, and allowed Mayling Soong's father to flourish as a businessman linking American and Chinese trade in Shanghai.[19]

In addition to foreign influence and a weakened government with spiraling taxes to pay the indemnities levied by the Western powers, subsequent popular uprisings and natural disasters encouraged some Chinese to emigrate. Recruited by labor agents and steamship companies, those who could afford to pay the fare went to the United States, where labor was needed to build the infrastructure of empire. Those who were less fortunate often entered into labor contracts with companies who would ship them to plantations in the tropical zones of Latin American or the Pacific Islands.[20] Those secure in their wealth and position or with no means at all remained in China.[21] This out-migration was primarily male. Thus Soong's father, Yao-ju Soong, followed the pattern of Chinese littoral migration along the southeastern coast of Asia, traveling first to Java and then to the United States. Similarly, Wong's father traveled with thousands of other Chinese males from southern China to northern California in the 1860s to prospect for gold.

Gendered and sexualized notions of China, already circulating in American culture through the press and theater, coincided with the specific conditions of Chinese males seeking employment abroad. Several circumstances, including family structure, economic conditions, and cultural expectations, resulted in most wives of Chinese laborers remaining in China. After the passage of the Page Law in 1875, U.S. immigration policy further contributed to an extreme gender imbalance among the Chinese immigrant community. The Page Law officially denied entry to any Chinese woman of immoral character and suspect virtue. In practice, it denied entry to virtually all Chinese women because they were *Chinese* (rather than because they were unfree or coolie labor). Those women traveling to the United States faced much stricter screening before they even left China and were again subject to questioning once they arrived

in the United States. The law succeeded beyond its stated intent in reducing the number of female Chinese immigrants, including those trying
to reunite with their spouses.[22]

The communities of Chinese working men who remained continued
to be perceived by Americans through the exoticizing and pathologizing
lens of orientalism, which incorporated the same fears and prejudices articulated in contemporaneous nativist movements against immigrants
from Ireland and eastern and southern Europe. Americans believed that
the existence of predominantly male communities suggested a moral inability to form and sustain families, a clear contrast with the heteronor-
mativity of American society.[23] Gender norms worked with perceived
racial distinctions to create a distinct category for all Chinese as inassimilable. The subsequent passage of the Chinese Exclusion Act in 1882
relied on racial arguments about the Chinese lack of character. Renewed
every ten years until its indefinite extension in 1904, this law denied Chinese laborers the right to enter the United States both because of their
purportedly unhealthy and immoral way of living and because of their
apparent threat to American labor. By the twentieth century, these restrictions related increasingly to nationality and to race, rather than to
class.

Ignoring its bias, the United States continued to see itself as a protec-
tor of China's interests against the imperialistic acquisitiveness of Britain,
France, Germany, and Russia after the Second Opium War. As the
United States entered into its own period of international growth during
the late nineteenth century, it stood in political opposition to European
empires and in cultural opposition to China and other Asian countries.
This positioning was important, because it allowed the United States to
claim a history of exceptionalism—an exception to the industrialized nations' legacies of imperialism and colonialism. This exceptionalism further affirmed what had been accepted as the nation's higher mandate—
its duty to civilize the North American continent and beyond, including
the Pacific Rim.

America's fondness for China was cultivated by the peculiarly "sentimental imperialist," the well-meaning missionary. Christianity often accompanied and sometimes justified American expansionism.[24] Missionaries to China extended America's "informal empire" to Asia, whether
they consciously intended to or not. American perceptions of China necessarily intersected with Americans' belief in their manifest destiny.
American missionaries prided themselves on protecting Chinese women
from the abuses of an archaic and patriarchal culture. By viewing itself

as a moral and political guardian of weaker countries like China, America could justify a "more humane" and in fact "necessary" form of global expansion.

The complementary discourses of American nationalism and orientalism, which together informed the mission of American evangelical Christianity at home and in China, both relied on characterizing women as moral or immoral. American women—who, according to American nationalism, constituted the moral center of the American nation—reflected the morality and character of the United States, whereas Chinese women, as seen through the lens of orientalism, were hypersexual and lacked maternal instinct, reflecting the lack of civilization and morality in China. Missions empowered women who participated in this evangelical enterprise: like other women missionaries, Buck and her mother could justify their activity beyond the home and into China as an extension of their feminine roles.

In return for relocating far beyond the borders of the United States and for the difficult work they did within the highly patriarchal missionary community, missionary women enjoyed a certain authority and status when they returned to the United States. Missionary women in China were often received as heroines in their home communities for braving a strange and exotic land, as well as for what they accomplished there.[25] Their reports in letters home and church presentations on furlough "created the images of China that were held by hundreds of thousands of Americans before World War II."[26] These images shaped Americans' expectations of Chinese American women in the United States and Chinese women in China. Anna May Wong and Mayling Soong found that American orientalism provided them justification to participate in public life, even as it limited the extent of their participation.

The effects of American orientalism established the foundations for further interactions between Americans and Chinese, with widely divergent consequences. The three women who are my subject were not the first to experience these border crossings or the complexities of ever-entangled international interests. Indeed, all three women were at least second-generation travelers between the United States and China. Yet the complex transnational relationships forged between China and the United States through immigration, missions, and diplomacy would fundamentally shape the context of each woman's identity and social location in relation to both nations. In turn, each of these women would help shape these transnational relationships.

# CHAPTER 2

# Pearl Sydenstricker Buck

In her life and in her career Buck epitomizes the dynamic history of American orientalism. Her perspectives about race, gender, nation, and power were formed on the mission field where, as a child and then a missionary, she witnessed dramatic changes in China over thirty years. Buck brought these perspectives with her when she relocated to the United States, where she gained prominence based on her intimate understanding of China and her fresh, critical perspectives on American society.

Buck's position as an authority on China allowed her to address American race relations in an international context. Her social critiques contributed to her growing prominence as a cultural mediator and political commentator during the 1930s and 1940s. Buck's ability to reorient Americans toward a more positive assessment of China without fully rejecting orientalism facilitated American's embrace of the China mystique; it also provided her with an opportunity to shape the international perspective with which Americans would increasingly view the United States and its emerging role in world affairs.

## LEGACIES

Pearl Sydenstricker Buck grew up in China. Nonetheless she was an American, owing to her parents' decision to return to the United States in order that their second child be born on American soil. This decision guaranteed Buck U.S. citizenship and allowed her to live in a country that was not her own, and to teach the Chinese about a religion that was not their own. Far inland from the hybrid treaty port cultures that nourished Soong, Buck experienced being an ethnic minority, a protected elite, and a despised Westerner during her China sojourn.

During her formative years, Buck knew China as reality and the United States as reflected in the memories and conversations of others. As a child, her family worked and socialized with other American missionaries. This community was united by their Christian faith and by the belief that Christianizing the Chinese was their divine appointment. As a young child within the Chinese community of American missionaries, Buck also absorbed the American missionary discourse of orientalism. Along with the message of salvation, American missionaries brought to China a belief in the cultural and racial superiority of American civilization, and an orientalist lens through which to view the Chinese. This lens gave missionaries of both genders a sense of power and accomplishment.

Buck's father, Absalom Sydenstricker, for example, felt strongly called to be a missionary in China; facing few prospects in the United States, he believed that in China, among the unsaved and uncivilized souls, he could accomplish something memorable and lasting. But if her father taught her to think of China as a new frontier, her mother provided her with an image of the United States. Carie Sydenstricker longed to go back to the States and reminded her children through her comments that the United States was home. Her mother's longing for "home" and her father's desire to nurture a human legacy in China indelibly shaped Buck's understanding of both countries. Her knowledge of China was gendered not only in witnessing her father's dominance and her mother's subordination within her home, but also through the work her mother and other women missionaries and she herself conducted among Chinese women (see figure 1, a family portrait).

Their American nationality guaranteed mother and daughter a status in China that they would not have enjoyed as farming or missionary women in the border state of Virginia. Within the United States gender intersected with race or ethnicity and socioeconomic status. At a time when working women were viewed with suspicion and resentment, missions represented one vocation for women that garnered respect and status. Women were encouraged to pursue it as an extension of their maternal and moral natures.[1] Christian women's associations and temperance unions in the United States likewise allowed white, middle-class, and Protestant women sanctioned access to the public sphere as social housekeepers. This access was facilitated by popular images of urban immigrant working women, including Chinese women immigrants targeted by the 1875 Page Law, as lacking proper womanly traits and values.[2] Similarly, American Protestant women—even lower-middle-class women like Buck and her mother—on missions to China achieved a higher status relative to the Chinese men and women to whom they proselytized by virtue of their nationality and religion.

Throughout her life Pearl Buck defined herself in relation to China: she left the United States as an infant and did not return until she was seventeen. Buck's letters from China to friends and family in the States contained stereotypically orientalist observations that compared Chinese culture unfavorably to American culture. But back home and faced with the realities of American life, Buck would frame China more positively through her childhood experiences. A look at Buck's diverse representations of China from her childhood memories through her married life reveals how the complementary ideologies of American orientalism, nationalism, and womanhood informed the missionary enterprise in China as well as her own identity.

## Childhood Memories

Because she left her homeland as a three-month-old infant, Buck came to take the American orientalism that explained her family's presence in China as a reference point for American society and culture. It defined the United States as an ideological and moral nation in opposition to China and Japan and thus justified the expansion and intervention of the United States into Asia. Similarly, the American missionary enterprise in China, described as an "ever more systematic attack on social as well as religious heresy" in China, perceived anything alien to American values as "heresy."[3]

Growing up among American missionaries who defined themselves and their homeland in opposition to the culture of the land in which they were stationed, Buck would often henceforth describe her experiences in China as the immediate world of reality. In a striking reversal of orientalism, the American life became "the dream world of the West."[4] Buck imagined the two countries in an oppositional binary relationship. And like other American missionaries, she experienced a dual nostalgia: she idealized the United States and romanticized her participation in China's spiritual and social development as benign.

Buck's memories of childhood reflect this neoimperialistic relationship of the United States and European powers with China. "I was a white child in a land of brown people, and they were all kind people, at least to me. I have no memory of ever seeing an angry brown face or of hearing a harsh Chinese voice directed toward me in my childhood." Although other children called her a "foreign white devil" when she visited the city, it was her Chinese amah (nurse) who defended her, comforted her, and scolded the Chinese children.[5] The security Buck enjoyed as a child revealed the Chinese awareness of their own vulnerability relative to any representative of Western nations. Buck's childhood in China, seemingly innocent, resulted from Western economic, social, and cultural dominance over China. Missionaries in China, no matter how much they might identify and sympathize with the Chinese people, "were a protected elite."[6] James Thomson writes that the new treaties of 1860, after the Second Opium War,

> bestowed on these foreign sojourners an automatic upper-class status, a cocoon of inviolability. Nor was it a status that could be shaken off even if one rejected it—as some, in much later decades of nationalist ferment, sought to do. For their peaceful invasion of the Chinese countryside had been won by force of arms. And their presence had behind it the flag of their nation and the threat of arms in the protection of their rights. Missionaries could renounce their consuls, but consuls—and eventually their gunboats—could not abandon the missionaries, for the prestige of the state was at stake.[7]

As a citizen of a dominant power, even as a child, Buck made every move under the auspices of the United States government. Chinese people and the government especially could not afford to forget that her treatment was a matter of international consequence, including further foreign intervention. The presence of white children, then, was not devoid of power dynamics, even though the children themselves might be unknowing participants in the enterprise of imperialism.

Euro-American families residing in the interior of China served as a constant reminder to the Chinese nationalists of the dominance of "the foreign white devil." Missionaries and their children became the objects of Chinese frustration and anger expressed against imperialist powers. Buck's "first great fear in China" occurred when, as a child, she experienced the Boxer uprisings against foreigners in 1900. The Boxers were a sect of Chinese who, with the encouragement of the empress dowager, attacked foreigners throughout China, especially missionaries. They identified Christianity with foreign attempts to change China to suit their own interests. Buck recalled,

White people there were being killed because some white people had done great wrong to the Chinese. . . . The missionaries, within their limitations, had done no harm, but they were killed and with them their little children who were entirely innocent. To me, then eight years old, it was a frightful revelation that children could be killed because of their parents, who in turn were killed because some entirely strange white people had been cruel and wicked. From that day on I felt less secure in my life. If such a thing could happen in China, where little children were much loved, it could happen anywhere.[8]

At the same time, Buck acknowledged that being a foreign child could in some contexts result in privileged access. She recalled being on equal terms with Chinese adults, even attributing to herself more moral responsibility (possessing the ability to know right from wrong) than they had. She noted that the Chinese behaved "in the freedom of their own ways" in front of a foreign child, but not in front of foreign adults. According to Buck, she *knew* of the worst of human behavior committed by the Chinese, "as a child I saw many things in Chinese homes and on the streets which I have never told anyone, and did not even tell my parents at the time. There were Chinese who behaved in the freedom of their own ways when no white person but a child was by[,] whom they knew very well and felt they could trust. I never have broken that trust and I never shall."[9]

By framing her experiences of China as childhood memories, Buck minimized the power of her whiteness and foreign nationality. Because she herself kept silent about some Chinese behavior, Buck presented herself as a true friend of the Chinese people. Yet Buck's privileged position relied on a coercive authority. Her selective memory suggests "imperial nostalgia," a term coined by the anthropologist Renato Rosaldo to describe films that portrayed the imperialist system of racial domination with a sense of loss and longing.[10] This representation allowed persons to "mourn the passing of what they themselves have transformed" and in so doing maintain a "pose of 'innocent' yearning."[11] Buck's missionary nostalgia is a variation on this theme.

When Buck left China in 1910 to attend college in the United States, her reference points and social position changed. As a white American, Buck easily reentered the United States to enroll at Randolph-Macon Woman's College in Lynchburg, Virginia. After that point, however, her status as an American brought her no special privileges. Moreover, at age eighteen Buck was a stranger to American culture, highly conscious of her lower socioeconomic status and her lack of literacy in American material culture among her classmates, the majority of them, like her, Euro-American. It is perhaps not surprising that after graduating from college, Buck returned to her mother and Grace, her younger sister, in China. One year after her mother's death in 1916, Buck wed a young missionary and agricultural specialist, J. Lossing Buck (see figure 2). They were assigned to rural northern China, where Buck began her life as a missionary's wife.

## Married Life and Manifest Domesticity

When Pearl and Lossing Buck arrived in northern China, Buck brought with her the expectation to be fulfilled as a wife and mother, the inherited orientalism of her parents, and optimism regarding what she and Lossing would accomplish in their work. The next two decades would force Buck to reassess all of her initial assumptions.

The moment Buck entered married life she also entered the field as a missionary in her own right. Buck fully embraced the American ideal of true womanhood, a Victorian-era construct of femininity in which the woman's role was to nurture her husband and children, and to accept his leadership over the family. In a glowing letter to her best friend and former college classmate, Emma Edmunds, she recommended marriage as "simply the *only* life for a woman . . . there is nothing like marriage and a home." Yet, as Buck had already witnessed in her mother's life, the missionary wife was involved in the mission field as much as the husband, without lessening her domestic responsibilities. In a letter to Edmunds, Buck soon acknowledged that her double day as "an assistant missionary" and wife was daunting. "I get oppressed, sometimes, with a realization of how awfully much there is to be done. I have *sole* charge of the evangelistic work for the women in a district of about two million people! . . . [Yet] I *can't* spend all my time on the work, because I owe it to Lossing to make his home cheerful and pleasant and be so myself."[12]

Indeed, the prospect of evangelism in a rural and isolated region was overwhelming. The number of Protestant missionaries in China, about 5,000 at this time despite a steady increase from the midnineteenth century, remained miniscule in relation to the number of Chinese souls yet to be saved.[13] Out of a general population of over 5,180,000, Chinese Christians in 1920 numbered only 320,000.[14] And the missionaries were widely separated from one another as well. In another letter to Edmunds, Buck mused, "Out here one's home means so much, especially in such a very isolated place as we live in—with only one other white family."[15]

A far greater rarity than the presence of other foreigners was Buck's status as a foreigner who could speak Chinese fluently. She continually negotiated her in-between status as a foreigner and as someone who had been raised in China. In a letter to her mother-in-law, Buck wrote, "We created a great sensation every where we went as I was the first foreign woman who had even been there."[16] Buck also was aware that her visible appearance and her ability to speak Chinese defied expectations. "The fact that I have lived all my life in China is always a bond of union, and they immediately say, 'Oh, you are not a real foreigner then'—which puts me in mind of a good lady in Virginia who once asked me in all earnestness whether or not my parents were full-blooded Chinese."[17] In a lighthearted manner, Buck reveals her liminal status of fitting neither in the United States nor in China.

Awareness of being "in-between" did not prevent Buck from asserting her moral and cultural superiority when she described her work to her church and family supporters. Viewing the Chinese through an orientalist lens, Buck deplored the "stupidity and barbarity" of the Chinese with whom she worked. She was especially critical of the women, because "practically all Chinese women are totally unaccustomed to using their minds for anything more difficult than gambling or their very simple housekeeping, and so a sermon is quite beyond their reach, often."[18] (Of course, most of these women had little interest in Christianity.)

Buck's focus on the treatment of Chinese women and the lack of femininity exhibited by Chinese women was a theme common to most foreign missionaries in China that pointed up fundamental cultural and moral differences.[19] Letters written by American missionaries to their supporters at "home" constituted key sources of information about lands and cultures unknown to them. The letters served as ethnographic reports (held to be authentic) about the practices of other peoples already defined as spiritually and morally inferior, and they perpetuated orientalist stereotypes. In letters to her family and friends—"Home-people," she called them—Buck affirmed their preconceived notions of China as barbaric and uncivilized when she described her work among Chinese women. For example, she reported her "plan . . . to start a mothers' club, or rather a course of lessons in the care and training of children," because Chinese mothers "are the worst possible. Any idea of inculcating any principles of good is quite unknown. . . . Even a merely animal maternal instinct is often lacking, for they throw away little unwanted girls."[20] Almost exactly one month later Buck lamented, "It is rather depressing to live among the

Chinese only. . . . They are so degraded and live so miserably that before one knows it one either gets unduly hardened and narrow or else
gets 'nerves.' "[21]

In addition to explaining the gospel, then, Buck actively taught the
tenets of American morality and womanhood. Buck formed a girls' club
with some schoolgirls, hoping to achieve "a definite and lasting hold" on
them and "to keep them from feeling the influence of heathen homes too
strongly." In letters home Buck provided examples of the ways in which
Christianity made a difference. "One of the greatest joys we have is to
see the Christian homes, and to see how there the parents welcome each
little one gladly, *whether son or daughter* and give them the best they
have of love and guidance and education. Anyone who has seen that
sight must see the worth-whileness of missions."[22] Her efforts to educate
young Chinese women paralleled efforts by middle-class Christian
women in the urban centers of the United States during this era, when
the desire to break old patterns of belief resulted in programs designed
to educate the children of immigrants and Americanize their parents.[23]
In fact, historians of American missions in China generally agree that the
largest and longest-lasting effect of the missionary efforts was through
education, particularly that of Chinese women. By 1925 Protestant missionaries had established over three hundred schools that taught over
twenty-six thousand students.[24] Missionaries set up schools for women
only and encouraged Chinese women to attend.[25] Descriptions about
how missionaries intervened in the maltreatment of Chinese women
made clear to Americans the need for missionaries to civilize and convert
China.

During this time Buck came to recognize the effects of patriarchy
within her family and within the church and missionary community. She
had witnessed her mother's continual catering to her father's wishes and
needs, and her mother's accession to the demands of the church and missionary community that she deny her desires and her own self as proof
of her faith and devotion to God. In 1936 well after her father's death,
she would write two semibiographical novels about her parents, *Fighting Angel* (1936) and *The Exile* (1936), which illustrated her perception
of how gender affected their opportunities and choices. Both novels suggest that her parents were exiles—one, the male head of the family, a vol-
untary exile, and the other, the wife and mother who maintained and
nurtured the vision of home, an involuntary exile. On these pages, Buck
described the moral rigidity of her father and the church, and the masculine superiority both exhibited. In *Fighting Angel,* a novel based on her

father's experiences in China, Buck described women's roles within the
church.

> They all knitted those women while their men gave reports and passed laws
> of the church and made prayers. Their strong hard fingers flew while they
> had to remain mute. Into these stitches went what curbed desires and stub-
> born wills and plans! They would have burst without that vent.[26]

Buck scathingly noted that "the inevitable result of this religious subjec-
tion of women was to breed in them an irrepressible independence and
desire for self-expression, born of their innate and unconscious sense of
injury and injustice. All subject women so suffer."[27]

Witnessing and experiencing the oppression of women within the missionary community raised fundamental questions in Buck's mind that
only increased over time. Her own faith was shaken in 1921 when she
gave birth to a child and was forced to have a complete hysterectomy. It
was shaken further later that year when she learned that the baby, Carol,
was mentally handicapped. Her personal doubts mirrored those she as-
cribes to her mother in *The Exile*, where she talks about finding poems
and clippings among her mother's belongings after her death. "They
were poems," she recalls, "about little dead children, about exiles far
from home, and over and over again about the God who must be taken
on faith because none has ever seen Him."[28] Over the next decade Buck's
faith in God and the church would be shaken even more by events in
China.

*Breaking with the Past*

Beginning in the 1920s, Buck faced challenges as a mother, a missionary,
a Christian, and a wife. As a result of these personal challenges, and reflecting the significant social changes in both Chinese and American society relating to women, the church and missions, and politics, Pearl
Buck would begin to reassess the relevance of missions to the lives of Chinese, and the role of missions within the American church.

By the 1920s the church no longer was as central to the lives of many
Americans. Social changes, including the growing culture of consumption, the increased prominence of the sciences, and the emergence of anthropology, also contributed to the decline of the church's social authority.[29] While church attendance declined, evangelism also declined.[30]
Donor fatigue on the part of Methodists and a doctrinal division among
the Presbyterians contributed to this malaise. The domestic disputes of

modernists, evangelicals, and conservatives—in which humanism and toleration were pitted against the traditional message of conversion, salvation, and redemption—additionally manifested themselves in mission work.[31]

Missions in China at this time primarily taught a social gospel that aimed to fulfill the material as well as spiritual needs of the Chinese—needs that included nutrition, hygiene and education. The social gospel emphasized social transformation, unlike evangelism, which emphasized individual conversion.[32] The Bucks' work in China reflected this shift. After a sabbatical in the United States to attend Cornell University, from where Buck and her husband earned master's degrees in English literature and agricultural science respectively in 1926, they returned to Nanking University where both taught students and Lossing conducted research.

Americans' increasing toleration of cultural differences further eroded the belief of home congregations and missionaries in the purpose of missions.[33] Influenced by anthropology and sociology, liberal theology accepted cultural differences and taught the ethics of living rather than the necessity of salvation. Although abstract ideas of salvation and love did not seem adequate to meet the needs of the mission field, mission boards still maintained that the primary purpose of missions was evangelism. Encountering overwhelming poverty and suffering in China challenged Buck's belief that Christianity addressed the immediate needs of the Chinese. The uprisings of Chinese against foreigners in China in May 1927 further challenged her faith in the American missionary enterprise.

During what is known as the Nanjing (Nanking) Incident of 1927, Chinese soldiers, students, and others began rioting against the foreign soldiers who occupied the city. The violence soon turned on foreigners, including missionaries. Pearl and Lossing Buck, her father, sister, brother-in-law, and their infant relied on their Chinese friends to hide them from the rioters. In a letter to Lossing's parents Buck referred to the experience. "Sometime . . . I am going to tell you *all* about those terrible days in Nanking. . . . We thought the end was very near for us all. My great anxiety was but the children should not be killed first, so that I might know they were safe, at least, out of the hands of people who would torture them."[34] Simultaneously, Buck was humbled by the fact that Chinese had saved their lives, "Personally we feel bound to China and the Chinese now as never before because we have seen of what splendid stuff our Chinese friends are made."[35] The family left for Japan but came back the next year; while her husband returned to Nanjing University, Buck and her children resided in Shanghai. Continued political unrest in China only heightened Buck's concerns that they again might be driven out or subject to violence.

The Chinese nationalism expressed in the 1927 violence against Nanjing missionaries forced Buck to recognize her differences from the people she was supposed to be serving. According to her sister's account, during this time Buck felt "more alien than ever before. Suddenly, she was more than ever conscious of America and being American."[36] Witnessing the hatred of some Chinese toward her and other foreigners also appears to have awakened in her a desire to return to her "homeland." She wrote to her closest friend, "My own advice to you, Emma, is to settle down in America for good." She went on to say,

> China is going to be unsafe for years to come—certainly until new treaties are made. The old fear of the foreigner has gone completely since no punitive measures have been taken for what has happened. . . . I would not live anywhere except in Shanghai now with children, and Shanghai is only fairly safe because of the foreign soldiers.[37]

Tellingly, Buck acknowledged how dependent she and other missionaries were on diplomatic treaties and gunboat diplomacy in China. She reported that corruption was widespread among *all* the Nationalist leaders, including Chiang Kai-shek. The consistent note she sounded in the year following the Nanjing Incident was one of moral reform. Of the disillusionment of "good and thinking Chinese," Buck opined, "this despair is a hopeful sign—it may force them . . . to realize that what they lack is moral bottom, and education and nothing else except moral soundness can solve their troubles. Chinese have never been willing to face their real faults."[38] Anxious for her family's safety and uncertain about the future, Buck spoke and wrote like the foreigner she was. In these letters, Buck admitted her outsider status in China. She acknowledged that any privilege and protection afforded her and other missionaries in China resulted from Western force and her American citizenship. Just as her vision of the United States evolved in relation to her growing dissatisfaction in China, however, Buck's opinions of China would again shift as she reassessed the American enterprise in China.

In the aftermath of the uprisings, Buck and other missionaries learned that the church would put missionaries' lives at risk in order to maintain a positive image for church members in the United States. According to the historian Shirley Stone Garrett, the self-interest of American Protestant churches forced missionaries to remain in China even in the face of obvious danger. "[B]y the late 1920s, sending the missionaries back [to China] was at least as necessary to the health of the churches in the United States as it was to the destinies of the churches in China." If the missionaries fled China, this would cast further doubts on evangelical Christianity.[39] The Methodist Mission Board repressed accounts written by missionaries about Nanjing and other riots, fearing that negative reports or criticisms of China's chaotic political situation would diminish its congregations' support for efforts to convert the Chinese. The Presbyterians, with whom the Bucks were affiliated, went even further. The board refused funds for its missionaries to return from China, fearing negative effects that might result for the Presbyterian Church from the stories missionaries would then relay of their experiences.[40] Buck felt herself doubly powerless, her desire to return to the United States dismissed by both the Presbyterian Mission Board and her husband, who wanted to remain in China to complete his research.

Facing a situation similar to that of her mother who suppressed her individual needs for that of her husband and the church, Buck began to focus on her own interests. She had been writing fiction and essays from an early age and continued to do so as an adult while stationed in China. Although she reportedly lost her first manuscript during the Nanjing uprisings, she wrote two manuscripts, "Winds of Heaven" and "Wang Lung," over the next three years.

ORIENTALIZING THE AMERICAN DREAM:
THE CREATION OF PEARL S. BUCK

During the thirties Pearl Buck's life would dramatically change with the success of her career as a writer. This change was shaped in part by expressions of Chinese and American nationalism at the turn of the decade. The success of her first novels set in China further perpetuated her image as an authority on China, and Buck increasingly cultivated her persona as someone who was more Chinese than American. Her ability to engage in such cultural passing is but one example of the ways in which Buck negotiated and appropriated American orientalism in the development of her public identity.

*An "Authentic" Chinese Voice*

Pearl Buck's first novel was published by the John Day Company in 1930, setting into motion a dramatic makeover of Buck's identity that would result in her returning permanently to the United States four years later. Published under the title *East Wind, West Wind,* Buck's first manuscript, "Winds of Heaven," required the editing out of American colloquialisms in order to preserve the "authentic" Chinese sensibility. Editorial comments observed that the first half was written in a manner "that is remarkably fresh and redolent of China" but that the author "seems to have tired somewhat and to have fallen into the use of Americanisms and trite phrase, which destroy the atmosphere."[41] Just as editorial changes could delete Americanisms, so could Buck refashion her own history for her American audiences.

Angling for customers in typical American fashion, the publishing industry during the 1920s relied on modern trends in advertising that appealed en masse to Americans' heightened fascination with "newness." Advertising raised Americans' awareness of needs for the latest items and supported the planned obsolescence that increased demand to absorb what the American industry was producing at unprecedented rates. As with any product, Richard J. Walsh, the editor and owner of the John Day Company, sought to publicize Pearl S. Buck as a new literary discovery to American readers. The success of Walsh's marketing strategy and the subsequent popularity of Buck's second novel, renamed *The Good Earth,* would reintroduce Buck to the United States.

Communicating with John Day from China, Buck represented herself as a modest individual who was more Chinese than American. When Walsh initially requested photographs and biographical information in order to publicize her books, she sought to distinguish herself as quite ordinary. She wrote, "I seem to have lived a very uneventful life in the midst of events, for certainly no one could say China was uneventful in these years of my life. Perhaps my difficulty in finding anything exciting in my life—for I am told Americans like things that are out of the ordinary—is that my interest has always centered on the normal life of human beings and not on the extra-ordinary circumstances of wars and great change and catastrophes." Even in noting the unique context for her ordinary life, Buck tried to dispel the events' import: "they have simply been the background of my life as they have been that also [for] the average Chinese."[42] In suggesting that she lived an ordinary *Chinese* life, Buck disingenuously highlighted how she indeed differed from most Americans.

Buck thus incorporated the mysteriousness Americans associated with China into her persona as an author distant from American modern culture. She refused to provide information to John Day about her personal life, "taking the lofty (and allegedly 'Chinese') position that the work was more important than the author." She relied on the imagined cultural distance between China and the United States to present herself as unfamiliar with American culture, even though she had been at Cornell University five years earlier. When notified that her second book had been chosen for Book-of-the-Month status, Buck wrote in reply, "Of course it is very good news that the book-of-the-month club likes my book. I do not know exactly what it means, since I do not belong to this club." She added that she had looked up an advertisement in the *Atlantic Monthly* and saw "a very imposing list of names there of well-known authors, and so I appreciate the fact that it must mean something for them to like my book well enough to put it on their list."[43] In relaying the news to her friend the very next day, however, Buck assessed its value. "I have just had a cable from my publishers that my new book, *The Good Earth*, is chosen by the book-of-the-month club for March which is good news of course. I am making a real beginning on my fund for Carol."[44] Buck may have been practicing feminine modesty in her reply to Walsh. Regardless, she found American orientalist assumptions about China being the opposite of the United States, distant and out of touch with the modern world and inscrutable, useful in constructing a marketable literary identity.

Pearl Buck's complex performance of writing about China as a Euro-American reveals her distaste for conspicuous orientalism. She adamantly differentiated her own portrayal of China and Chinese from popular American images of China as a larger version of Chinatown peopled with exotic and strange characters, such as those enacted by Anna May Wong in Hollywood films. In presenting herself as an inhabitant of rural China who knew very little about America, Buck made her portrayal of China seem more valid. Even after the American success of her novels, Buck sought the affirmation of Chinese readers in order to assure herself of the accuracy of her portrayal. And she again wrote to Walsh about the positive reviews she had received. "I have been so extremely pleased by the uniformly fine reviews that Chinese papers have given to *The Good Earth* that I am giving below two quotations that are typical. . . . I send these because doubtless many Americans are asking and wondering how true the books are to life here and what the Chinese themselves think of them." She added, "Since very naturally I consider the Chinese as my most important and indeed my final critics, you will understand my satisfaction in such reviews."[45]

John Day's publicity for this second novel in 1931 fixed on the author's own experience in China to emphasize the novel's realistic image of that country.[46] In a four-page pamphlet under the subtitle "Some facts about the author," it described Buck as someone who had lived most of her life in China, and who "from childhood wore Chinese dress at times and lives in the Chinese fashion."[47] These details, meant to emphasize Buck's authenticity, further demonstrate how the appropriation of cultural knowledge in modern American society could equal consumption of the other in fashion and style.[48] Just as an actor is identified from film to film with certain character types in the film industry, Buck's image similarly became synonymous with the books she authored.[49] Buck's firsthand knowledge of China promised American readers a glimpse into "real" China.

While she earned acclaim for introducing Americans to "real" China and the Chinese, Buck sustained public attention by engaging American orientalism in unexpected ways. In this second and most famous novel she would explore the traditional theme of man's individual struggle with the land, natural forces, and change, but from the uncommon perspective of a Chinese farmer.

## The Good Earth *and American Society*

The novelty of an American woman author emerging from northern China increased Buck's cultural currency in an American society that desired vicarious experience. Until the mid-1920s, missionaries had been heroic and revered models in their Christian communities. Pearl Buck and her publisher parlayed her missionary heritage of growing up in China into a unique and privileged status that resonated in the secular marketplace of American culture.[50] Buck's humble background as a missionary living the simple life in rural China highlighted even more dramatically her discovery by the publisher, as well as her rapid ascent to best-selling status with her second novel in modern America. *The Good Earth* brought readers not only an "authentic" China, but also a new and unlikely "American success story."

In 1931 *The Good Earth* drew China into the orbit of American attention and preoccupation with tradition and myth as the United States was recovering from economic collapse.[51] In plain, unadorned language, the novel tells the story of Wang Lung, an ambitious and proud Chinese farmer. It chronicles Wang Lung's continual adjustment to changes in his socioeconomic status, his family, and the expectations of his educated sons. He does not love his homely first wife, O-lan, who works equally hard beside him on the land, helping amass a fortune with which he eventually purchases a second, more beautiful wife. Wang realizes only after O-lan dies what the readers knew all along—that *she* was his good fortune. At the end of the novel, Wang's prosperity has distanced him from his land and his sons, who now have more modern ambitions in the city and away from the land.

The authority of Buck's experience and her effective use of realism dramatically contributed to the transformation of American orientalism into more positive yet still distorted perceptions of China and the Chinese. Buck received particular praise for her straightforward account of O-lan giving birth. This scene, written in detached prose that echoed contemporary anthropological accounts of "primitive" societies, had a realism rendered more acceptable to American readers by its focus on a foreign body in a foreign location. She thus perpetuated to a degree the conceit that Americans could possess intimate knowledge about China and the Chinese. When the Book-of-the-Month Club panel of literary experts chose *The Good Earth* as a featured selection (and ensured its bestseller status), one of the judges, Dorothy Canfield Fisher, observed that, "Most Oriental novels, you know, are for Americans really only curiosities, travelbooks of the mind, so to speak." Buck's novel, however, "makes us belong to the Chinese family as if they were cousins and neighbors."[52] Although China was still "half a world" away, Chinese were now likened to neighbors, their struggle to live off the land parallel to the struggle of the American heartland. Buck presented her protagonists in a style of realism that, for a novel set in China, starkly contrasted with the foreign and orientalized images of China and Chinese that populated American culture.

Buck hoped that the film version of *The Good Earth* might feature realistic portrayals of Chinese and inform American perceptions of China. Thus when Metro-Goldwyn-Mayer purchased the film rights to *The Good Earth* and began preproduction in 1932, Buck sought to ensure that the film would be an accurate portrayal of her China and urged the studio to employ an all-Chinese cast. In 1934 she sent to MGM executives a list of suggestions about filming her novel. MGM had been investigating the possibility of filming the movie in China, and Buck listed specific locations for certain scenes and suggested names of Chinese actors for different roles.[53] She did not suggest any American actors like Anna May Wong, whom she considered—somewhat disdainfully—more American than Chinese. The prospect of an all-Chinese cast on location in China had certain drawbacks for MGM: the Chinese Nationalist government seemed too eager to dictate the course of the film's production and storyline, and employing an all-Chinese cast would require MGM to negotiate the restrictions of the Chinese exclusion laws.[54] Whether MGM concluded that Chinese actors would not appeal to American audiences, or that the cost and trouble of casting and relocating a Chinese cast to the United States would be prohibitive, filming was delayed for the next two years and two director changes. By the time a third director, Sidney Franklin, started production on the film in 1935, Metro-Goldwyn-Mayer chose to cast European American actors in the lead roles, with Paul Muni as Wang Lung, Luise Rainer as O-lan, and the Chinese American Keye Luke as Elder Son.[55]

MGM's screen version of *The Good Earth* opened in 1937 to positive reviews and tremendous box office. *Film Daily* proclaimed, "The dominant quality of the visualized 'Good Earth' is its honesty. . . . It is China seen through Chinese eyes this 'Good Earth.' Or such, at least, is the half-mesmeric conviction one can carry away from the screening."[56] The film's focus on the everyday lives of Chinese peasants indeed represented a breakthrough in American representations of Chinese, and in greater opportunities for a new generation of Chinese American actors. For Pearl Buck, however, the epic film was disappointingly far from what she had envisioned as a realistic, human portrayal of a Chinese farmer and his wife. She and others believed that hers was a more honest portrayal of China because it drew on what she had seen and known.

Yet even though Buck had lived in China for nearly thirty years, her experience and knowledge of China had been informed by American orientalism and limited by the boundaries of her nationality, gender, and race. Thus both her and MGM's characterizations of O-lan as the long-suffering Chinese wife and mother—described in the book as in the souvenir program: like an animal, simple, and seeking only the approval of her husband—simply confirmed for American audiences their perceptions of the poor treatment and submissiveness of Chinese females, the amorality and untrustworthiness of the males, and the agrarian timelessness of Chinese culture.[57] Buck's portrayal of O-lan, and Rainer's passive and emotionless portrayal of her in the 1937 film, would have a lasting effect on Americans' perception of Chinese society and culture. Indeed, Buck's "honest" portrayal of the Chinese would contribute to reconfiguring an orientalist aesthetic, putting aside ancient and mysterious China in favor of a narrative about a changing China that reflected contemporary tensions in American society. In the numerous essays and speeches she wrote in the thirties, Buck referenced popular orientalist images of China as ancient, primitive, and slow, to contextualize her observations of the rapid pace of modern American society. Her exploration of modernity resonated with other Americans also coming to terms with the shifting dynamics of social communication and interaction.

## A Mirror of Modernity

The timing of *The Good Earth* provided another layer of interpretation to the novel about a Chinese farmer and his wife. Buck's success occurred during the Great Depression, when Americans confronted great technological advance and social and economic insecurity. Their confidence dramatically shaken, they turned with renewed appreciation to common sense and a shared heritage of national myths.[58] Buck's subject matter thus paralleled a prominent concept in depression America, that of returning to the land. Central to the concept of American nationhood were the role of the frontier and the heritage of those who worked the land. American farmers and their relation to the heartland were celebrated in the Farm Security Administration photographs of Dorothea Lange and James Agee's *Let Us Now Praise Famous Men,* and in films such as King Vidor's *Our Daily Bread* (1934) and John Steinbeck's *The Grapes of Wrath* (1940). All of these consciously portrayed the "realistic" relation between Americans and the land.[59] Moviegoers and readers related to the Chinese family confronting challenges and struggles and thus contributed to *The Good Earth*'s best-selling status.

Buck's portrayal of Chinese toiling on the farm, or of American missionaries forging new spiritual territory in China's hinterland, also fit into the genre of the frontier novel, a popular form of women's fiction from the turn of the century that was popular again in the twenties and thirties. Likewise, Patricia Raub classifies O-lan as a "sacrificial wife" similar to the twenties and thirties literary characterizations of a "good wife" who achieves success for her husband and family at great cost to herself.[60] A number of best-sellers in the thirties featured women protagonists in rural locations. For example, Gladys Hasty Carrol's *As the Earth Turns,* set in rural Maine, placed second on the 1933 best-seller list and was a Book-of-the-Month Club selection; and Laura Ingalls Wilder's *Little House in the Big Woods,* published in 1932, was a nostalgic, fictionalized memoir of a simpler, though difficult, life. In the context of the modernization wrought by technology, increasingly complex relations, and a population shift toward urban areas, these novels represented a reaction against social change.[61] Buck's *The Exile* (1936) clearly reflected this experience, with a lone American woman confronting the rough and imposing frontier of China, as well as the uncertainty of changing gender roles.

Whereas imaginings of an ornate and exotic China earlier had affirmed Americans' perception of the United States as moral and progressive civilization, this new image of China was nourished by Americans' need to reflect on the shift from agrarian to urban life in their own society. This expression, moreover, was not limited to literature. The choreographer and dancer Martha Graham, widely known for her modernist, abstract forms of dance, also returned to images of America's past. Her 1935 piece, entitled *Frontier,* depicted Graham's "all-encompassing view of the Midwest. . . . *Frontier* was pure Americana: forthright, free—the very spirit of an indomitable westward-moving people."[62] The program notes tellingly describe the piece as "a tribute to the vision, and independence of the pioneer woman. It portrays her strength, and tenderness, her determination and jubilation at overcoming the hazards of the land."[63]

## An American Pioneer

The best-selling success of *The Good Earth* introduced Buck on two separate occasions in 1931 and 1932 to the American media and a whirlwind of publicity regarding her "American success story." American society and culture for Buck represented a new frontier in which to make her mark. In a brief publicity tour of New York, Buck made it her mission to address the racial prejudice and discrimination directed at African Americans. Focusing on China enabled Buck to address issues of racial discrimination and national displacement away from the immediate tensions within the United States. For, she claimed, Chinese did not exhibit racial prejudice.

The issue of racial inequality had deeply affected her during her 1931 book tour to publicize *The Good Earth.* During the tour she accepted an invitation to speak with a group of African American women in New York. With these women, Buck discussed her own experience of being different and treated as alien in China. Sharing her difficulties as a white minority in China, she believed, forged a connection between herself and her audience. This first experience in Harlem provided Buck with a new mission on her return to America, one she would pursue with characteristic zeal and energy. "I made up my mind," she stated, "that if I ever returned to America to live, I would make these people my first concern.'"[64]

By 1932 Buck's concern over racial inequality and her willingness to speak out were growing. Elmer Carter, the chairman of the National Urban League invited Buck to address a small group of African American women in Harlem, at "the Opportunity Tea." Her decision to speak was at the urging of her publisher, Richard J. Walsh, who noted "there are not enough people who give practical encouragement to the aspirations of the Negroes."[65] During her talk, Buck incorporated the multiple influences of ancestral tradition, impressions of American arrogance in China, and the knowledge of what it was like to be despised because of her whiteness, into an espousal of liberal politics and racial equality. Living among another race, Buck noted, "has given me invaluable training in detachment, so that I am able to look at white people as though I were not one of them. Indeed, there have been times when I wished I were not one of them." Yet China also provided "that strange and terrible experience of facing death because of my color." She argued that race pride, or consciousness, was "a deadly and poisonous emotion, the foe to humanity." Buck, however, was strictly a moderate liberal. She strongly opposed revolution of any kind, believing it to be unjustifiable. Intelligent people had to fight this war not with arms, but with "the weapons of solid achievement, which *prove* your reality to all races and your special superiorities, those special gifts which each race has to bring to others." Adding "I would not dare to be so presumptuous as to give my counsel if I had not experienced in my own way some of those wrongs," Buck concluded by asking forgiveness on behalf of "my race."[66] Already Buck was establishing a reputation for her willingness to confront racial tensions and to take on unspoken subjects in American society. I expand on both issues below.

### "Is There a Case for Foreign Missions?"

In addition to race relations, Buck chose to voice her ambivalence about the American church's missionary work in China and distorted perceptions of China when she was invited to address a conference about missions to China in 1932, at the height of her celebrity. She seized this public opportunity to pose the question, "Is there a case for foreign missions?" to the missions board and evangelical Christianity in general. In her speech Buck rejected the Protestant formulation of America's "special responsibility" to China. China, she stated throughout her speech, did not *need* American help but rather *desired* the best of what Americans could offer. She described the cultural arrogance and insensitivity

of the American missionary, characterizing him as "being too often a little man" who, lacking support, clung to rigid doctrine and moral standards. "It is not to be wondered at that he clings jealously to his little idea
of God, fearing lest he lose it, fearing to see if it be true knowledge or
not."[67] The choice of gender was deliberate. Instead of the patriarchal
and ethnocentric bias of evangelical Protestant Christianity and missions, Buck championed empathy and interaction (stereotypically feminine forms of communication). She concluded that foreign missions
could be justified so long as missionaries interacted with Chinese and
learned Chinese culture, rather than demanding that Chinese become
more American.

Buck's questioning of Christian missions, missionaries, and theology
did not please the Presbyterian Missions Board.[68] The board demanded
that she revise her statements, particularly her implication that profession of faith in Jesus Christ was not necessary for conversion. No longer
dependent on the missions board for financial support or vocation, Buck
responded in the confidence of her newfound career and identity. "I cannot honestly modify what I have said or written, nor can I agree to bind
myself as to what I shall or shall not say or write in the future. I believe
I have the right to this freedom."[69] In 1933 Buck successfully requested
to be relieved of her commission.[70] Soon thereafter she asked her husband for a divorce, relocated to the United States, and married her publisher, Richard J. Walsh.[71]

The unusual context for her permanent removal from China pro-
foundly influenced Buck's self-representation and her perspective about
the United States and China. Her story was the material of American
dreams: a modest Christian missionary in China writes a national best-
seller and travels from obscurity in rural China to fame in urban New
York. Not having experienced the Depression herself, Buck had every
reason to feel more optimistic about her future in the United States, particularly after her harrowing experiences in revolution-torn China.[72]
Thus emboldened, Buck published prodigiously during the late thirties
and forties, and the accompanying publicity issued by the John Day
Company about her life experience in China perpetuated her image as an
authority on China (see figure 3, a publicity photo). Her many publications in magazines and the publicity she garnered through MGM's film
versions of *The Good Earth* (1937) and *Dragon Seed* (1944) enhanced
Buck's status as a celebrity—an unknown and outsider who became a
success.

*A Missionary in Reverse: Pearl Buck and the American Gospel*

Pearl Buck's views of the Chinese people, and the ways in which she positioned herself in relation to China and the Chinese, were complicated. Buck understood and even criticized the inequalities of power between the United States and China. She was less aware of how she benefited from being an American and how her speaking for Chinese might even perpetuate that inequality. Buck's sincere intentions, and the absence of challengers to her proclaimed knowledge of China and the Chinese, may explain why she felt comfortable speaking for Chinese and China on returning to the States.

A missionary at heart, Buck made it her mandate to demystify the Chinese and humanize them in terms accessible to average Americans. Sometimes she succeeded admirably: "The Chinese are not 'poor.' They are a strong, brave, superior people. . . . I want my children to grow up thinking of Chinese as their equals, not as people fit only for China."[73] More often than not, she romanticized China as a site of timelessness and dislocation with comments such as "The Chinese thinks instinctively in terms of centuries and he sees himself as a particle in time."[74] Even at her most laudatory, Buck presented China in these nostalgic terms. "To that peace table let us hope that China will be allowed to bring her unchanged self, that self which has already lived through ten thousand changes, and can live through ten thousand more."[75]

Against the panorama of an unchanging China, Pearl S. Buck constructed her America. On her return to the United States, she observed, "Accustomed to China's timelessness and to the illimitable breadth of the Chinese outlook upon all human beings and endeavor, I have at times been baffled and dismayed by the momentary quality of my own country and by the narrowness of our experience and human understanding, mentally and spiritually."[76] Buck's elaborations of travel, distance, and change between China and America served as a metaphor for an American society looking to the past for inspiration while undergoing dramatic transformation. Buck expressed nostalgia for the "unwesternized" and "authentic" China that, realistically, she could not have known—in order to make sense of the American present to which she was yet a stranger. In her books she mourned changes in Chinese society that had been wrought largely through the Western influence of missionaries such as herself.[77]

Buck was able use what ordinarily might have made her seem less

American—her lack of knowledge about her homeland, the United States—to establish her status as a prophet of American democracy. This is particularly apparent in her 1937 essay "On Discovering America."

> I had lived all my life an American away from America. Then I returned, a sort of immigrant among immigrants, except that I came to my native land. But it was as new to me as though I came from Sweden or from Italy or Greece. . . . Some of us, like me, came because we wanted to come home . . . having lived always among an alien race, spoken a foreign tongue and walked the streets and roads of every day as a foreigner.[78]

Buck also recalled how astounded she was by the racial prejudice evidenced by black and white Americans, native-born and foreign-born, and how she "began to delve into the dark feeling which few Americans, it seems to me, are willing to face and acknowledge" of prejudice.[79] She received an overwhelmingly positive response to this essay.[80] Buck had seemingly captured the common experience of being American, of "being restless" and in constant motion in her celebration of "Americans all." Furthermore, the fact that she was an American who experienced immigration to America seemed to give her critique of American society a certain weight that other immigrant groups and liberals in America could not have.

Her initial, disingenuous claim to be ignorant about American culture and society, and her willingness to speak out "as a Chinese," allowed Buck a public platform that faced few challenges. Curiosity about China had enabled Buck and other missionaries to command interest about their mission activities; now this same curiosity with China enhanced the interest in her novels and social vision. The cultivation of Pearl S. Buck's image as one who intimately understood China and who brought an outsider's fresh and critical perspective to the United States contributed to her growing prominence as a cultural mediator and political commentator (see figure 4, taken at a China relief fund-raiser).

In 1938 she received the Nobel Prize in literature. Although this prestigious award contributed to her popularity, it also heightened Buck's alienation from intellectuals and literati, who did not view her with equal respect. In response, Buck increasingly sought legitimacy in her unique position as the intermediary between the United States and China. Pearl Buck's willingness to publicly negotiate the cultural ambiguity of her own life challenged oriental stereotypes and provided Americans with a more complex understanding about cultural differences. As Pearl Buck's biographer Peter Conn has demonstrated in great detail, Buck subsequently invested much of her time and energy into organizations that sought to achieve equality for African Americans in the United States, to writing and addressing essays condemning racism as well as legislation like the Chinese exclusion laws, and to behind-the-scenes lobbying of government officials regarding the social inequities facing nonwhites.[81]

## NEGOTIATING AMERICAN ORIENTALISM AND NATIONALISM

Even though Buck's writings were located within the intellectual discourse of her time, she chose to publicly identify herself with "everyday people." Buck's prolific contributions to widely circulated magazines and her broad appeal may have given her words a more pronounced effect than those of intellectuals when she stated, "The future of America depends on immigration. . . . We all have a right here, for America from the very first has had her beginning in all peoples, and her strength is drawn from all peoples and her future depends on us all."[82] Thus Buck voiced ideas already expressed throughout the twenties and thirties by many intellectuals, including Horace Kallen, who advocated cultural pluralism, and Randolph S. Bourne, who offered immigrants a transnational model as a means to be fully American and fully other.

Pearl Buck's geographic displacement and subsequent transnational identity informed her enthusiasm for Bourne's cosmopolitan ideal. He envisioned a transnational alternative to the nativist, 100 percent Americanism he witnessed in 1916, during the First World War. Basing it on a diversity of geographic locations and ethnic identifications, he proposed "a 'trans-national' federal culture of hyphenate dual citizens that could 'unite and not divide' the world." This vision contributed to what David A. Hollinger describes as "the emergence of a national, secular, ethnically diverse, left-of-center intelligentsia" that flourished in the forties among those who considered themselves intellectuals.[83] During the Second World War Pearl Buck would embrace this idealistic vision as well.

### Internationalizing American Nationalism

During the late 1930s Buck increasingly drew on her multiple identities as a woman, a Chinese, and an American to differentiate herself as one of the few public intellectuals with any experience or knowledge about Asia and women's experiences. Even though she did not necessarily focus on China or Asia, Buck continually adopted an international—often Chinese or Asian—context. Discussing American social locations from an international perspective thus normalized China for those Americans who read her work. Buck, moreover, emphasized individual effort and individual cosmopolitan experience as socially transformative. This cosmopolitan ideal, however, would be used by Euro-Americans whose white ethnicity allowed them to unite with other white ethnics, and whose socioeconomic mobility enhanced their transnational mobility. On the one hand Pearl Buck's cosmopolitan idealism allowed her to disseminate the values of diversity, but on the other it served as a cultural blinder to the specific contexts in which others lacked mobility and the ability to fit themselves into any given geographic location or cultural context.

Buck thus romanticized both her experience in China and the possibilities of equality and success in United States society, believing that individuals' risk taking would earn appropriate compensation, including economic security, political empowerment, or recognition. Framing citizenship, Protestant style, as entirely volitional and made concrete through action reveals the ways in which Pearl Buck's expectations of marginalized groups came about. If she, a white woman, was able to successfully make her home among the Chinese, what prevented others from being successful at whatever they needed to be? Although she rejected the patriarchal structure of American society and the church, Buck nonetheless highly valued the ideal of the "rugged individualist"—the missionary who "tamed" the hinterland, who "knew" the "unknown." In many ways she applied the same individualist expectations she had of missionaries to those structurally disadvantaged in American society. When she spoke and wrote about social equality, Buck assumed that, because equality existed as an ideal, individuals only had to *claim* and demonstrate that equality in order to attain it.

Indeed, the long-standing assumption among Americans that China was vastly unlike their country in politics, ideology, religion, and social norms further legitimized Pearl Buck's status as someone who could assess the United States from a distanced, objective standpoint. Buck claimed an awareness of being a foreigner and a sensibility of being Chinese, blurring the boundary of insider and outsider. She reversed the common orientalist paradigm understood by many Americans by placing herself squarely at the intersection of East-West polarities: an Anglo-Protestant American woman of Southern heritage, she had experienced what it felt to be unaccepted by schoolmates, to be different. Where

China was a mysterious culture to many Americans, it was the most immediate culture she had known.

The noted anthropologist Margaret Mead herself remarked on Buck's unique perspective regarding the United States: "Pearl Buck, returning to a world which she had dreamed of as a true democracy, saw, with a sharpness denied to most of those who have lived in America instead of having heard about America in China, how far from her dream—our dream—we were." Buck became a "missionary in reverse," proclaiming the gospel of American democracy, freedom, and opportunity to her fellow citizens.[84] With the passion of a new convert, Buck openly expressed her puzzlement over the social malaise she encountered. "Why are so many Americans sour, when we have the most beautiful and wonderful country in the world? And the easiest, richest life? And freedom? . . . It seems to me life here is perfect. And yet I never saw so many acid people, cruel in their envy, cruel in their spoken and written judgements, so much prejudice."[85] Buck emphasized her lack of knowledge about her homeland and her many years in China—a position as an outsider that allowed her to raise awareness about social issues.[86] Buck thus relied on the binary oppositions with which Americans perceived the United States and China in order to challenge Americans to reexamine themselves as a national community.

Buck developed this oppositional international argument in a 1939 article she wrote about gender inequality in American society for *Harper's Magazine*. Buck argued that the material comforts of the United States had "spoiled" women so that they exerted their abilities less than men.[87] In other countries around the world, she emphasized (albeit without evidence), women did not have the luxuries that American women had and thus enjoyed more respect. Buck espoused what Nancy Cott has termed a "womanist" ideology—she believed that women contribute to society within their particular gendered realms of expertise—"[but] women must be trained to see this and to be willing to take their place in the world as citizens and workers and thinkers."[88] Buck argued, "Thanks to our privileges which compel us to no effort, it is the truth that men go beyond us in everything except childbearing, and doubtless if men had to bear children they would soon find some better way of doing that."[89] Buck's analysis clearly overlooked working-class women, as well as structural barriers in society that contributed to women's being prevented from pursuing their roles in the public sphere.

## Assimilating Differences

Buck likewise exhibited little patience for ethnic or racial separatism on the part of marginalized groups. She still appeared to favor a volitional form of assimilation in which individuals maintained their ethnic diversity but on entering the United States sought to "become more like" native Americans in outlook, values, and actions.[90] Just as she had called on women to earn their equality with men, Buck argued that in order to make the United States truly "their country," and to contribute toward the end of racist and prejudicial attitudes, those who were marginalized because of their ethnicity had the responsibility to participate in American public discourse and to take an active role in educating white Americans.

For example, in 1939, Buck submitted a story outline in which she addressed "the Jewish problem" in Europe at the time through a character's refusal to marry another Jew. She explained, "they must give up being Jews as quickly as possible. It's been wrong to do as they have done—maintain their own country and religion and tradition wherever they were. They have no country and they must belong wherever they happen to be. And they must lose their very blood as quickly as they can. If two generations are not enough, then four, or eight or whatever is needed until they are lost—lost and safe. Only thus can there cease to be persecution of the Jews."[91] Buck's response to the anti-Semitism of Nazi Germany disturbingly suggests that Jewish people should abandon their ethnic identity, in a self-induced ethnic cleansing. Buck expressed her personal frustrations in a letter she wrote to Freda Utley in September 1940. "I am afraid that I have come to feel that one can expect nothing else just now from a Jew. . . . [I]t all goes to prove that they are first Jews and second citizens of whatever country they happen to be in."[92]

It appears that Buck's self-proclaimed race-blindness contributed to her anti-Semitism and American ethnocentrism—that those who want to retain their ethnic identities essentially contribute to their persecution. Applying her own particular and privileged experience as a missionary to China, Buck apparently expected that all people could easily move between existing cultural locations; she had little awareness of how borders develop as a form of survival and protection.

## Pearl Buck's Chinese Americans

Although Buck wrote several essays addressing institutionalized racism and its specific impact on Chinese Americans, she created few fictional

Chinese American characters. Buck set some of these characters into short stories she wrote for magazines when the China mystique was emerging during the late thirties. One of these stories, "His Own Country" engages most directly the China mystique.[93] This story addresses the trend of American-born Chinese returning to China to work for the betterment of their "homeland" during the early to mid-1930s. Notably, "His Own Country" first appeared in the British periodical the *Argosy* in 1939 and was not widely accessible to an American audience until 1941 as part of *Today and Forever* and the basis of a radio play. This date suggests that Buck, her literary agent, or magazine editors did not believe American readers would be as receptive to this story when it was first written.

Indeed, Buck begins the story by portraying the United States through the eyes of a young man alienated by American society, which rejects him because of his race. The radio play narration describes the "restless" plight of John Dewey Chang, born in New York's Chinatown but never feeling "at home."

> John Dewey Chang had always known that Mott Street, New York, was not his country. Even though he had been born in the crowded lively streets of Chinatown, and had never seen anything else, still he knew this was not his country. The first time he knew this was when he went to school and had to walk in line alone because no one else would be his partner. This was the beginning of his education in America.[94]

In this story, Buck captures his romanticized views of China as "home." Buck's story did not represent new information to those familiar with data from social science on immigrant children or to those acquainted with the Chinese American community. However, Buck was able to disseminate this knowledge more widely through popular fiction.

"His Own Country" refutes popular notions that racial heritage conveys innate cultural knowledge. Buck emphasizes that her American-born Chinese protagonists were indeed American and as ignorant of China as any other Americans. John and Ruth, his wife-to-be, hold opposing views of China, reflecting the bifurcated attitudes of Americans in general toward China. John, seeking recognition and belonging, decides to return to his parents' homeland and to work for modernizing China. He believes in the China mystique—a new, idealized, and romanticized view of China. "Slangy, lively, noisy" Ruth Kin, like "Anna May Wong" an American-born, assimilated Chinese girl who exhibits few stereotypically "Chinese" characteristics, does not want to leave

America; it is her home.[95] (Buck's allusion to Anna May Wong suggests that she was familiar with Anna May Wong's publicized trip to China three years earlier.) Ruth views China as old, backward, and inconvenient compared to the United States.

The narrative emphasizes the significance of experience as a form of knowledge; John and Ruth's respective views of China dramatically shift when they travel to China after their marriage. John expects a quiet, pastoral *Good Earth* setting but instead finds China as noisy and crowded as New York. Nor is John received as an enlightened American bringing with him the hope of Western culture to transform China. Faced by indifference, he begins to despise the "backward" China he encounters. John cannot reconcile his romanticized notions of China and his experience of China. He realizes that his own country is not China, but the United States. Indeed, he decides to return home to the United States.

In a plot twist, Ruth—a modern American girl who resists moving to China—befriends the Chinese and convinces John to remain in China. Just as her Biblical prototype forsook her people and promised her mother-in-law that "your people shall be my people," so Ruth Kin makes China her country and the Chinese her people. Her willingness to interact with the Chinese and to participate in their community changes her perception of China and allows her to appreciate this country. In turn, Ruth is able to show John the common humanity of the Chinese. Ruth's kinship with the Chinese (a not so subtle play on Ruth's last name) eventually brings John into the community as well, enabling him to accept China as it is, and to claim it as his own country.

This story about identification and belonging thus incorporates Buck's critical views about gender and power with China's growing popularity, Chinese Americans' alienation and search for inclusion, and American nationalism. The ideology of whiteness that informs American democracy alienates John, and he looks to China in his search for significance. China represents the homeland—a place of belonging—for the Chinese American immigrant community. John doubly romanticizes China as a place to belong, and a place that needs and welcomes him as someone who can bring that change. Buck strikingly portrays John as she did her father in *Fighting Angel*—a man seeking individual recognition—only this time instead of American evangelical Christianity he is bringing American liberal democracy to China. Buck thus suggests that the China's allure for Americans is as a location where an individual might transform his surroundings and in the process be transformed into full American masculinity. She also implies that China cannot fulfill these expectations for individuals or for the United States as a nation; John only claims his American identity in the process of confronting his unrealistic expectations of China.

Likewise, Buck suggests that men and women experience border crossings differently; whereas men strive to prove themselves in destinations abroad, women consistently attempt to create a community wherever they are. Buck's critique of this secular version of American nationalism abroad again parallels her earlier critique of American missions: a masculine, intellectual tendency to avoid interpersonal communication versus a more adaptive, resilient, and nurturing feminine attempt to gain a truer knowledge of a culture and people through cross cultural relations.

As she did throughout the 1930s, Buck thus asserts her common theme that one must make one's country wherever one is, that one's present location and cultural knowledge are more significant than one's place of birth or racial identity. In another ironic allusion—this time to what John Dewey termed "the individual meshing with social improvement and national cohesion"[96]—Buck contrasts her protagonist's encounter with Chinese reality to Dewey's lectures in China from 1919 to 1920 on education as the way to develop a civically engaged citizenry. On his return Dewey interpreted China to Americans.[97] He did not interact with "the masses," as Buck had in her "assistant missionary" work. Instead, he socialized with the educated elite and mostly stayed within the culture of the often Western-modeled universities.[98]

Buck nonetheless echoed the vision of John Dewey, describing China as a potential democracy and arguing that, because true American nationality was inclusive of all identities, the actual American possessed a "cosmopolitan dual nationality."[99] In her story, she stresses the idea of reciprocation through cultural exposure. Buck acknowledges the painful consequences of racism but suggests that individuals must take on the responsibility to extend themselves beyond the pain of rejection to become a part of the national community that rejects them. Taking her protagonist out of one context of racial prejudice in the United States , she forces him to confront his own prejudice against the Chinese in China. Yet the issue of racial prejudice in the United States remains unchallenged. Buck suggests a fluid and flexible stance—an easy shedding of affiliations and allegiances, locations, and identities. In both cases, a willingness to leave provides the solution to racial prejudice; and a willingness to give up one's claimed identity in order to take on a new identity as required by one's immediate location "solves" the "problems" of displacement.

Buck's fictional stories of Chinese Americans returning to China and effecting positive change among "their own people" are consistent with her wartime speeches encouraging African Americans and Japanese Americans to be a bridge between cultures. She argued for treating Japanese Americans fairly during the war because she assumed that this group ideally "would" return to Japan after the war and proclaim the ideals of American democracy. Her argument, one articulated by social scientists and other intellectuals, presumed an inherent association of the individual to her culture based on her ethnic descent and racial heritage. This correlation of descent to consent, moreover, assumed that an individual was predisposed by descent to a particular culture regardless of where he had lived his entire life. Buck did not take into account that immigrants in the second and third generations might have barriers of language and culture and might furthermore not be accepted readily by Asian communities abroad. Nor did Buck seem to understand the specific contexts that might encourage some communities and individuals to hold fast to cultural traditions.

Buck emphasized the authority of experience in opposing ways. While her image as someone who had authentic knowledge of China resulted in positive stereotypes of China, her later stories appear to caution against relying on images and stereotypes. While she used her own experiences of cultural adaptation to condemn the Jewish community, she also suggested that Chinese Americans might be able to contribute to China because of their affinity—even if imagined—with China.

Her contradictory perspectives on diversity and assimilation reflected the ideological tension underlying American society at this time. On the one hand, Buck held individuals responsible for participating in the structures of their national communities rather than taking a separatist stance. On the other, she charged the United States with complicity in the Western nations' domination and exploitation of non-Euro-American, nonwhite peoples and challenged Americans to fulfill their national ideals. The two constants of Buck's apparently contradictory stance are her emphasis on individual merit, action, and accountability—witness her blunt address on racism in the United States—and her fundamental belief in American liberalism and democracy as universal, human ideals—witness her ambivalent critique of American nationalism. Tolerant of diverse perspectives, experiences, and ethnicities so long as these ultimately affirmed the American nation, she endorsed the dominant ideology of cultural pluralism: in theory it valued diversity while in reality seeking an ideological consensus based on American values of freedom, equality, and democracy.[100]

Because Buck could not fully acknowledge the privilege of her position as a Euro-American foreign missionary in China, she did not fully recognize the intersections of multiple factors that worked together to disadvantage individuals and communities. From the late thirties on Buck would continue to rely on her own experiences to interpret American society. She internationalized for the American public the concept of cultural pluralism, providing her readers with a cosmopolitan context for the United States' increasing role in international affairs. By incorporating China into a vision of a diverse international cultures sharing in a common democratic and liberal ideological vision, Buck contributed to popular understandings of the United States as a beacon of light and freedom for the world.

## THE MOST CHINESE AMERICAN?
## PEARL BUCK AND WORLD WAR II

When the United States entered the Second World War and joined forces with China against Japan, both news and popular media looked to a select few persons who had experiences in China for their insights about the alliance.[101] Most prominent among the second generation of those supporting China throughout the 1930s were Pearl S. Buck and Henry Luce, also the child of missionaries who had been stationed in China.[102] As the publisher of *Time* magazine (and later *Life* magazine) and as producer of the *March of Time* dramas-newsreels, Luce wielded considerable influence in shaping Americans' perceptions of China. He applied his experiences and reputation in corporate America to organize China relief efforts during the 1930s and onward.[103]

Their political views differed, but Buck and Luce shared a commitment to China during its war of resistance. Buck was one of the founding members of the China Emergency Relief Committee, which was formed in 1938 and raised funds to send to China before the United States acknowledged the war between Japan and China. After seven major China relief agencies incorporated as United China Relief (UCR), Buck would continue to devote her name and considerable energy to raise funds for numerous relief projects in China.

### Through "Chinese-Trained" Eyes

In her public proclamations and critiques, Pearl S. Buck located herself on the margins as a somewhat distanced and objective observer of American culture. As such, she and others who possessed a more global perspective were granted greater credibility to comment about American society. Margaret Mead, for example, returned to the United States from field research in the Pacific and brought with her a "certain way of looking at peoples." In her 1942 *Keep Your Powder Dry,* subtitled "An Anthropologist Looks At America," Mead discussed the American national character with the perspective of some years' absence from her homeland. Anna Louise Strong's account of traveling and exploring America's heritage was published in 1940 as *My Native Land.* In the midst of shifting interpretive emphases from racial "types" to national or ethnic cultures, Buck differentiated herself from these authors by virtue of her apparently seamless identification with the Chinese. Her unique position contributed to her role as an important commentator during World War II.

Buck believed that the war would test the consistency and integrity of the United States' professed ideals of democracy and equality. She repeatedly warned that the minority races would not accept continued imperial domination in the postwar world, further establishing herself as a champion of racial equality in the minds of many Americans. Through her magazine articles, essays, and books Buck earned the respect of a large number of Americans. Herbert Agar's review of her 1942 collection of essays on democracy and the war, *American Unity and Asia,* even suggested that Pearl Buck might "turn out to be the Tom Paine of our worldwide civil war."

During this "new era of nationalism" occasioned by the American involvement in a "war for freedom," Buck challenged Americans to fulfill their democratic ideals.[104] Her experience in China, she claimed, had provided her with a unique worldview that could help prepare Americans to be international leaders. She warned that the United States was under close scrutiny, and that the rhetoric of freedom and democracy had to be put into action as well.

Citing her personal knowledge of China's less developed political and social system, Buck assured her readers that the level of "civilization" they enjoyed in the United States exemplified the "advanced" state of the system of American government and democratic ideals compared to other places in the world. Thus, Americans had a duty to respond to the needs of other countries that lacked this system: "millions of people in India and China and other parts of the world," Buck noted, "are waiting for us to take the lead for democracy, and are growing disheartened and discouraged because of our delay."[105]

From this international perspective she applauded the U.S. government's desire to incorporate immigrants and ethnic minorities into its national community. She shared the fears of officials, intellectuals, and other liberals that blacks and other ethnic groups in the United States might support a Japanese victory as a victory for all peoples of color in the world. While the assumption that blacks would have more of an affinity for the Japanese was yet another manifestation of racism, Buck attempted to demonstrate why some black Americans might be swayed by Japan's rhetoric of a race war, linking it the history of racism in the United States. She repeatedly warned that minorities would no longer tolerate discrimination and prejudice from a dominant white race, and that if racial equality was not an outcome of this war, future conflict was inevitable. Thus Buck strongly urged an argument voiced by numerous progressive groups: social welfare and increased law enforcement did not adequately address the status of African Americans in the United States— the source of economic deprivation lay in American racial prejudice.

In advocating for change, Buck shrewdly appealed to the American conceit that the United States was a more modern and progressive society—and more open to change—than China, which was still perceived as "old" and "backward." If China, a more "primitive" culture, exhibited no racial prejudice, then how could Americans—boasting the most advanced political system in the world—justify the existence of racial inequality in the United States? Using China as a point of comparison, Buck argued that American fears of diversity were unfounded because the United States boasted the unifying system of democracy. In a 1942 guide on books about Asia that Buck included in *Asia Magazine,* Buck remarkably asserted, "It would be easy . . . to become a Chinese" due to China's homogeneous, unified culture.

> China is half again as big as the United States and has four times as many people. But China is more of a unit, its people of one general race, its history long and continued upon one piece of ground, its language, in spite of its dialects, the same and especially the same in its sources, and its civilization built out of common roots. The Chinese are people peculiarly unified in all but the western political sense.[106]

In contrast, the United States boasted a central governing system of democracy. Despite rapid changes in society and the growing diversity of the national community, the United States had at its core a fundamental political and ideological unity that allowed for stability, while China's lack of political uniformity resulted in internal factions and conflict. Buck thus employed an oppositional image of China to encourage her readers to focus their energy on strengthening American democracy by embracing diversity and rejecting prejudice.

Alluding to the current war, Buck called for a return to the true democracy of America and not the subjugation of minorities. "Cruel as [Nazism] is, and dangerous as it is to civilization, it is less cruel, and it may be even less dangerous in the need, than the sort of democracy which is not real enough or strong enough to practice what it preaches." "Is democracy right or wrong?" she challenged, already having dismissed the "wearisome defense" of miscegenation. "If it is right, then let us dare to make it true."[107] The circumstance of the United States being at war with Japan, and the positioning of United States democracy against the authoritarian governments of Germany and Japan, converged with Buck's unique status of being a popularly read author and someone associated with another culture. In this "in-between" space, Buck delivered critiques of American society with her "Chinese-trained eyes" while at the same time expecting ethnic and racial minorities—who she assumed shared her experience—to follow her example.[108]

## The Burden of Interpretation

Just as she had earlier argued that her life in China had made her Chinese and ignorant of most things American, so Buck now claimed knowledge about American race relations on the basis of her family's regional origins, and an understanding of racial prejudice based on her upbringing in China. Buck first circulated her argument in her November 15, 1941 letter to the editor of the *New York Times,* responding to a November 12 editorial, "The Other Side of Harlem." She stated, "I am, I think, realistic and objective on this matter of race, having lived most of my life among coloured peoples. My own ancestry is entirely Southern," she added, "and I am very familiar with the problems of white and coloured in the South."[109] In a commencement address at Howard University in June 1942 Buck took up the issue of racism facing the African American graduates and noted its absence from her China experiences. "I confess . . . I have been completely perplexed by this race prejudice in my own country." It was only on her return to the States in the 1930s that she "came to understand the full reality of race prejudice and its effect on both colored and white people."[110]

Buck applied her dual perspective in directly addressing a very touchy issue in American society. Contrary to white supremacist ideologies, Buck proposed that black Americans should lead the ideological war against racial inequality. At the height of the war, Buck took the unusual step of sending a "Letter to Colored Americans" to every black newspaper in the United States to be published on February 28, 1942. Her open letter also enjoyed circulation in newspapers like the *New York Herald-Tribune*. According to John Day's publicity for a subsequent collection of essays, Buck's letter appeared "as front page and feature articles in almost every colored paper, in many with eight column headlines, and with much editorial comment."[111] Confident of her reputation for speaking out on racial prejudice Buck began, "Some of you may know how frankly and constantly I have spoken to white people about their obligations to you. Now I should like to speak to you of the responsibility resting at this moment upon the coloured Americans for the survival of human freedom." According to Buck, blacks in America were symbols for the people of the world, including the people of India and "peoples of all colonies in Asia and Africa," some not under foreign rule but "ruled without freedom by certain classes and groups of their own race and kind." Nonetheless, Japan and Germany did not offer true freedom. If they were victorious, "The freedom of coloured and white together would then be lost."[112]

Buck asked her black audience to help fulfill the United States' unique potential to lead the postwar world to freedom.

> I tried to think as one of the minority—not difficult, because in China I had all my life belonged to a minority race—there the white race—and as a white, in spite of my very close relations and even integration into Chinese life, I had suffered some of the inevitable experiences of those who are in the minority in any country. But I had to think newly. What, I asked myself, would I do if I belonged to a group in my own country against which race prejudice worked?[113]

Although she admitted that nothing could excuse past wrongs and cruelties, Buck urged blacks to be the better humans, to respond not with vengeance but with courage and resolve. "I ask you, coloured people of the United States, to stand by this great mass of your white countrymen in this imperfect democracy of ours, where nevertheless the hope of democracy is still clearest. They need your help. . . . Every time one of you conducts himself, with honesty and magnanimity and dignity, you are helping white men and women toward a real democracy."[114] Throughout her commentary on race relations, Buck took care to refute the need for a separate African American culture, a viewpoint championed by W. E. B. DuBois among others. She called on the African Americans to "[c]ome out of that little world of your own and take your place in America as interpreters of the colored peoples of the world."

Some African Americans appear to have accepted Buck's claims to understand them; they appreciated her efforts to confront the American majority about existing racial inequality. In 1943 the *Defender* named Buck "Woman of the Year" for "meritorious service to the Negro by a member of the white race. The world famous novelist undoubtedly did the outstanding job of the year in helping break down racial prejudice in America." Citing her many articles, books and speeches, the article praised Buck for confronting "fake racial theories of superiority" and bringing to Americans "a complete picture of the racial problem from a worldview."[115] The honor came to her as "a member of the white race." Although her stance seems rather conservative today, Pearl Buck's willingness to acknowledge the responsibility of white Americans in perpetuating racial inequality was radical for its time and its context. Risking her reputation and popularity at the height of American patriotism and nationalism during the war, she worked to ensure that popular wartime discourse about America's international role did not overlook the inequities remaining within the United States as well as abroad.

*Knowledge as Power*

Pearl Buck's attempts to institutionalize internationalism at a popular level in the United States both reflect the power of the China mystique and reveal American orientalism's imprint on her China experience. Circumstances during World War II inspired cross-cultural educational efforts on an international scale. From the beginning of the war, the consensus among officials, educators, and intellectuals was that Americans knew very little about China. Thus Buck enjoyed recognition and status as a result of her knowledge about China and her ability to communicate this knowledge to other Americans. Through her publications, and with the conspicuous guidance of the American and Chinese governments, Americans began to perceive similarities between their values and history and those of the Chinese.

Thousands of American soldiers and service people had been posted overseas; their wartime letters brought snippets of new cultures into the lives of families and friends back home. As they came home on leave, Buck noted, they "will come back to us with a curious partial knowledge of those peoples . . . and yet that experience will change them into different men." To Buck, that experience of cultural differences and similarities was useful, valuable knowledge. Thus in 1941 Buck and her husband, Richard J. Walsh, founded the East West Association (EWA), where travelers and "plain people" could exchange and share their experiences, personalizing and dissipating the mystery of foreignness. As she declared, "We are all mysterious only because we are unknown."[116]

The EWA intended to educate people.[117] It reflects Buck's conceit that her knowledge of China could demystify the mysteries of Asia. Knowledge constituted a form of power in itself. According to Buck, the EWA "came out of the conviction of a few persons like myself, whose lives have been divided between the Far or Near East and the United States. We have lived since childhood among two peoples" and the experience of similarities and differences among cultures impressed on these people that both hemispheres of the world must overcome their ignorance of the other.[118] As a result, most of those "ordinary" people from distant countries who appeared in EWA programs were themselves transnationals. For example, the speakers for a ten-day forum, "Peoples of the Pacific," featured professors from China and a Wellesley graduate, Chandralekha Pandit, the niece of Jawaharlal Nehru.[119]

The EWA also demonstrates the ways in which Buck believed in popularizing and demystifying knowledge in American society. Perhaps more than any other prominent advocate of cosmopolitan and democratic ideals, she tried to make knowledge more accessible to all. In the process, however, Buck's rhetoric also exhibited a telling shift. In expounding her form of American nationalism, she claimed more and more often to speak for "everyday Americans," a "majority of persons" who lacked privilege because of their minority, national, or political status. Being closely identified with the transition from American orientalism to the China mystique, Buck could likewise locate her outsider status at the center of the internationalized national ethos and facilitate everyday Americans' negotiations of their nation's emergence as a global power.

### A Conflict Transcending Nations

Buck extended her critique of domestic race relations to imperial relations abroad, seeking to clarify what was at stake for multiple interests in this world conflict. She emphasized national unity in spite of diverse interests, articulating for the American public the rapidly changing national and global contexts it could not ignore. "Perhaps one reason why this war has been so difficult to focus in our minds has been because the boundaries to which we have long been accustomed have faded. . . . This war is at the same time a dozen civil wars, an interracial war, and an international war of the widest scope yet known." Anyone who fights for a particular group, "be that group national or racial or political," Buck added pointedly, "is the enemy." After the war, she argued, the United States and all world governments must change: no one race should dominate but freedom must be accessible to all. Buck provided examples of common struggles linking Americans to other nations. "We Americans have exactly the same task as India. Our people have political freedom, but not human equality. Our civil war rid us of the slave system, but it did not give the freed human equality. The people of China have human equality but not political equality. We are all only partial democracies, and we cannot be sure of victory until we are made whole."[120]

While Buck's moral idealism during the war served the interest of the federal government in emphasizing the necessity of national unity, her attempts to emphasize the connections between racism and imperialism within a time of carefully cultivated wartime propaganda nonetheless challenged the government. Ida Pruitt, the coordinator of INDUSCO—an American organization dedicated to empowering Chinese through developing local industries—wrote to Buck expressing her gratitude for "saying these things that need so terribly to be said. There was no man to get up and say them six months ago, but we are thankful there is a woman to get up and say them now, a woman who is, thank God, listened to by so many of the people of this country."[121]

Government officials could ignore neither Buck's status as a China authority nor her prolific output of commentary. Chester Kerr, the chief of the Office of War Information's Book Division, considered *American Unity and Asia* so important that he circulated a report throughout government offices suggesting it to others.[122] He then ordered more copies to distribute, believing that it "should be read by every member of this Government who has a hand in shaping American opinion."[123] *The New Leader* proclaimed of this 1942 collection of Buck's wartime speeches and writings about the wartime and postwar contexts of American international relations: "With her special knowledge of Asiatic countries and inherent and deep sense of democracy, Mrs. Buck herself is now and doubtless will continue to be one of the key persons in furthering ties of understanding between the Asiatic peoples and Americans. . . . The current world crisis is apt to turn her into a world leader."[124]

Buck's claim to being culturally both Chinese and American reflects the fluidity of ethnic and racial identities at this time, and particularly the ways in which social scientists had begun to replace racial categories with ethnic and cultural categories. Just because the American media afforded Buck the space to speak as both Chinese and American, it did not necessarily mean that she spoke for American Chinese. Nonetheless, she occupied what little political space was afforded to minorities—particularly Chinese Americans—in the American public discourse of identity (see figure 5 of Buck at home). Buck's increasingly visible and vocal role raises questions about how someone gains an authoritative voice to speak for a particular community.

## Pearl Buck and a "Structuring Absence"

Pearl Buck benefited from a "structuring absence" of Chinese Americans and African Americans in popular discussions about race relations taking place throughout the United States. During the late 1930s and through the 1940s, the popularity of "blackface" carried over from its nineteenth-century vaudeville stage traditions into film musicals. There was a sense among white upper-class liberals during the 1920s and 1930s that black culture, exemplified by Harlem, was more natural and emotionally expressive and hence more inviting and intriguing than the sterile, albeit more advanced, middle- and upper-class white culture. Yet each had its place. Ella Shohat and Robert Stam write, "In a power-inflected form of ambivalence, the same dominant society that 'loves' ornamental snippets of Black culture excludes the Black performers who might best incarnate it." In other words, those in control of the production of popular culture are able to control the visibility of "otherness" or "others," in order to contain their possible meanings as "a kind of structuring absence."[125] The same mechanism applies to Chinese Americans as well.

In 1942 the Office of War Information (OWI) began to promote the idea of China as a "fighting ally" and hence increased the popular consumption of the China mystique even more. Independent of Buck's publishing interests, the sociologist Bruno Lasker also noted the growing market for magazine material on China in 1941.[126] In the arena of popular culture, voices are ordered according to marketability, which is in turn determined by consumption on both a domestic and an international scale. Similarly, in the arena of foreign relations, nations and their representatives are ordered by protocol according to their economic and military power. Pearl Buck demonstrated China's marketability, and the consumption of Buck's China further enhanced her value as an authority on China. Even so, the popularity of *The Good Earth* did not result in the sustained popularity of novels or movies featuring Chinese characters. In 1944 the market for Chinese fictional subjects remained unfavorable.

Racism and ignorance limited the market for Chinese-based fiction during the war. The few stories set in China justified the lack of accessibility for other Chinese (American) voices. In other words, the "structuring absence" of representatives in support of the interests of their respective communities was a fiction based on the perceived "reality" of the marketplace.[127] For example, the lack of Chinese American voices in popular culture could be cited to justify the marketing of Buck as a "Chinese and American" voice, even though the market itself allowed no access to Chinese American voices. And in turn the absence of Chinese Americans in public space "necessitated" the presence of articulate and active China experts, who spoke on behalf of the communities and appropriated aspects of the communities' defining knowledge and expertise.

Buck chose to locate herself on the margins when discussing American nationalism, first as a "Chinese" American and increasingly in her identification with African Americans after her relocation to United States during the 1930s and early 1940s. As a white woman, she could unthreateningly claim to speak for marginalized communities, positioning her self relative to widespread American ignorance and the absences allowed by prejudice as an "all-knowing" interpreter. She also could present herself as a liberal benefactor to the groups she claimed to know. Buck at times also romanticized Chinese culture in contrast to United States' social ills: at one point she suggested that Chinese held no prejudice against the Jews in China and would not hold prejudice against blacks. The purpose of such an unfounded and distorted claim makes no sense unless it was to allow Buck to claim an innocence she falsely credited to Chinese culture. As one of few foreigners who had traveled to the remote northern part of China, Buck could create her own mythical past. Moreover, Buck's inability to see her limitations as a foreign-born white woman, like her attribution of her American and Chinese views primarily to hard work and effort, blinded her to the ways in which she silenced the very communities she believed she was empowering.

Pearl Buck's success in constructing her image against the presumed lack of Chinese voices in the mainstream public reflects the extent to which American orientalism had succeeded in rendering Chinese Americans invisible in American society except in its elaborate productions of otherness. Constructing her image around her knowledge about China thus also created a dilemma of authenticity for Buck when someone more Chinese threatened her authority. When Madame Chi-

ang Kai-shek (Mayling Soong), for example, threatened to overshadow
Buck's role and undermine her legitimacy as a representative of China,
Buck claimed behind the scenes to be a true representative of "the Chinese people" who were abused by corrupt and elite Nationalist interests. In many ways, Buck's critique was accurate and her advice sound.
Yet she framed her critique of the Nationalists in a way that emphasized her own authority on both the United States and China. In a letter to Eleanor Roosevelt regarding the first lady's possible trip to
China, she wrote disparagingly, "I do not believe that Madame Chiang ever had the impulses of real democracy toward her own people."
She added, "I wish that if you went to China you could get to know
the real people. . . . My faith in people is constantly renewed because
of . . . what I have myself seen of the way the plain Chinese people
lived and died in this war. . . . Take for example the new drama. I
asked Madame Chiang about it and she knew nothing of it."[128]

Although Buck credited the experience of being white in China with
her ability to sympathize with the marginalized, her writings suggest that
an equally, if not more, significant experience was witnessing the treatment of women within her own family. Buck took her first public stand
against the American Protestant church, a patriarchal institution that
replicated its hierarchy on the mission field. Having discovered her own
sense of purpose and a sense of self in her writing, Buck left the church,
China, and her husband all at once. But she did not turn away from or
condemn patriarchy altogether, only those structures in which its purpose had been corrupted. In many ways Buck never shed the evangelical
Protestantism and social reform of her upbringing, instead taking up the
evangelism of liberal cosmopolitanism and American nationalism.

## Pearl Buck and China's Feminized Mystique

Pearl Buck benefited from the intersection of her personal identity and
experiences at a time when common knowledge about China was rare in
the United States at all levels of the government. She enjoyed the valid-
ity of being a white citizen in the United States, the authority of being one
of a few white female missionaries in the interior of China, the visibility
of having authored a best-selling, naturalistic novel about a Chinese
farming family, and, of equal value, the prominence of being outspoken
about American international and domestic issues at a time when American middle-class women were being encouraged to participate more ac-

tively in the polity. Finally, Pearl Buck as a woman benefited from the American popular culture's feminization of the China mystique.

Even when celebrated as an emergent, modern world power, China remained feminized as it had been throughout its relationship with the United States. Although Japan had been perceived more favorably by Americans as a result of its rapid modernization since the turn of the century, its aggressive imperialism during the 1930s and its hostile confrontation with the United States in 1941 was now reinterpreted through the lens of American orientalism.[129] Japan's rise to power occurred without a corresponding development in civilization; thus, Japan used the technology of modern warfare in a manner betraying its continued barbarism. As a result of geopolitical necessity and the popularity of Mayling Soong, the American-educated wife of the Chinese Nationalist leader Chiang Kai-shek, China was perceived to be more benign. China as a nation now relied on the guidance of the United States to prevail against Japan and also to develop a modern government and economy. In this subordinate relationship, Chinese nationalism did not threaten but rather affirmed the United States' role as a leader of a new, democratic world order.

The gendering of this particular geopolitical alliance allowed Buck to represent China to the American public. Prominent Euro-American male supporters of China such as Wendell Willkie, a 1944 presidential candidate, and Henry Luce, a powerful cultural and political broker, were never identified as closely with China as was Pearl Buck. As leaders of American institutions of power, their cultural identity remained firmly American. Pearl Buck, in contrast, was produced by her publisher (although she enjoyed a greater degree of control over her production because she was married to him) and could only informally participate in the American discourse of diplomacy and politics through her influence in the realm of popular culture.

"Being Chinese," moreover, allowed Buck to take on the feminized aspects of China in relation to the masculinized role of the United States in her critiques of American society. Buck described her experiences within China primarily as a foreigner and an American, yet these experiences were largely shaped by her gender—as a missionary, a wife, and self-described confidante to various Chinese. Uncomfortable with traditional male forms of power, she consciously distanced herself from such institutions. She did so, however, not as a female but by "being Chinese." By remaining within her Chinese persona—and in the position of defining China for Americans throughout the thirties and early forties—

she was largely able to define herself. Buck lacked the power to define "feminist" on her own terms.[130] "Feminist" was (and still is) a political label; "Chinese" was perceived to be cultural and thus less open to dismissal. So she retained a unique marginality by conflating her identification of gender with that of culture. "Being Chinese" provided Buck with a prominent position of authority from which to vocalize her critiques of male-dominated institutions of power. In terms of actual practice, Buck was able to maintain a position of power from a marginal position through her affiliation with China and the Chinese, not through her gender.[131]

Consistently throughout her career as an author, Pearl Buck displayed an acute ability to assume multiple perspectives. Keeping a critical distance from nationalism, she embraced internationalism, a cosmopolitan ideal. She recognized the dangers of a democracy that did not meet its own standard, and the ominous breach that existed between its educated elite and subjugated minority peoples. She viewed the latter as unwilling or fearful, hence unable to take on their responsibilities in a democracy.

The numerous editorials, essays, and speeches that Buck wrote or delivered during the late thirties and early forties, along with her activities in various educational associations, underscore her realization that fiction was not the most effective way to raise critical awareness about key issues in American society. Popular magazines made decisions based on profits, not morals, and editors reminded Buck's literary agent David Lloyd that most readers did not wish to be reminded of unpleasant or anxiety-inducing subjects, no matter how pressing. Her nonfiction pieces were considered based more on her personal observations and experiences than on "facts." Her work illustrates what feminist scholars, including Patricia Hill Collins and Gloria Anzaldúa, would elucidate: European-based forms of "objective," empirical knowledge have been privileged over lived experiences.[132] This hierarchy often silences or renders invisible women at all levels of society, as Buck observed in her wartime writings. Yet unlike these feminist writers of color, Buck claimed that her experience in China as a foreigner allowed her to understand what it meant to be a woman of color.

Hence Buck's construction of her cosmopolitan self in terms of ethnicity and culture in itself constitutes a political act. Many feminist scholars of color have explored the ways in which women's self-definition in opposition to gendered constructions of racial identity demonstrates a dual or oppositional consciousness necessary to their survival in the United States.[133] Although Pearl Buck herself was a white woman of European descent, her choosing to locate herself on the margins of American society through her identification with Chinese in international affairs and African Americans within domestic affairs can be interpreted as her construction of self. Thus Buck's ability to understand the oppression of women illuminated the oppression of other peoples based on race, and she attempted to turn her privileged position as a celebrated author into a tool of social transformation.

Buck translated the oppression she experienced as a woman into the language of race, culture, and power. Buck thus engaged in a form of "passing as other" to negotiate her position as a woman in American society and to achieve a public platform that otherwise would have been denied her due to her gender. Her experiences in China provided her with a legitimacy to speak out in public about United States–China relations, Chinese politics, and domestic race relations. However, her ability to negotiate multiple perspectives in order to maintain her public image in American culture was equaled by an inability to recognize how her public image relied on stereotypical assumptions about Chinese and African Americans and the lack of visibility afforded both communities in American society. Pearl Buck, along with many other well intentioned Euro-American liberals of her time, faced substantial obstacles in confronting racial prejudice, particularly her own. Her message was diminished by her own inability to examine the privilege of her position and to question more probingly the circumstances of her transnational, cosmopolitan identity.

Because of her position as a white middle-class woman, Pearl Buck was able to shape American perceptions of China more effectively and positively than either Wong or Soong. Buck's willingness to negotiate the difficult landscape of race relations, and her demand that race relations be understood within the context of Western imperialism and colonization, pushed Americans to reflect on their own national community, rather than define themselves in contrast to China, for example. Buck engaged American orientalism in ways that normalized China and made China more familiar and comfortable as a concept for the public. Her willingness to edit her childhood memories ultimately contributed to the paternalist image of American orientalism. At the same time, Buck's articulation of American nationalism in constant reference to China also contributed to a new mythology of the China mystique, presenting China as a reflection of American values and society.

1. Portrait of the Sydenstricker family in China, ca. 1900. Buck stands, Grace sits in their mother's lap; the amah is in the background—Edgar is not pictured. (Courtesy of Pearl S. Buck International, www.pearlsbuck.org)

2. Wedding photograph of Pearl and J. Lossing Buck, 1916. (Courtesy of Pearl S. Buck International, www.pearlsbuck.org)

3. Pearl S. Buck, 1932. From an article in her college yearbook, which had a *Good Earth* theme. (1932 *Helianthus,* Lipscomb Library, Randolph-Macon Woman's College)

4. Pearl S. Buck and Eleanor Roosevelt at a China relief fund-raising event, 1936. (Reproduced from the collections of the Franklin D. Roosevelt Presidential Library)

5. Pearl S. Buck at home, 1943. She looks up at a work of Chinese calligraphy by Li Chengmou. (By Peter Stackpole for Time-Life. © Getty Images)

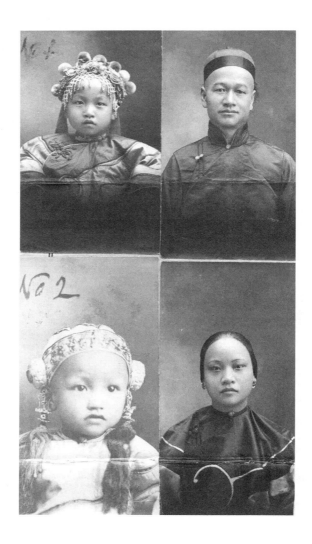

6. Photographs of the Wong family, ca. 1906 or 1907. Anna May Wong is at the lower left, LuLu above her; such photos served to identify and verify the relationship of individuals claiming kinship. (Courtesy of National Archives and Records Administration, Seattle, WA)

7. Anna May Wong as Annabelle Wu in *Forty Winks*, 1925. (Reproduced from the British Film Institute's Stills and Photograph Collection)

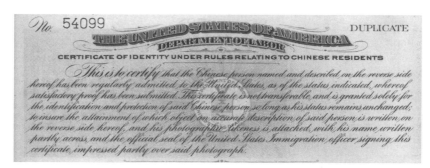

8. Anna May Wong's certificate of U.S. citizenship, 1924, as required under Chinese exclusion legislation. (Courtesy of National Archives and Records Administration, San Bruno, CA, and Vincent Chin)

9. Anna May Wong with beauty pageant contestants at the Moon Festival in Los Angeles, January 1941. (By Hansel Mieth for Time-Life Pictures. © Getty Images)

10. Photograph from Mayling Soong's certification of student status, presented to immigration officials in Seattle, Washington, 1907. (Courtesy of National Archives and Records Administration, Seattle, WA)

11. Wedding portrait of Mayling Soong and Chiang Kai-shek, 1927. (Courtesy of Wellesley College Archives)

12. Mayling Soong visits schoolchildren in China, ca 1936. (Courtesy of Wellesley College Archives)

13. "China's Madame Chiang" on the cover of *Life Magazine,* June 30, 1941.
(By Margaret Bourke-White for Time-Life. © Getty Images).

14. Eleanor Roosevelt and Mayling Soong at the White House, 1942. (Reproduced from the collections of the Library of Congress)

15. Mayling Soong and Capt. Mildred H. McAfee at Wellesley College, 1943. A short time later the college lifted its restriction on women's public appearance in pants. (By Cosmades. Courtesy of Wellesley College Archives)

華美 **CHINESE DIGEST** 週刊

COMMENT · · SOCIAL · · SPORTS
NEWS · · CULTURE · · LITERATURE    SAN FRANCISCO, CALIFORNIA

ol. 3, No. 3                     March, 1937                     Ten Ce

## "GOOD EARTH" NUMBER

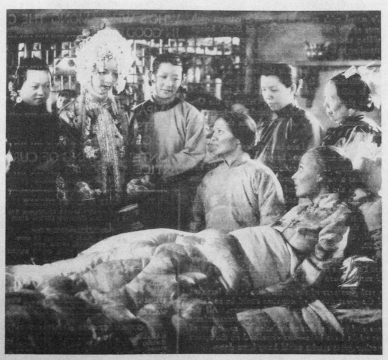

**O-LAN SEES HER FIRST DAUGHTER-IN-LAW** As her second son takes unto himself a wife, O-Lan, the mother and heroine of "The Good Earth," lay dying in her bed, while those partaking in the marriage feast make merry outside her room. This is the climax of the motion picture version of Pearl S. Buck's world famous novel. Luise Rainer plays O-Lan, and Mary Wong is the Little Bride. This production is now released after three years' preparation.

16. *The Good Earth* issue of *Chinese Digest,* March 1937. (By Amy Lonetree and Myla Vicenti Carpio. Reproduced from the collections of the San Francisco History Center, San Francisco Public Library)

17. Anna May Wong posing for photographs with Chinese American children at the Moon Festival in Los Angeles, 1941. (United Service to China Archives, Princeton University Library)

18. Chinese American boy selling special "Welcome Madame Chiang Kai-shek" edition of the *Chinese Press* in San Francisco, 1943. (Hansel Mieth Collection, © Center for Creative Photography, University of Arizona Foundation)

# Anna May Wong

As an American-born female of Chinese ancestry, Anna May Wong experienced the legacies of American orientalism: spatially, in the social geography of Los Angeles; socioeconomically, within the Chinese American community; and culturally, in the images of Asia that saturated American popular culture. Her status complicated the orientalist assumption that Asian identity was diametrically opposed to American identity.

Unlike Pearl Buck or Mayling Soong, who could reside in each other's countries without losing claim to their national status, Wong confronted ambivalence in both the United States and China because of the seeming ambiguity of her identity; her U.S. citizenship was always in question because of her racial heritage. As someone who portrayed the perpetual foreigner in Hollywood films, Wong constantly redefined herself as a Chinese American in relation to shifting international relationships and competing national interests within the film industry.

Her choice of acting as a career in itself challenged preconceived notions of what it meant to be a Chinese American woman, and Wong knew that to attain recognition as an actor and a private person she would have to fulfill public expectations in both roles. Balancing the constraints that racial prejudice put on her career and her desire for visibility required her to perform oriental femininity for public consumption. At times she intervened in these cultural productions to provide alternate readings and insights about American orientalism and its effects on American society and the Chinese American community.

Wong's career and life choices were also deeply affected by changes in the United States' national identity and relations with China, which in turn resulted in changing popular portrayals of China. Her negotiations of the transition from American orientalism to the China mystique reflect and emphasize the interdependence between the production of popular culture and America's national identity.

## LEGACIES

From the mid-nineteenth century, when Chinese immigrants first arrived in the United States, Chinese in America confronted American orientalism. Because national prejudices presumed that Chinese were less civilized and less moral than Americans, if Chinese immigrants made their way past national borders policed by immigration officials armed with discriminatory laws, they often endured legal and extralegal harassment or even violence where they tried to settle. In the face of this endemic racism, Chinese American communities developed as places of shared culture and safety. Yet as a result of discriminatory immigration laws, these communities had dramatically imbalanced gender ratios.[1] And the lack of Chinese women immigrants resulted in a small number of American-born Chinese. Anna May Wong's childhood reflects these demographic consequences, even as her family history highlights the effects this discrimination had on the Chinese American community.

One effect of legal constraints on Chinese immigration is particularly evident in Wong's family history. According to one account her mother, Lee Gon Toy, had been born in Oakland and her father, Sam Sing Wong, in Sacramento. In earlier accounts Wong stated that her parents were from China. The legacy of Chinese exclusion and the lingering shame within the Chinese community even today make the accounts difficult to untangle.[2] Recent studies of Chinese immigration and the 1950s "confession" program confirmed the suspicions of many United States immigrant officers—the majority of Chinese claiming to be U.S. citizens by birth entered under fraudulent names of lineage, as "paper" sons, and even daughters.[3] During a 1924 interview, as required of Chinese Americans when they exited and when they reentered the United States, Wong stated that her father had been born in China; in later interviews she said that he had been born in California but had grown up in China and married before returning to the United States. Inconsistencies in her accounts raise the possibility that either or both of Wong's parents were not born in the United States. But whether her parents were American-born or not, Wong herself grew up among second-generation Chinese Americans and this clearly shaped her perception of what it meant to be Chinese American. (See figure 6, from immigration records on the family.)

When Anna May Wong's parents relocated from northern California to Los Angeles during the late nineteenth century, they were part of a larger Chinese American migration southward, motivated by anti-Chinese violence. Although nationwide this Chinese-born population decreased from the 1880s through the 1890s—a result of return migration and restrictive immigration laws—the community in Los Angeles actually increased.[4] Yet as American natives of Chinese descent, Wong and her siblings were among the minority within their community. In 1910 the United States Census identified only seventy-seven American-born females of Chinese ancestry in Los Angeles, including a five-year-old girl listed as "Anna."[5]

Owing to anti-Chinese hostilities, economic necessity, and restrictive housing ordinances, the majority of Chinese Americans resided in what were popularly known as Chinatowns. The social and economic marginalization of Chinese immigrants in the western United States manifested itself in the marginal location and condition of these Chinatowns, which were often crowded, poor, and crime-ridden.[6] For many Chinese immigrants however, living with other Chinese provided a sense of safety and protection. Those who did not live within the borders of Chinatown still actively participated in the community, visiting to hear Cantonese spoken, purchasing Chinese vegetables, and celebrating Chinese traditions.

The Wong family lived in an ethnically diverse neighborhood just outside Chinatown, near their business. They first lived behind their laundry on Figueroa Street and eventually moved to a house on Flower Street. According to census reports, this neighborhood in 1910 was inhabited primarily by middle-class immigrants who came from central or northern Europe but also from Mexico, eastern Europe, and China. Within a span of ten years the Wongs' immediate neighbors changed: the majority of residents were now first- and second-generation immigrants from Mexico or eastern Europe and of working-class status, and the Wongs were the sole Chinese family on the block.[7] Anna May Wong and her siblings thus grew up in a culturally diverse neighborhood, but one in which they stood out.

The entire family worked in their family-owned laundry, with the children contributing their labor from an early age and coming in after school as they grew older. The need to help their parents with the laundry provided Wong and her sisters more freedom of movement than was otherwise allowed most Chinese American daughters, who were expected to remain within the home.[8] Wong interacted regularly with non-Chinese in her neighborhood when she picked up and delivered customers' laundry. In this way Wong first met Rob Wagner, a customer of the laundry, a writer for the *Saturday Evening Post,* and the eventual editor of *Beverly Hills Script* magazine, who encouraged her interest first in writing and then in acting. This friendship was somewhat unusual.[9] But her early interactions with Euro-Americans were not always pleasant.

*Learning Differences: An American Education*

Growing up outside Chinatown in some ways rendered Wong and her siblings more vulnerable to the challenges of being a minority among the increasingly diverse Los Angeles population. Wong's recounting of her first experience with racism reveals the painful education in difference that schools in immigrant communities provided children, introducing them not only to American values but also to a keen awareness of being different. Education also contributed to differences in culture and values between the children and their parents, as each generation, according to gender, responded differently to social pressures to fit in and be American.

Wong and her older sister, Lin Ying, called "LuLu," initially attended the California Street School in downtown Los Angeles, which reflected the city's diversity with a majority of Hispanic and white students, and a very small number of Chinese students. Wong recalled how she enjoyed school and looked forward to making new friends, even though she was a shy child. But "[t]hen came the knife stab, which, even today, has left a scar on my heart." She and her sister found themselves surrounded by a group of young male schoolmates, who "pulled our hair, which we wore in long braids down our backs. They shoved us off the sidewalk, pushing us this way that, and all the time keeping up their chant: 'Chink, Chink, Chinaman. Chink, Chink, Chinaman!' " The teasing only intensified, as other boys and girls joined in, "We felt that we were suddenly thrust into a new terrifying world. The great game was to gather around my sister and myself and torment us."[10] Sam Wong, according to Wong, told his daughters, "we must be proud always of our people and our race. But," he added, "our position in the

American community must at times be a difficult one."[11] Shortly later their parents transferred LuLu and Wong to the Chinese Mission School. It had been founded in Chinatown to educate the children of Chinese immigrants and to meet the mandate of the social gospel, in which progressivism and spirituality merged in "a new view of missions as a humanitarian agency."[12] Ironically, this American missionary discourse about China contributed to the racism that led so many Chinese immigrants to live together in Chinatowns equally orientalized as exotic, strange, and dangerous. Pearl Buck tried to change Chinese values and habits through instructing not only Chinese mothers but their daughters, and the mission schools also hoped to influence the Chinese immigrant community by educating its children.[13]

As with other Chinatown schools run by Catholic and Protestant churches nationwide, this school served a population that was ostracized elsewhere and had sought refuge living together in marginal urban spaces. Wong described the difference that attending the Chinatown school made to her own sense of security. "Here though our teachers were American, all our schoolmates were Chinese. We were among our own people. We were not tormented any longer."[14] The school constituted a safe space and community, though the neighborhood typified the communities targeted by American evangelical churches for their evangelical and reform efforts.

Free public education in the United States was accessible to Chinese American girls and boys, representing a key shift in cultural expectations. And as a result of attending school, Wong recalled feeling increasingly alienated from Chinese traditions: "Outside of our own home, we were thoroughly American in dress, action, speech and thought. Right and left we were smashing the traditions of our forebearers. . . . What was America doing to me, that at so early an age I shared a marked tendency to forget all my parents' teachings? There is no question I was changing rapidly." [15] In response, the parents employed a strategy used by many Chinese parents to maintain their homeland culture and enrolled the children in Chinese language school to learn to speak, read, and write Chinese.[16]

Anna May Wong's school activities—playing baseball or marbles, and refusing to attend the school's sewing circle—already defied traditional expectations for young women of any ethnicity. Nonetheless her subsequent pursuit of a film career was a dramatic departure from the expectations of her parents and community. The majority of Chinese American females sixteen years and older in Los Angeles were married; those who were not married found work mostly in the service sector as domestic workers or seamstresses.[17] First-generation Chinese American parents' expectations that their daughters conform to Chinese tradition were further normalized by the relatively high ratio of Chinese-born to U.S.-born members of the Los Angeles Chinese American community in the first third of the twentieth century. According to the 1930 census, fewer than one thousand Chinese American women held salaried positions.[18]

Significantly, Wong associated her fascination with movies with being American. Wong explained that "playing hooky" was evidence of her Americanization. "I was learning to think and act for myself. It is this trait of independence which sets me apart, perhaps more than anything else, from other Chinese girls, most of whom obey their parents blindly all their lives."[19] Wong believed that her portrayal of highly exoticized and sexualized Oriental roles—directly associated with perceptions of her as Chinese—actually evidenced her increasingly American perspective.

### Pursuing a Film Career

Anna May Wong's fascination with Hollywood movies shaped her own idea of China. Hollywood's China served as a magnet for criminals, alienated persons, and cynics. It could also represent a place of transformation. One script writer explained the importance of "the East" as an extension of the frontier: "the Orient is a place where people can go in the hope of a second chance. . . . It gives a sort of pioneering spirit in a new country."[20] A character could choose to discard the moral ambiguity of China and participate actively in Western society.

Chinatown—exotic, strange, and dangerous as it appeared to outsiders—constituted evidence for many Americans of the inability and unwillingness of Chinese to assimilate and leave their Chinese culture behind. Hollywood films perpetuated the view of Chinese Americans as foreigners more at home in China by shooting on location in Chinatown to recreate the atmosphere of "the Orient" and hiring extras from Chinatown to populate the foreign locale. Their popular misperception, of course, meant extra income for Chinatown's residents as extras or in bit roles (those involving more prominent acting or lines). Ironically, Wong's very American choice of an acting career developed because of Hollywood filmmakers' stereotypical ideas about China and Chinese people. The conflation of China and Chinatowns gave Wong the opportunity to leave Chinatown and its more obvious socioeconomic constraints behind. She began skipping school to watch film crews on location in Chinatown or enjoy Ruth Roland and Pearl White serials at the theater on Main Street, nearer her home. In 1919 when Nazimova's *The Red Lantern* was filming in Chinatown and required 300 local Chinese for atmosphere, Wong enjoyed her first opportunity to be an extra.[21]

The decision to pursue acting meant that Wong would have little choice but to portray stereotypical images of Oriental women. In 1921, for example, Wong portrayed a Christian female convert, Chu Ying, in one of a series of three vignettes set in Chinatown. Chu Ying is abused in the shadowy depths of Chinatown by her opium-addicted husband in *Bits of Life* but eventually impales her husband's skull with a crucifix. The mass circulation of such lurid images only reinforced orientalist perceptions that Chinese immigrants were inassimilable to American values and would always be foreigners.

Her performance as Chu Ying caught the attention of producer Joseph Schenk and enabled Wong to leave Chinatown for her next role as a featured player in a short film. Schenk cast Wong as Lotus Flower in *Toll of the Sea*, a low-budget, nonoperatic rendition of Puccini's *Madama Butterfly*. Because the film was demonstrating a new colorizing process called Technicolor, Wong's vivid acting in the 1922 short film was viewed by many in the film industry, including the actor Douglas Fairbanks, who cast her as the treacherous Mongol slave girl in 1924 for his first film as producer and director, *The Thief of Baghdad*.[22] Wong's expressive performance, striking appearance, and highly revealing costume resulted in several more bit roles.[23]

From Chinatown to China to the Middle East, Wong's early extra and bit roles spanned the spectrum of the oriental imaginary and adorned the fantastic and highly orientalized sets of Hollywood's silent films. The amorality Americans associated with China and Chinese Americans translated into the racial, moral, and gender ambiguity of her onscreen characters.

VISIBILITY AND THE LIMITS OF REPRESENTATION

Wong's visible Chinese heritage sharply limited the parts she could play. As one of a handful of Asian or Asian American actors considered for any feature roles, we might assume that Wong would be in demand. This was not the case, however, as Euro-American actors continued to be cast in any feature female roles of almost any race during the 1920s. Makeup could allow a Euro-American actor to perform Asian femininity, but makeup could not overcome Wong's racial identity.

## Hollywood's Racial Logic

Hollywood's racial logic informed casting decisions as well as plot nar‐
ratives. Its inability to categorize Wong according to strictly black and
white binary terms allowed her the flexibility to portray an assortment
of Hollywood's "Oriental" female characters, including an Indian and
an Eskimo. Wong's characters may have been in different locations and
of different cultural backgrounds but nonetheless had similar fates. For
example, as tomboyish Tiger Lily in Paramount's *Peter Pan* (1924), Anna
May Wong boisterously leads the Lost Boys in ambushing the English
and virginal Wendy—which might be read as an attempt of the racially
othered woman seeking to overcome Anglo femininity and thus gain ac‐
cess to the whiteness associated with white masculinity. This attack fails
and relegates her to Never-Never Land, the sole female among primitive
boy-men. Just as the Lost Boys never become men, Tiger Lily never be‐
comes truly feminine. In addition, Tiger Lily's implied identity as an
American Indian female within the masculine frontier includes the char‐
acteristics of a primitive, aggressive, and uncivilized female.

Chu Ying, the Mongol Slave, Lotus Flower, and Tiger Lily represented
the majority of roles that were available to Wong throughout the early
1930s. In many of her early bit parts, Wong reprised the Mongol Slave,
embodying the exotic and highly sexualized female. Her several roles as
a dancer—in *Piccadilly, Daughter of Shanghai, Chu Chin Chow,* and
*Hai Tang,* to name just her feature roles—allowed the camera's gaze to
focus on her body. With feature roles, like Lotus Flower, Wong often
portrayed the tragic Oriental beauty who falls in love with a Euro-
American male and either kills herself out of love to erase the potential
for miscegenation from the plot (as Lan Ying did in *Dangerous to Know*)
or threatens to kill the Euro-American female who is the object of her
love's desire (as Princess Taou Yuen did in *Java Head*). In other cases,
Wong's characters reveal their ruthless and treacherous Oriental nature,
such as Chu Ying or the manipulative and scheming Annabelle Wu in
*Forty Winks.* Even supposedly sympathetic roles, such as Wong's club
owner in *Tiger Bay* (1933), laughs maniacally as she hurls a knife into a
thug to protect the orphan in her care and then kills herself so her ward
may marry a respectable young Englishman; and her Chinese prostitute
stabs a corrupt Chinese general in *Shanghai Express* (1932) and steps
stoically into the background.

By the 1930s, Wong's visibility and unique presence in films shaped
American expectations of what Chinese females should look and act like.

The Chinese American Florence Jung recalled auditioning for a part where the producer was looking for "someone who looked like Anna May Wong." Jung recalled the process: "They look you over, 'No, she doesn't have Oriental eyes, and doesn't have this pug nose.' . . . [T]hey expect . . . everybody to look like Anna May Wong."[24]

After Wong's highly visible role in Paramount's *Daughter of the Dragon* (1931), the *Hollywood Reporter* predicted that Wong had "put herself in line for larger and better things," and suggested that Wong presented "one of the most startling and different of exotic screen personalities."[25] However, the lack of potential romance continued to limit Wong's opportunities well into the 1930s. Because she was allowed to portray only supporting roles and never the romantic lead, the development of her role required those producing the film to care enough to develop her role beyond a stock supporting character. Wong enjoyed such a role when she was cast as Hui Fei in the German director Josef von Sternberg's 1932 *Shanghai Express,* a Marlene Dietrich vehicle for Paramount Pictures. This film, set in 1920s China in the midst of civil chaos, featured corrupt Chinese officials, lawless Chinese guerrillas, assorted Europeans on a train, and romantic intrigue. Wong's Hui Fei and Dietrich's Shanghai Lily, both women of considerable disrepute, share a compartment on the Shanghai Express train, which is attacked by Chinese guerrillas. Hui Fei ultimately saves the day as well as the white heterosexual romance between Dietrich and Clive Barker through her "Oriental cunning" and skill at using the knife hidden in her sleeve. Under the direction of von Sternberg, Wong portrayed the stereotypical role of the stoic Chinese prostitute with passion; expressing inner strength and depth beneath the seemingly placid visage, she stole scenes from Dietrich. After this point in her career, Wong's roles would revert to the "B" films with little dramatic potential.

## Third Beginning

A drought of roles during the middle of the decade ended in the late 1930s, with what Wong herself referred to as the "third beginning" of her career.[26] China's war of resistance against Japan and increasing American sympathies for China resulted not only in additional roles, but in positive portrayals of Chinese Americans. *Daughter of Shanghai* (1937) and *King of Chinatown* (1939) featured accomplished, independent Chinese American women. In *Daughter of Shanghai,* Wong's character, Lan Ying, aided Philip Ahn's Chinese American FBI agent Kim

Lee in breaking up an Irish smuggling ring. Playing with racial stereotypes, the Chinese American protagonists with the aid of an Irish American cop put an end to the nefarious machinations of a San Francisco society matron and her (white) cronies. Groundbreaking and provocative
as the plot and casting were, the film's lackluster script and poor production values were serious drawbacks.

Wong's determination to find positive roles manifested itself in her
next Paramount feature, *King of Chinatown*. She portrayed a Chinese
American woman physician in San Francisco, Dr. Mary Ling, raising
funds for Chinese victims of famine and war.[27] In another example of
Hollywood's inclusion of positive Chinese American depictions, Wong in
1938 signed a contract with Warner Brothers to develop a film series for
herself as an Oriental detective. She developed and starred in the quirky
*When Were You Born?* for Warner Brothers in 1939, playing an eccen-
tric Chinese astrologer who unravels mysteries.[28]

Hollywood's interest in positive portrayals of China reflected international relations with China rather than audience demand. As a result,
the studios' minimal commitment to portraying Chinese more positively
was short lived. While Wong was praised for "a very creditable performance" in *When Were You Born?,* Warner did not choose to develop
a series with her astrologer, Mary Lee Ling.[29] Publicity efforts for these
movies, furthermore, undermined these film's more positive characterizations of some of its Asian characters. Posters for *Where Were You
Born?* represented Wong as a dark, hovering, and ominous backdrop
against which the two "star-crossed" (Euro-American) lovers were
posed. Even the publicity for *King of Chinatown*, which claimed to feature Wong's "most action-filled role of her career as the strong-willed
woman-surgeon whose unwavering devotion to her profession and Oriental ingenuity succeed in getting the better of gangland's cleverest
leader and trapping criminal whom even the police can't track down,"
simultaneously relied on the usual characterizations of Wong as a "Chinese Charmer."[30]

Wong's two remaining pictures with Paramount, *Dangerous to Know*
(1938) and *Island of Lost Men* (1939), reverted to recycled plots with
standard Oriental characters, and Wong was relegated to smaller supporting roles. Wong seemed to have difficulty in killing off the spurned
Chinese mistress she portrayed in *Dangerous to Know*. This may have
been the last film in which her character committed suicide, and there
were clear signs she was tired of her characters dying on screen so fre-
quently. According to the movie press kit in a press release, morbidly en-

titled, "PRACTICE MAKES WONG'S SUICIDE ALMOST PERFECT," the director, Robert Foley, had to play a recording of Grieg's "Faces of Death" to help Wong "face death more resolutely" in nineteen takes.[31]

Wong rarely enjoyed opportunities to portray the female protagonist until the late 1930s and early 1940s and primarily portrayed characters whose stories were secondary to the romantic narrative central to so many Hollywood films.[32] Of course, her Chinese heritage was part of why Wong received as much international interest and exposure as she did and may have distinguished her from other "B" or even would-be actors in Hollywood. Wong seemed to understand that, in order to "succeed" as an actor—one whose livelihood depended on her ability to project a commodifiable, easily identified image—she would be limited to less desirable, morally questionable characters. She put it succinctly: "As to the medium I am playing in, I have no choice in the matter. One has to take that which is available."[33]

## WHITENESS, ORIENTALISM, AND NATIONALISM

Reflecting the racism and sexism Wong encountered as a Chinese American, the legacies of American orientalism shaped her everyday life. As someone who was so publicly identified with China, moreover, Wong faced the additional impact of international developments, specifically those related to China. The development of Chinese nationalism resulted in more vocal international protests during the 1930s against American and European stereotypes of China and the Chinese that Wong was up against in Hollywood. The complex negotiations of these stereotypes inflected Wong's choices in unexpected ways.

Like that of others, Wong's performance of American orientalism articulated an oppositional cultural identity. It simultaneously enacted the containment of nonwhiteness and the superiority of whiteness. Wong's wry observation about the propensity of her characters to die young and tragically illuminates how Hollywood's racial logic policed interactions between white and nonwhite actors as well as their characters' fate.

### Hollywood's Narrative of White Heterosexual Romance

Hollywood's most established and popular plot narrative is that of the white heterosexual romance—white boy meets white girl, loses girl, wins girl back, and lives with her happily ever after. According to Hollywood's racial logic, and that of American society in general, nonwhites naturally desired whites, while those whites who desired nonwhites were obviously morally and emotionally deficient. Interracial erotic attraction—which was never honest, but based on deception, threats, or violence—inevitably complicated the plot. This diversion from the ultimate "happy ending" consummation of white heterosexual romance was only temporary, however. The white male protagonist's discipline—his mastery over his own or the nonwhite male's deviant desires—ultimately would triumph, demonstrating his moral right to the white female protagonist. As a Chinese American, Anna May Wong was not able to participate fully in portrayals of American femininity and whiteness; true womanhood continued to be defined as white and virtuous, and American orientalism assumed that Chinese (American) women lacked virtue.

Such was the case in Paramount's *Forty Winks* (1925), in which Anna May Wong earned a feature role as the pivotal character, Annabelle Wu (see figure 7). Wu's desire to be white and to win the love of a white man is a central theme in the story, further emphasizing whiteness as fundamental to the central romance between the American heroine and English hero. The screenplay makes stunningly clear the author's perception of a "typical" Asian woman in the scene where Annabelle Wu first appears:

> We intend to characterize Anna as a girl who would give her last drop of blood to be considered a "white" girl. She loves to think of herself as looking thoroughly American. To point this [out], we must make certain that all her dress (negligees, etc.) and her head-dress, in fact everything intimate and personal about her be done in American fashion. [But h]er instinctive reactions are *always* Oriental.[34]

These "Oriental" reactions, according to the screenplay, include wanting to be white and acting in a conniving and duplicitous matter. Yet no matter how much she strives to fashion herself as American in dress and makeup, Anna—as Annabelle appears in the scenario—will always remain innately Oriental.

In one revealing scene, Anna peers into the mirror, then looks intently at the magazine on her dressing room table. An advertisement on the open page promises, "For the thoroughbred American GIRL—a skin as white as milk! You can have it!," and features a full-length figure of the "Typical" American young woman on the margin. Her gaze drawn back to her reflection, Anna frowns at her "brown" arm and, directing her attention again to the mirror, attempts to "massage out her Oriental lines." Finally she reaches for a bottle of lotion, "Malhofsky's Milk-White Magic." Gazing in the mirror, she imitates the pose of the "Typical American girl" pictured on the lotion's label. Annabelle Wu hopes that by achieving whiteness she will also win the love and adoration of Le Sage. But this cannot be. After Le Sage realizes she has failed him in his attempt to blackmail the heroine into marriage, he is furious. "You yellow fool! Do you know what this means to me? It means prison—for life!" When Anna hysterically indicates that they should flee together, his response, as written in the scenario, is to fling her from himself and out of the picture. "You! I hope I may never see your stupid, slant-eyed face again—you damned Chink!"[35]

As the scenario suggests, definitions of femininity and whiteness mutually reinforce each other. White females—with the aid of cosmetics, fashion, and women's magazines—demonstrate femininity in their appearance, dress, and manners.[36] The culmination of white femininity is to be desired by a white Euro-American male who is equally accessible for a heterosexual, romantic relationship and the security of marriage. The screenplay also exemplifies the racial violence that Wong, as the Oriental subject of the camera's gaze, regularly experienced. One film critic ruefully observed that Wong's complexion directly reflected the character of the women she portrayed: "Miss Wong is invariably conscripted when a moving picture demands Oriental intrigue. Her dark beauty appeared sinister by contrast with Nordic fairness of Laura La Plante in *The Chinese Parrot* and Dolores Gatella in *Old San Francisco*. She has been a villainess and a vampire, *but her appearance will never let her be heroine, although occasionally she manages to achieve a sympathetic role.*"[37]

### The Intertextual Oriental

The celebrity-making apparatus of Hollywood extended Wong's romantic life offscreen to "an existence already laid out in films."[38] Wong's hybrid identity formed the basis of her unique star personality: she was the one recognizably Chinese American female in films during the twenties and thirties.[39] Her publicized "personal" life, an essential ingredient of celebrity, only confirmed and entrenched expectations from producers (and possibly even audiences) of the characters Wong could convincingly portray. Wong's conflict of cultures and her attempt to reconcile her American and Chinese backgrounds were central to her picture personality as developed in movie magazines and in her film roles. Articles about Wong in film magazines, then, emphasized similarities, or intertextuality, between Wong's celebrity personality and the characters.

By the 1920s movie magazines marketed at movie fans constituted a particularly important mechanism for perpetuating personalities.[40] Articles about film personalities promised their readers a glimpse into the real life of celebrity and a virtual relationship with particular actors inside and outside the movie theater. Interviews and articles "revealed" personal details of the star's ostensibly private life, individualizing his or her identity. "Reality" in star discourse, as Richard de Cordova notes, is constructed in concert with the fabricated image of the star herself. The actor's thoughts and feelings enter the public sphere only as they are channeled through the star system and subjected to its requirements.[41] Hence publicists serve up stories to fulfill the audience's perceived desire to focus on, and identify with, the celebrity, to find out what made the individual unique and what kept her ordinary.

In this way, they projected onto Wong's private life Americans' fascination with Oriental exoticism and the stereotypical "all-American" (heterosexual) girl's desires of love, romance, and marriage. Discussions of her "real-life" cultural conflict set up a divergence of Chinese and American identities for Wong and the fanzine reader. For example, Wong discussed her family's reaction to her rather un-Chinese choice to become a film actor.[42] "[My father] said I was disgracing his family and all that sort of thing, but I told him that I was determined to be independent some day, that I just couldn't be like the girls who live in China and it was no use trying to make me over."[43] On the one hand, readers might partly identify with Wong's story of wanting to make choices independent of her parents. On the other hand, few readers could identify with the object of Wong's conflict—her Chinese ancestry.

These publications consciously appealed to middle-class and white adolescent women, who constituted the target audience for their advertisers' health and beauty products.[44] Features about Wong affirmed white privilege and heterosexual same-race romantic relationships. The authors—many of them Euro-American women—implied that not being white resulted in suffering, and that any subsequent interracial relationships would be unfulfilling and tragic. In contrast to most movie magazine features, which focused on successful romances, features about Anna May Wong emphasized her romantic failures. A magazine article titled "The Tragic Real Life Story of Anna May Wong," was subtitled "Oriental Beauty Compelled to Choose Between Heritage of Race and Her Preference for an American Husband." Throughout this article the question of why Wong had to choose between race and nationality never presented itself. A caption in the same article read, "Anna May Wong

finds it difficult to keep *her real Chinese self* separate from her westernized personality."[45]

The conspicuous absence of publicized romance, a topic that immediately connoted a private life, became the core of Wong's public image.
Discussions about Wong's romantic life emphasized gendered difference
between the cultures of the West and those of the East. Helen Carlisle of
*Motion Picture Magazine* reported Wong's conjectures about her marital status, heightening her privileged status as confidante and Wong's
Oriental status. "In a burst of confidence, exceedingly rare among her
people, she said to me one day: 'I don't suppose I'll ever marry. Whom
could I marry? Not a man of your race, for he would lose caste among
his people and I among mine.' " Another writer noted that this "strange
problem," which "seemingly has no solution," fastened itself to Wong's
image. "Yet, Hollywood wonders, what true romance—and romance
should go hand in hand with youth—can come to this girl who is a part,
yet not a part?"[46] Melodramatic articles portrayed her as continually divided and terribly lonely. The taboo against interracial romance offscreen translated into the prohibition of on-screen interracial romance
and suggested that Hollywood's form of fulfillment was accessible only
within the discourse of whiteness.

*Performing Orientals*

Wong herself recognized a key distinction between her own embodiment
of difference and Euro-American actors who performed Asians. Discussing her desire to portray the Asian wife of an Englishman in *Java
Head,* she explained, "I know I will never play it. The captain, you see,
*marries* the woman. . . . But no film lovers can ever marry me. If they got
an American actress to slant her eyes and eyebrows and wear a stiff black
wig and dress in Chinese culture, it would be allright. But me? I am really Chinese. So I must always die in the movies, so that the white girl
with the yellow hair may get the man."[47] As Wong acknowledged, her
presence in a film as a publicly and visibly Chinese American actor maintained the distinctions of white/nonwhite in the midst of a perpetual play
on appearance and served as a reminder that markers of Oriental exot-
ica might adorn a non-Asian actor's body but not ultimately affect his or
her innate identity or character.

Hollywood's practice of *yellowface,* or making up Euro-American actors to "look Oriental," manifests another way in which whiteness constrained her opportunities in film. The ideology of whiteness as mani-

fested in the film industry assumed that Euro-American actors were talented enough to perform roles that did not reflect their own identities or experiences; it also assumed that nonwhite actors could not perform roles beyond their social identities and lived experiences. In addition to competing with Euro-American actors for any Asian female protagonist roles, Wong also confronted the devaluation of her performance. For example, when Loretta Young played the Chinese ingenue and protagonist in First National's *The Hatchet Man* (1932), *Photoplay* featured a full-page photo spread, "Loretta Goes Oriental." "Intimate portraits of a smart, young American girl being turned into a Chinese woman" showed Young with adhesive and "fish skin" pulling back her eyes. The caption suggested, "The finished job might make you think Loretta was Anna May Wong." Additional captions explained that it was not necessary to cast a real Chinese "girl" like Anna May Wong because Loretta, who was already under contract with Republic, had made "tests . . . as excellent as the make-up, so they thought you wouldn't know the difference." Yet "they"—the studio—clearly wanted "you"—the audience—to know the difference. The magazine hence discussed and displayed the two-hour process for its readers, differentiating the actor—"a smart, young American girl"—from the Chinese woman she portrayed on screen.[48] Silk robes and a fan complemented Young's makeup of slanted eyes, pale skin, and black hair. These pan-Asian cues—music, lighting, scenery, costumes, and accents—all conveyed an Oriental aesthetic. The feature thus emphasized Young's acting capabilities as an actor and her embodiment of white femininity while simultaneously undermining Wong's acting ability by focusing on her racial identity, implying that Anna May Wong could not overcome the limitations of her racial identity but Young could.

The structuring absence of Chinese American voices in American society that allowed Pearl Buck to locate herself, a Euro-American woman who had lived in China, within the space of being Chinese American functioned similarly in Hollywood. The use of yellowface continued the film industry's tendency to cast Euro-American actors as persons of African, Asian, or Latino heritage. The notion that Euro-American actors could reproduce any culture and ethnicity also presumed cultural superiority: members of "more civilized" cultures could pass as racialized others, but members of "primitive" or "backward" cultures could only *attempt* to do so, with either tragic or comic results, as was the case with Annabelle Wu. Indeed, one of Wong's greatest frustrations was repeatedly witnessing how the few female Asian roles available were awarded to Euro-Americans. For example, although Anna May Wong reportedly was the leading contender for the starring role in the screen adaptation of *The Son-Daughter,* the role was awarded to Helen Hayes.[49]

Moreover, even when Wong gained a role, she was pressed to play it according to directors' preconceptions of Asian mannerisms. Bessie Loo, a Chinese American woman who also worked in the film industry during the thirties and forties, recalled, "there were no important parts . . . for Chinese because they thought Chinese were passive, they did not have any emotions."[50] In most of her speaking roles Wong appeared stiff, her expressions inscrutable, and her voice a monotone.[51] Perceptions about Asian behavior influenced how non-Asian actors portrayed Asian characters as well. Myrna Loy portrayed an "Oriental" slave girl opposite Wong, her fellow inmate of the House of a Thousand Daggers, in the silent film *Crimson City* (1928). Loy, who is not at all inanimate in other roles, appears to have been directed to express little feeling. One reviewer even observed, "Miss Loy has the sloe eyes, the exotic feature which, it would seem, would make her well suited for her role. However, she is strangely unemotional."[52]

American expectations about "Oriental" behavior thus reached beyond casting decisions to restrain Anna May Wong's moving and talking image onscreen. In silent films like *Piccadilly* or *Toll of the Sea,* Wong's expressiveness had distinguished her performances. A change in her carriage and presentation accompanied Wong's transition to the talkies. Wong's acting ability is undeniable in *Shanghai Express,* which provided one of Wong's few sympathetic, complex, and almost heroic roles. Paramount invested this film with the time and resources that would befit a celebrated actor, Dietrich, and an equally respected director, von Sternberg. As a result, Wong's character is more fully developed, providing Wong with the material for one of her best performances.

### The Global Politics of Film Representations

The glowing reviews Wong enjoyed for her work in *Shanghai Express* came from American film critics comfortable with China as a space of marginal morality. Wong confronted different reviews from Chinese already critical of Hollywood and American attitudes toward China. Chinese nationalism became even more internationally focused in the aftermath of the Mukden (Shenyang) Incident of 1931, when Japan occupied Manchuria in northeastern China. In January 1932 the United States, deeply mired in the Depression and isolationism, stated its "Non-Recog-

nition Doctrine," asserting that it would not take sides. In March, Japan
created a puppet state called Manchukuo (Dongbei) and even displayed
Pu Yi, the last Qing emperor, as the head of state. While the League of
Nations did not recognize Manchukuo as an independent state, the
league did not actively oppose Japan's aggression.[53]

Demonstrations against imperialism increasingly pointed out the presence of Western culture that depicted China in less than flattering ways.
Chinese worldwide angrily sought to halt the film depictions of China's
civil strife as a backdrop to foreign romance and adventure. Demonstrations took place in the streets of Chinese cities, and in the campuses
of schools, and in movie theaters. During the filming of *Shanghai Express* one 1932 Chinese newspaper editorial decried that the film, "when
completed, will further expose all evils of Chinese society, and as the Occident knows very little of Chinese and always entertains a contempt for
things Chinese, the pictures always exaggerate the truth." This article entitled, "Paramount Utilizes Anna May Wong to Produce Picture to Disgrace China," reserved its most scathing criticism for Wong. "The Oriental star in Hollywood, Anna May Wong, is working as a featured
player in America. Her specialty is to expose the conduct of the very low
caste of Chinese, such as when she played the part of a half-robed Chinese maid in *The Thief of Bagdad [sic]*. Although she is deficient in artistic portrayal, she has done more than enough to disgrace the Chinese
race."[54]

Chinese officials had long complained about China's depiction by
Hollywood (as early as Harold Lloyd's work in silent films), but Anna
May Wong was the target of particular ire because she herself was Chinese. Chinese speaking the language of nationalism were particularly fluent in translating the effect of gendered images. Half-dressed women
prostitutes reflected on a nation's morals. Just as imperialism relied on
ideas of proper feminine behavior to legitimize colonization as a civilizing project, some Chinese Nationalists—many themselves the products
of Western education and thus doubly inculcated with norms of "proper
civilization"—sought to legitimize the new, modern China through the
representation of Chinese women. As Cynthia Enloe has noted, many
communities seeking to affirm their national stature assign "ideological
weight" to women's clothing, behavior, and sexuality, precisely because
women are viewed as possessions of community, transmitters of culture,
and mothers of the nation.[55]

Hollywood and British film executives assumed that audiences expected a certain representation of Asian women. Because she was of Chi-

nese descent, however, some Chinese interpreted Wong's representation, specifically her sexuality and ethnicity, as a reflection on China. According to Chinese officials, Wong's roles onscreen perpetuated negative stereotypes of Chinese women and damaged China's international reputation. Stereotypes propagated by missionaries in China—that the Chinese hated baby girls, abused and exploited women, and were immoral—flourished in Americans' imaginations. When asked how Wong was perceived in China, General Tu, the Chinese government's official advisor to MGM for *The Good Earth,* replied, "Very bad. Whenever she appears in a film, the newspapers print her picture with the caption: "Anna May Wong again loses face for China." The general himself added, "I feel sorry for her . . . because I realize that she has to play the part assigned her. It is the *parts* China objects to. She is always a slave—*a very undressed slave.* China resents having its womanhood so represented."[56]

As a Chinese American woman performing American orientalism, Wong was caught in crosscurrents of nationalism, racism, and sexism. Paralleling the imperial culture that Helen Callaway describes as functioning through "its cognitive dimension," the American film industry circulated its hierarchy of race and nationhood worldwide through the technology of mass culture and the dominant status of its government.[57] In an attempt to refute negative historical perceptions and images, some Chinese critics further entrenched the gendered division of a masculine nationalism and a feminine propriety and civility.[58]

### An Orientalism Out of Style

Chinese nationalism flourished internationally almost at the same time that Americans were introduced to a different, more intimate and familiar, portrayal of Chinese. The popularity of Pearl Buck's *The Good Earth* and the developing sympathy for Chinese in their struggle against Japan offered Anna May Wong the possibility of more positive, realistic roles. Even so, Wong's own film history, the configuration of race within Hollywood, and the Chinese Nationalist government's international activism prevented Wong from taking advantage of increasingly positive American attitudes toward China.

Unlike the actively manipulative Chinese or Asian temptress, Buck's female protagonist, O-lan, is a loyal peasant who suppresses her private needs to meet those of her family and provides the novel's moral center. In 1933 rumors circulated in the Los Angeles papers that Wong would portray O-lan. Instead the 1935 film production featured the white actors Paul Muni and Luise Rainer as Wang Lung and his wife O-lan. Wong was invited to audition only for the role of Lotus, the manipulative song girl who enthralls Wang Lung, enters O-lan's home as the second wife, seduces the eldest son, and contributes to the disintegration of Wang's family.

Lotus was the epitome of orientalized womanhood, as described in the casting notes: "A very beautiful and sensuous girl of twenty. And let's have her sensuous. Most stunning figure in the picture." In contrast, O-lan, the role Wong wanted to play, was "By no means a beautiful woman, but with kindly eyes and mouth. A slave girl type."[59] Had Wong been cast as Lotus, her location as a Chinese American within the film's hierarchy of actors would have remained the same as her previous roles. Not only would Wong's character threaten the marriage of O-lan and Wang Lung, but as an actor of Chinese descent, she also would threaten the racial unity of Muni and Rainer. For the film audience, Wong's previous roles as an Asian woman trying through feminine and Oriental cunning to ensnare the (often white) male protagonist—would provide the audience enough context to define the character of Lotus.

Reports regarding the casting of Lotus differ.[60] After her return from China, Wong claimed that she refused to play "the only unsympathetic role in a picture featuring an all-American cast portraying Chinese characters."[61] Still, notes from the first screen test were less than glowing: Wong was "a little disappointing as to looks. Does not seem beautiful enough to make Wang' [sic] infatuation convincing."[62] A second test report four days later sympathetically stated that Wong "[d]eserves serious consideration as possibility for Lotus—[but] NOT as beautiful as she might be."[63] Regina Crewe, film editor and critic for the *New York American* suggested that Wong was not offered the role, observing, "While she doesn't say so, it must have been a keen disappointment to Anna May Wong. After taking dozens of tests for the role of the Second Wife in *The Good Earth*, the role was given to [the German actor] Tilly Losch. The producer said Anna May Wong wasn't the type."[64]

Although Wong attempted to develop her own films set in China, potential censorship by the Chinese Nationalist government proved a deterrent to Hollywood studios. From 1936 through 1938, Chinese Nationalist officials filed numerous complaints with United States consulate in China protesting Hollywood's depiction of immoral females, lawless bandits, and corrupt officials. Censorship, boycotts, or an outright ban of Hollywood films targeted the economic stake American studios had in the global distribution of their films.[65] Repeated threats by the Chinese

Nationalist Board of Film Censors to prohibit American films after *The General Died at Dawn, The Bitter Tea of General Yen,* and *Oil for the Lamps of China* resulted in Paramount, Universal, and other studios' shying away from producing films set in Asia. Whereas Hollywood studios protested that depictions of Chinese bandits, rebels, and traitors were not specifically meant to reflect on China as a nation, Wong defended the Chinese officials' concerns. "I can understand why the government officials are so earnest about this censorship idea . . . because they are self-conscious and want people to see their best side, not their worst."[66] However, the studios' hesitation to produce films set in China and Asia even further limited potential roles for Wong.

Chinese nationalism and Hollywood ageism converged to prevent Wong from portraying the positive Chinese roles she had lobbied for and sought out during much of her career. At the age of thirty she was no longer considered beautiful enough to play the song girl Lotus but was too overexposed as an exotic Oriental beauty to portray the peasant O-lan. Nor could Wong easily shift from ingenue to mature roles: Hollywood's Chinese female roles were either highly sexualized as young femme fatales and seductresses or defeminized as overbearing and manipulative dowagers. Wong could not convincingly play either.

## TRANSFORMATIONS

To achieve her goal of acting in films, Wong put aside her views and participated in Hollywood's representations of China and Chinese. She dutifully fulfilled the publicity demands of her film career by describing what it was like to be Chinese for the movie-going public. Wong's comments were mediated by interviewers, editors, and film studio publicists. Wong's recollections in her stylized autobiographical articles and early interviews strikingly emphasize her attempts to define her American identity in reaction to her Chinese heritage. Yet certain patterns emerge. Reflecting orientalist perceptions that one could not be both Chinese and American simultaneously, Wong early in her career described her identity in dichotomous terms. She was becoming less "Chinese" and assimilating as an American. Indeed, entering the film industry was a central part of her increasing Americanization.

### Becoming Chinese American

Socialization, assimilation, and orientalism figure in Anna May Wong's own narratives of development. Read as autobiography, interviews and

articles in motion picture magazines from the 1920s to 1930s trace Anna
May Wong's negotiations of American orientalism, Hollywood celebrity,
and Chinese American femininity. These stories constitute one of the ear-
liest autobiographical accounts of an American-born woman of Chinese
descent published for mass circulation.[67] Wong's insights reflect the pop-
ularization of *assimilation* as a concept that explained generational differences in self-identity according to cultural heritage or place of birth.

Wong's discussions about her family, coupled with a critique of male
privilege in Chinese tradition, challenge the patterns of silence and assimilation associated with the Chinese American community.[68] At the beginning of her film career in the 1920s, Anna May Wong's ambivalence
toward her Chinese heritage often emerged in her refusal to accept what
she understood to be traditional and Chinese gender norms. One of the
Chinese traditions she emphasized was the importance placed on having
sons.[69] "[W]hen father found out that his first child was a girl he was so
disgusted that he didn't come home for days, mother says!" Wong also
critiqued the cultural expectations regarding women within the Chinese
American community. Because a majority of first- and second-generation
Chinese American men, wanting a "traditional wife," married women
born in China, marital prospects for Chinese American women were limited. Wong explained to one journalist, "A Chinese friend, American-
trained, told me he'll never marry anyone except a native Chinese
woman, 'because I want a real wife!' There you have it. The two women
are miles apart. The men choose the hausfrau rather than the companion."[70] Additionally, racism manifest in antimiscegenation laws discouraged marriage between Chinese American women and Euro-
American men, further limiting the women's marriage prospects.

The differences between the daughter and her parents were yet another manifestation of the conflicts brought on by different degrees of acculturation, as well as changing expectations of women's roles. Anna
May Wong rarely spoke about her mother in an active sense and credited family decisions and discipline to her father. She recognized that her
goals and opportunities in life would be very different from her mother's.
Lee Gon Toy was very young when a marriage broker in San Francisco
picked her to be Sam Sing Wong's second wife.[71] As second wife, she may
have wielded less authority in family matters than her husband's first
wife and first son, even though that wife and Wong's half brother remained in China. Like other first-generation Chinese female immigrants
in Los Angeles, Toy worked very hard and experienced a growing distance between her and her Americanized children. Her primary role car-

ing for the children, maintaining the household, and helping her husband with the laundry monopolized her time. Chinese cultural expectations that women remain secluded from the public eye limited her ability to learn English. Her children translated American society and culture for her, but ultimately their different experiences would widen the gap. Wong was sure her mother "was content to have us grow up as Americanized-children, but father wasn't," and yet her mother was deeply concerned about her daughter wanting to be in front of the cameras—which Wong attributed to cultural superstitions.[72] The communication gap between her and her children paralleled the age gap between her and her husband. Based on the 1910 and 1920 censuses, Wong's parents were over two decades apart in age.[73]

Early in her career, Wong demonstrated her fluency in the popular rhetoric of marginality often imposed on the children of immigrants and even more so on those perceived as racially different. Exposed to the changing gender expectations in American society, she expressed her desire for independence and a companionate marriage.[74] Wong contrasted her ideal marriage with her parent's marriage, incorporating popular images of Chinese women to distinguish between Chinese and American romantic relationships. "I have never found a Chinese man whom I could love. With us, the woman is slave, the man master. I've been educated as American girls are. My work has fostered independence in me. I couldn't live as my mother always has, under the domination of my father. I don't believe that woman is an inferior creature. How can I?"[75] In this interview, Wong affirmed for mainstream audiences the American discourse of orientalism that idealized U.S. women's independence by contrasting them to the slavish position of women in China. Her comments about her mother, both sympathetic and critical, unmistakably reflect the influence of the American society in which she participated.

Wong's public critiques of Chinese male privilege and her declarations of individual freedom also alienated her from some within her ethnic community. Her presumed insider's pronouncements on Chinese culture often echoed mainstream American perceptions and seemed to justify continued prejudice against Chinese Americans. For example, she reinforced the perception of Chinese males as domestic despots and Chinese females as long-suffering, passive wives. Wong's observations of male favoritism within the Chinese family were published in newspapers' arts and entertainment sections or movie magazines. As a female in a "disgraceful" profession, Wong was not recognized as someone who had the right to speak for the Chinese American community. Yet she enjoyed access to mainstream America that was unattainable to most Chinese Americans or Chinese until the Second World War. San Francisco Chinese American leaders, in fact, founded their own English-language newspaper, the *Chinese Press,* in response to the neglect of the mainstream press.[76]

## Claiming Rights and Freedoms

The historian Sucheng Chan has suggested that, in the Chinese American community, second-generation males viewed their experiences in terms of "rights" whereas second-generation females viewed their experiences in terms of "freedom," incorporating the appropriate language of "American-ness" according to their respective gender.[77] For Anna May Wong, her father's attempts to discipline her and her mother's own isolation represented the lack of freedom for Chinese women. Wong's career as an actor, however, also challenged the rights allowed Chinese Americans in American society. Her ability to comment publicly about these issues, even if obliquely, reflected her particular location as an actor of Chinese descent. Female film actors necessarily negotiated public expectations of femininity and womanhood both on- and offscreen. As a Chinese American actor whose career was shaped by and relied on a visible public presence, Wong additionally confronted the withholding of certain rights allowed to Chinese Americans in public discourse and civic life.

Critical of both Chinese expectations of gender and American expectations of race, Wong revealed a heightened consciousness of her Chinese American identity and the ways in which this identity had been shaped by dominant perceptions. In a 1926 interview she addressed distorted American perceptions of Chinese Americans. Wong acknowledged that most Americans perceived Chinatowns to be mysterious but noted that, because, "I mingled with the people there. . . . I accepted it as a matter of course." She reminded readers that Chinatowns were neighborhoods with people, not exotic, mysterious locales. "I was glad my parents didn't live in Chinatown," she admitted, "but only as any child might be glad to live in a house with lawns and gardens around it rather than a crowded tenement."[78] By naming Chinatown as a crowded tenement, Wong humanized the community by comparing it to other urban immigrant enclaves and drew attention to the economic circumstances that forced many recent immigrants to live in densely populated urban communities. Wong additionally normalized what was familiarly an exotic site for most readers.

As her film career continued but substantial roles failed to materialize, Wong began to question the constraints of American orientalism and to complicate her narrative of freedoms some Chinese American women experienced with a discussion of rights denied to Chinese American women and men because of racism. Unable to articulate these questions in her acting, Wong instead turned to the very film magazines that helped establish her identity as a Chinese American celebrity. With the access her visibility accorded, Wong inserted her own voice into the discourse of American orientalism.

### Questioning Images

Throughout the 1930s Anna May Wong increasingly challenged the conventions of celebrity by using her personal interviews to counter the assumptions inherent in her own films. In an interview with an American journalist about her experiences in Europe, Wong commented on race prejudice in the United States when she explained why she enjoyed Europe so much—she "found absolutely no race prejudice in Europe. That's one reason why I was so happy there." Wong added, "there everyone was lovely to me. That is not always true of America."[79]

Indeed, Wong's first Hollywood film on her return from London was Paramount's *Daughter of the Dragon* (1931), which yet again focused on her character's forbidden love for an Englishman. In an interview with the magazine writer Audrey Rivers, however, Wong framed the film's conclusion in a radically different way by emphasizing that she had been forbidden from sharing a kiss onscreen with her English co-star, because "it is *against the law*." Wong's discussion of California's antimiscegenation law, effective since 1880, countered the film's message that Chinese culture was too alien to allow a happy ending. Rivers sympathetically noted the irony of Wong's "inability" to be kissed on film because of her race, "even though she has become so Westernized that she is now almost a stranger to her own race. She thinks in terms of penthouses and speeding cars, not in terms of bamboo huts and ox-carts. She revels in the freedom of the Western woman—in clothes, in habits, in speech."[80] While Rivers deployed Oriental tropes of primitive technology and female subordination to describe Wong's "race," Wong's comments about the forbidden kiss provided a critique of institutionalized racism: even if a Chinese American woman enjoyed the cultural freedom to marry whomever she chose, racist state laws restricted her legal right to marry a white person. Wong thus maintained a boundary between her roles as Asian female victims and her identity as a Chinese American woman who valued independence.

By 1933 Wong also challenged the cultural norm of marriage constituting the primary goal for women. Publicly stating her age as twenty-six—well past the age at which women were expected to marry but two years younger than her actual age—Wong denied speculation that her single status was the tragic result of her seemingly alien status. Significantly, Wong neither relied on Chinese stereotypes nor expressed her independent status in terms of Americanization. She explained her single status as an expression of freedom from gender norms in both the Chinese and American communities. "This is the way I feel about it. Either you settle down and make a home or you don't, in which case it is better not to marry, I think, for it is hardly fair to the man or yourself to live impermanently and always with another interest which must come first. I still want to rove a bit."[81] Remaining single for the sake of one's individual fulfillment did not impart the melodrama of forbidden romance and challenged traditional Chinese and American notions of femininity and womanhood.

Wong also became increasingly frank about her film roles and the ways in which they disrupted the plot. One London journalist, for example, included Wong's theory on why she had to die so often. "Because," Wong explained, "on the screen it is very necessary to do something conclusive with any personality that's all glamorous or exotic. One cannot leave them just floating around. They are *too* definite."[82] Wong recognized that the marketability of her image relied on the glamour, mystery, and allure associated with her racial identity. Since racial difference rendered her characters inassimilable and threatened the white heterosexual narrative of romance featured in a majority of Hollywood films, her characters had to be eliminated.

In 1933 before going to England for another assignment, Wong expressed her frustration over the limited and poor quality of the roles offered to her. "After going through so many experiences of roles that don't appeal to me, I have come to the point of finding it all pretty futile to repeat poor things. I feel that by now I have earned the right to have a little choice in the parts I play."[83] Wong reportedly told reporters she "would never play again in a film which showed the Chinese in an unsympathetic light." In London for the filming of *Tiger Bay*, a Wyndham Films film that reportedly featured "her first sympathetic part," Wong aired her grievances in an exclusive interview with the respected British film journalist Doris Mackie.[84] This article, assertively titled "I Protest," allowed the actor to articulate her frustration with Hollywood. "You see I was so tired of the parts I had to play. . . . Why is it that the screen Chinese is nearly always the villain of the piece? . . . Why should we always scheme-rob-kill? I got so weary of it all—of the scenarist's conception of Chinese character—that I told myself I was done with the films forever."[85]

Nonetheless, Anna May Wong continued to seek opportunities for herself. A frequent traveler to Europe, and a well-traveled celebrity worldwide, she found more receptive audiences and in the process recreated her image and kept up her visibility within American society. Her adept fashioning of herself in relation to American cultural trends enabled her, in a limited way, to circumvent American orientalism.

AN OCCIDENTAL ASIAN

Anna May Wong joined an out-migration of performers of color when she traveled abroad. From the 1920s American culture infused by the Harlem Renaissance expanded its horizons artistically as well as geographically. The resulting outflow of talent consisted primarily of African Americans, most notably artists like Josephine Baker and Paul Robeson, who similarly performed throughout Europe before more appreciative audiences. Within this transatlantic flow of talent, Wong distinguished herself with her unique status of "being Oriental" and American at the same time, continually surpassing expectations with her modern flapper style and wry sense of humor.[86]

*Travel*

Anna May Wong first discovered travel's transformative potential in the late 1920s. According to Wong's account, she met Dr. Karl Vollmoller, a German author, in Hollywood. After he returned to Berlin in 1927 Vollmoller arranged for a German studio to hire her for a feature role. Wong traveled outside the United States for the first time in 1928 when she sailed to Germany. There she starred in three silent films.[87] After completing those films, Wong sailed to England in late 1928 to star in *Piccadilly* for British International.[88]

*Piccadilly* was a triumph for Wong as well as for the British film in-

dustry. This 1929 silent black and white film received accolades as one
of the best British films yet produced. Wong's animated performance in
*Piccadilly* as the sensuous dancer who eventually is murdered also received great praise. British film magazine writers congratulated themselves on appreciating Wong and wondered at the racism of Hollywood
for overlooking her ability. Their country had little experience of Chinese immigration, and this attractive Chinese American woman posed no
economic or social threat. The British journalist E. O. Hoppe described
her as both "essentially Chinese," and "an American citizen," which
most British journalists found intriguing.[89] Thus the racial difference that
marginalized Wong in Hollywood contributed to her greater visibility
within the British film industry.[90]

Still, Anna May Wong's popularity in Britain owed as much to the politics of the film industry as it did to her talent at marketing herself as a
unique personality. From the 1910s onward American film studios had
been staking greater claims in the global market and, by the 1920s, dominated almost all foreign markets. The popular belief in film's power to
shape perceptions and attitudes gave the prominence of American films
added weight. The high quality of production and the well established
celebrity-making machine of Hollywood would not be easily shaken, so
foreign governments increasingly began to create their own censorship
bureaus to screen films and to delay distribution to theaters in their respective nations until Hollywood studios met their demands to amend
anything that might be offensive to their audiences. Because the cost to
studios of reshooting or paying the screening fees to qualify for exhibition in foreign markets, including China, Italy, Germany, and Great
Britain, was prohibitive, economic factors gave those governments' representatives to Hollywood leverage to influence derogatory depictions of
their nations and peoples during film production. In addition, as European, Asian, and Latin American nationalism thrived, and concerns over
the power of films in shaping social interactions and values increased,
governments developed national film boards to encourage the production
of films that would affirm the culture and values of their own nations.[91]

As early as the mid-1920s, only 5 percent of films exhibited in British
territories had been produced in Britain. In addition to challenging national values, foreign-made films constituted threats to the domestic
economy—particularly American films that flaunted American consumerism and advertised American-made products. In 1927 Parliament
passed the Cinematograph Films Act, requiring that a certain number of
British films be shown in British theaters.[92] In response to this political

and economic measure, British theater owners demanded more films from British studios. The determination of British film studios to compete with American films in Britain provided a wealth of opportunities for Wong in London. In this context, Wong was able to employ her race, gender, and nationality to achieve in Europe—especially Great Britain— a celebrity status that had eluded her in Hollywood. It would in turn bring her better film roles in the United States.

Wong's critiques of American racism in the British press, as accurate as they may have been, also served the ideological needs of the British state. British journalists' emphasis on an American's experience of American racism obscured Great Britain's imperial practice of colonization and equally racist attitudes. Representing the largest share of the U.S. foreign market for film distribution and exhibition with its aggregate colonies—by the early thirties, for example, Britain represented 30 percent of Hollywood's foreign market[93]—British authorities had considerable influence on Hollywood's standards of morality. In 1928, for example, the Hong Kong censor banned any film subjects that included anti-British propaganda or depicted white men "using violence or in a state of degradation in native surroundings," or in "equivocal situations between men of one race and girls of another race." The racism and sexism that Wong criticized in Hollywood films was apparently as transnational as the film industry itself.

## European Style

Yet unlike Americans, who viewed her Chinese American identity as a liability, European audiences seemed to appreciate the complexity of her identity. When she made her London stage debut in *Circle of Chalk* in 1929 and was criticized for her flat voice, Wong worked with a vocal coach to improve her speaking voice and adopted a cultured English accent in the process.[94] During Wong's return to England in 1930 the columnist Margery Collier observed that Wong combined stereotypes of both Chinese and American women and featured "the face and figure of a Chinese girl and the mind of an American flapper."[95] The novelty of exotic appearance, careful speech, and carefree manner contributed to Europeans' fascination with Anna May Wong. Ironically, while Wong's celebrity inspired Oriental fashions in England, with women powdering their faces to "get the 'Wong complexion' " and "[g]orgeously-embroidered coolie coats" became the rage among the theater set, Wong herself wore "the smartest Paris clothes."[96] Photographs of Wong in Berlin and

in London show her continental attire and elegant companions; her
scrapbooks indicate an avid social life, attending sports events and the
theater. She was a modern cosmopolitan whose hybridity could not be
easily categorized.

Whereas audiences in Europe marveled at her ability to be simultaneously American and Chinese, those in the United States perceived
her as more cultured, sophisticated, and Western after her sojourn in
Europe. Wong confided to American movie magazine writers how
people told her she had "changed so much since my European experience, and that I don't look like a Chinese girl anymore. . . . My face
has changed because my soul has changed. I think like the people of
the West."[97] Another article credited Europe with transforming her.
"The Chinese flapper has an English accent now. She thinks in Western terms. Her manners, her dress, her humor, her attitude, are Western. She loves tea—but an English brand. Her face no longer looks
very Chinese."[98]

The cosmopolitan cachet that attached itself to Wong's image after
her success in Europe and England appealed to Americans' nouveau-
riche consumerism. A long fascination with Europe as more cultured
and sophisticated than the United States, and many Americans' emotional bond with England as their country's ideological and cultural
predecessor made Wong a star worthy of attention in the United
States. And it certainly enhanced her appeal in Hollywood. Thus
Paramount signed her to star in its 1931 film, *The Daughter of the
Dragon.* An article announcing her return to Hollywood stated that
"Wong was the toast of the continent, according to stories brought
back by film players who visited Europe. She made appearances in England, Germany and France."[99] *Picturegoer Weekly* also featured a
story on her return from Europe, declaring, "After playing subordinate parts in many American silent films this child of squalid Chinatown, who later became the glamorous toast of Europe, has returned
to Hollywood to try her luck in Talkies."[100] Throughout her career
Wong traveled between Europe and the United States. At the end of
1931 she recrossed the Atlantic to spend a year and a half in England
and other parts of Europe, performing vaudeville throughout the
British Isles and making four films. In 1934, after making only one
film in the United States, the disappointing *Limehouse Blues,* Wong
once again returned to Europe, where she already enjoyed popularity
and recognition.

*Oriental Mystique*

On this return trip to England, Wong consciously chose to exoticize herself even more as an "Oriental" celebrity. After *Picturegoer* reported that Wong received (but refused) an offer from "an Eastern plastic surgeon, who said he could take the slant out of her eyes, thereby allowing her to play European roles," perhaps it made sense to transform what some perceived as her "liability" into marketability.[101] One of her mentors, Rob Wagner, had suggested that Wong could actively increase her value in the culture of film and celebrity by "being different." "Among other things," Wagner recalled, "I urged her to 'can' her Hollywood feathers and be Chinese. I suggested that she even burn incense in her hotel room, to add to her exotic charm."[102] Wong followed Wagner's advice and, by all accounts, provoked curiosity, attention, and acclaim in Europe.

Rejecting the pathologies the American public associated with the Chinese, Wong drew on more exotic qualities in her self-representation. Vivien North described for the British readers of *Picturegoer Weekly* the mysterious quality surrounding the actor, "sitting there against the Oriental background of her room, with its bowls of big flowers, its mirrors and soft lighting, her hands—with their lacquered finger nails matching the Chinese red of her jumper—folded, her ankles crossed and every feature composed—almost physically feeling her complete stillness."[103] John K. Newnham noted Wong's ability to emphasize both the American and Chinese aspects of her identity in her self-promotion and suggested that Wong's unique combination of American initiative and Asian allure enabled her to "play Hollywood's game well. She retains a deliberate atmosphere of subtle mystery. There is always a faint aroma of perfume about her. But in her conversation and outlook on life, she is smartly Western. No genuine Chinese woman could boast the attribute she possesses: women haven't been emancipated long enough in China. So you can see," Newnham continued, "why Anna May Wong is so unique and why she can always step back to starring roles. She has a corner which is uniquely her own."[104]

Newnham's shrewd analysis suggested that Wong succeeded because she could use her multiple identifications to locate herself in the unique position of representing Chinese even as she maintained a Western outlook. Presenting herself in self-consciously orientalist fashion, Wong relied on a racialized identity to establish the uniqueness of her star persona. Although this strategy appears to contradict her earlier claims of realistically portraying China, Wong may also have persuaded herself that the exotic China she evoked was indeed authentic.[105] Wong's willing participation in the Occident's orientalism provided her with a public platform in London from which to critique the treatment and perceptions of Chinese Americans in the United States.

*Performing American*

On her stage tours throughout Europe, Wong exploited her perceived hybridity, exotic orientalism, and marginal status in Hollywood in order to appeal to the audiences' ambivalent fascination with American culture.[106] On the European stage, Wong performed vaudeville, cabaret, and dramatic monologues, many of which referred to "the Orient." She performed a scene from *Madama Butterfly*, for example, and made witty observations about the racism she faced in Hollywood. She then would sing Noël Coward's "Half-Caste Woman," the first-person lament of a Eurasian woman whose livelihood is based on prostitution and who is valued solely for her sexuality.[107] She ended her performance with a dramatic monologue inspired by her role as a Chinese courtesan in *Shanghai Express*. The choice of songs and monologues illustrates how Wong incorporated audiences' perceptions of her as a celebrity into her performance.

In Europe Wong enjoyed better production values and more studio attention to her as a "star." Her privileged status as a celebrity in Great Britain may have led her to assume that there was very little racism in British society itself. But British studios did not challenge dominant white fantasies. The "more humane characters" that she portrayed—with deeply expressed love, loyalty unto death—enjoyed feature status and more screen time without altering her ultimately treacherous or sinister Oriental nature. During the 1930s, however, with British-produced films no longer protected by British law, Wong's British roles would plummet. Simultaneously, the politics of Hollywood's foreign markets in Asia would lead most American film studios to halt any projects set in China.

BACK TO CHINA

In 1935, after she was turned down for *The Good Earth*, Wong again turned to travel to refashion her career. This time, in an attempt to capitalize on the growing popularity of China in the United States, Wong decided to visit China. On December 16, less than two days after her second casting test for *The Good Earth,* Wong applied for a reentry certificate (required of all American-born Chinese on their return to the United States) at the Immigration and Naturalization Service in San Pedro. In a letter written December 28, 1935, to a devoted fan, Wong reported, "I am leaving for China on the 21st of January to stay there a year and study the Mandarin dialect and Chinese Theatre, and I hope that I will be able to bring back something quite unusual."[108] Wong told an interviewer that she needed to "find out if my interpretations of China were truly Chinese."[109] It appears that Anna May Wong decided to develop her roles on her own terms and gain the legitimacy to do so through experiencing China firsthand.

## Returning to "the Homeland"

Anna May Wong's visit to China in 1936 reflected a trend among second-generation Chinese Americans who left the economically depressed United States for China in order to improve their professional careers. Modernizing China offered possibilities for career development that the United States, through a combination of racial prejudice and a weak economy, could not. Like other Chinese Americans, Wong's connection to China was shaped by the widespread feeling that Chinese were not citizens but temporary visitors who would return to China. While en route she wrote, "I am going to a strange country, and yet, in a way, I am going home. I have never seen China, but somehow I have always known it. . . . Chinese in the United States suffer from a lifelong homesickness, and this somehow is communicated to their children, even though the children know nothing about their ancestral homeland."[110] Her father's immigrant nostalgia for "home" had led him to retire in China and further inspired his daughter to follow him there.

In traveling to China, Wong—like other Chinese Americans—was understandably uneasy. "I'm awful anxious to visit my ancestral town. It will be a strange experience—my native Chinese feelings and my acquired American feelings. In a way I'll be more of a foreigner there than a full-blooded American."[111] The marginalization of Chinese Americans in the United States encouraged them to "return" to China in the hope of better opportunities and lives, of finding a place to belong. An estimated one-fifth of American-born Chinese traveled to China during the 1930s, intending to apply their professional training to the building of new China.[112]

Wong's alienation from the Chinese American community and Chinese culture also contributed to her ambivalence. She once voiced a reluctance to visit the homeland. "It would be rather embarrassing," she said, "because in China actors are regarded as the lowest note in the human scale—lower than coolies."[113] At a farewell dinner right before the trip, Wong recalled what she termed "strong race memories." Not only had her father repeatedly told her that actors were held in low regard, "most degrading of all, she had appeared in pictures nearly nude. Even old Wong [her father] was distressed over that. So her feelings were very mixed."[114]

When Wong traveled to China, she invited the American public also to discover China through the eyes of the media. Photographers snapped pictures of her setting sail, newsreel cameras captured her leaving the ship, and the *New York Herald Tribune* published a series of six columns she wrote about her first experiences traveling through Asia. Wong's retelling suggests that the journey was about seeking her own identity, propelled by the feeling that she did not fully belong to the American society in which she had been born and lived her life. "I am very proud of being an American; for years," she added, "when people have asked me to describe 'my' native country, I've surprised them by saying it is a democracy composed of forty-eight states. But I've always been aware of another country, just as I have never forgotten that my real name is Wong Lui [sic] Tsong, which means 'Frosted Yellow Willow.'"[115] In Hawaii, Wong noted "how happy the Chinese residents are . . . and how freely they share in community life." In contrast, Wong remarked, Chinese in America "often are isolated, not because of any deep prejudice, but because Americans regard them as a dark, mysterious race, impossible to understand."[116]

Yet Wong's expectations of China were just as distorted as those of most Americans and her hopes of finding a China opposite to the modernity of the United States were not immediately fulfilled. On the ship's second stop, in Tokyo, Wong admitted that she was "conscious of a growing nostalgia for the East I failed to find." Instead, she encountered automobiles on crowded city streets and modern department stores. When she finally came upon a Buddhist temple, its priest wore "a very foreign frock coat" and she could hear a "strangely familiar . . . 'Onward Christian Soldier,' adapted to Japanese words." Surprised by the manifestations of modernity and Western culture, Wong decided that she had "not yet found the serene spiritual tempo I had hoped to discern in the East."[117]

The locale imagined by some Americans, including Wong herself, as "the East"—inspired by Pearl Buck's writings in the 1930s—did not exist. The ocean liner that transported Wong followed established routes that had already facilitated the exchange of technology and culture. Indeed, Wong wrote of her second night in Shanghai at the Cathay Tower: "The nightclub is managed by a German, who proudly produced autographs of Marlene Dietrich and Lillian Harvey. There was an American orchestra and the star entertainer was a Filipino. So, this was China!" Wong's travelogue, begun as one "feeling suspended between two worlds," now seemed a trip from the familiar to more—even an excess—of the same. "Blinking with astonishment I'm hastily revising my early mental pictures," Wong admitted. "But undoubtedly," she added with some hope, "the hinterland is still true to ancient ways."[118]

While in China, Wong confronted the limits of her identification with China. Greeted at Shanghai by reporters, Wong, who did not speak Mandarin but Cantonese, "had the strange experience of talking to my own people through an interpreter."[119] In many ways, her imagined China was a China imagined by her fellow Americans—an alternative to the "modernity" of the West, a sense of timelessness expressed by novelists like Pearl Buck or a site of primitive simplicity evoked by some missionaries and diplomats. Wong's bewilderment at the modernity manifested by "the East"—the factories and pollution of Tokyo, Kyoto, and Shanghai, the cosmopolitanism of the cities and sophistication of their inhabitants—demonstrates how American orientalism could not imagine China's confronting the same issues of urbanization and industrialization as the United States.

Yet even the hinterland had surprises in store. On arriving at the small town where her father lived, at some distance from the cities and their international milieu, Anna May Wong discovered that he was now "homesick for America." She remarked, "Can you imagine Dad, who was supposed to be an old-fashioned Chinaman, impatient to teach the villagers American ways?" Her father found that what he thought he desired was no longer what he wanted. While some Chinese returned to China to retire, others, like the elder Wong, found the "homeland" jarringly unfamiliar. As Wong insisted, "I did not go to *see* China, but to *feel* it."[120] The "homeland" served an emotional and psychological need so long as it was indeed imagined to remain familiar and the same, always offering an alternative to one's present circumstances.

## An American in China

A newspaper account confirmed Wong's anxieties: the homeland did not recognize her as Chinese. "Although Anna May was born in California, she felt that her first visit to Cathay was going home. She soon found, however, that in the 'flowery Republic' she was regarded as an American, just as in Hollywood she is considered an Oriental."[121] Even though she was the daughter of a Chinese laundryman and had not completed high school, Wong had achieved the socioeconomic level of Chinese elite. Lacking a formal education, she purportedly mastered several languages and kept herself informed on political and social issues. In America, her rise from humble beginnings was perceived as positive and embedded into Wong's public history, her celebrity myth. In China, Wong's less than illustrious pedigree, hybrid-national status, and profession—to say nothing of her roles—probably lowered her status among government officials, who tended to come from wealthy families and received college educations abroad at prestigious institutions. Wong's global celebrity status, then, was viewed as particularly odd, peculiarly American, and somewhat offensive by the Chinese elites who, although Westernized in many ways, maintained a quasi-nationalism based almost as much in elitism as in national pride.

Additionally, Wong's celluloid image had preceded her and now influenced how she was received in China as a Chinese American actor. The Kuomintang (KMT) government issued an invitation for Wong to visit the Department of Cinematography in Nanjing, where KMT officials censored Hollywood and other foreign films. Wong wrote with enthusiasm, "This is an unusual honor and one which I shall certainly accept."[122] Again, what she found there startled her. Even though she was presumably a "guest of honor" of government officials in Nanjing, they did not simply welcome her to China. "They made speeches that lasted for four hours. . . . They all took turns berating me for the roles I had played." Wong apparently did not protest their complaints; she herself had expressed frustration at American films' unsympathetic portrayal of Chinese. "I told them that when a person is trying to get established in a profession, he can't choose parts. He had to take what is offered. I said I had come to China to learn, and that I hoped I would be able to interpret our country in a better light. It all ended with their apologizing to me!"[123]

But Wong also noted a double standard held by the Chinese officials toward Hollywood and herself. As an actor of Chinese descent, Wong realized she had been singled out by Chinese officials for seeming to legit-imize the negative caricatures of Chinese on film. As a woman of Chi-nese descent Wong faced the burden of being taken seriously as an actor and as a Chinese American she faced the additional obstacle of being typecast in roles that played up Western stereotypes of China. She ob-served that the Swedish actor Warner Oland had received a very differ-ent reception when he arrived in China. "No one thought of bringing up his evil past as a Chinese villain . . . in *Daughter of the Dragon*," she pointed out. Oland benefited from portraying a popular, intelligent, al-beit somewhat effeminate and highly orientalized Chinese sleuth, Char-lie Chan. Yet as an actor of non-Chinese descent, he clearly was per-forming a role.

American concerns with race and Chinese concerns with nationalism converged to pick apart Anna May Wong's image. Wong knew that American audiences might not be prepared to see a different side of the Chinese than they expected or were accustomed to, and that studios might not be willing to invest the time and effort necessary to produce alternative perceptions of the Chinese. At the same time her own posi-tion in China was equivocal. As one of the few Chinese American women known worldwide, Wong perpetuated images of the Chinese that her hosts deplored; yet their reception of her implicitly acknowl-edged that power to influence audiences worldwide. Intent on main-taining national prestige and honor, the Chinese officials were fasci-nated by American celebrity and cosmopolitan society. Wong's international visibility as an actor of Hollywood was an asset to the Na-tionalist government, and she encountered official receptions through-out China.[124]

## Embodying New China

On returning to the United States in 1936, Wong incorporated China's critique of Hollywood portrayals into her American image, both behav-ing and appearing more decorously and visibly Chinese. When she re-turned from China, as a symbol of cultural pride she abandoned the lat-est American or European fashions in favor of gowns that Chinese women were wearing.[125] She continued to sign her name in Chinese char-acters—no longer as a means of exoticizing her image, but now as an ex-pression of pride in her Chinese heritage.

At the same time Americans expressed increasingly positive atti-tudes toward China. The image of the Chinese had improved as a re-

sult of positive portrayals in Pearl Buck's novels, the positive response
to China's struggle against the Japanese, and the efforts of missionaries returned from China.[126] Hollywood's transition from Fu Manchu
to Charlie Chan in 1931 illustrates the shift.[127] More human characterizations of Chinese Americans emerged: Charlie Chan's eldest son,
the Chinese American Lee Chan (played by the Chinese American
actor Keye Luke), was introduced to the profitable Chan series in
1935. Still the most well known Chinese American actor of her era,
Wong and Paramount Studies signed a multi-film contract that would
result in her portraying relatively modernized, proactive Chinese
American female characters in two films, *Daughter of Shanghai* and
*King of Chinatown.* The Chinese consul to Los Angeles, T. K. Chang,
had approved the final script for both Paramount productions. Wong
linked her own desire for more positive and interesting acting roles
with China's desire for more positive portrayals. Wong remarked of
*Daughter of Shanghai,* "I like my part in this picture better than any
I've had before . . . because this picture gives Chinese a break—we
have sympathetic parts for a change! To me that means a great
deal."[128]

Wong's trip to China thus marked a significant turning point in her career; she would now attempt to use the fame she had earned through portraying stereotypical Chinese roles to publicize the "real China."
Whereas her travels to Europe had contributed to her American and Oriental image simultaneously, her trip to China allowed her to recreate herself as Chinese and American.

NEGOTIATING NATIONALISM

After 1939 Anna May Wong would not appear onscreen for four years,
well into the war. Those years, paradoxically, mark the full emergence
of the China mystique, in which Americans increasingly romanticized
China and portrayed it as a reflection of their own national aspirations
and identity. During these four years, however, Wong participated in
public stagings of Chinese American identity in ways that had previ-
ously been inaccessible to Chinese Americans because of their exclusion from the national community. She nonetheless continued to confront the burden of American orientalism—never displaced but
rearranged with the China mystique—while also performing her American patriotism.

## Homeland Survival

Although Euro-Americans became increasingly aware of international
conflict during the late 1930s, Chinese Americans had been following the
course of China's resistance to Japan from the beginning of the decade.
As early as 1931, Chinese immigrant and Chinese American women
throughout the States had organized to support China's war efforts
against Japan. From 1937 to 1941 as China's resistance to Japan continued, Chinese Americans increasingly participated in activities to raise
awareness and funds for China relief. They were assisted in these efforts
by former "China hands." Pearl Buck and Henry Luce, for example,
were increasingly active in fund-raising activities. Several humanitarian
organizations joined in these efforts, particularly organizations raising
funds to send to aid China in the face of floods, famine, and war. Wong
involved herself in these efforts as well. In June 1938 the *New York
Times* reported that Wong planned to auction her movie costumes to
raise funds.[129] A New England paper described Wong as "having helped
China to the best of her ability. The star lives in a $60 a month apart-
ment, sends all her money to China, and has even turned her Oriental
costumes and jewels into cash for the cause."[130] In October 1938 the
Chinese Benevolent Association of California acknowledged Wong's
contribution to Chinese refugees.[131]

Wong's celebrity presence at China relief fund-raisers also served to
glamorize the proceedings and legitimize the events as worthy of attention. The Moon Festival in October 1938 was organized by the Hollywood and Los Angeles UCR chapters.[132] It took place in old Chinatown
with the participation of the Chinese Consolidated Benevolent Association and featured numerous activities such as a Lion Dance, Shadow
Boxing, a Fashion Show and Chinese Drama at the Chinese School, and
a concert featuring "China's Bing Crosby." The publicity for the event
promised the appearance of numerous Hollywood stars amid the Chinese festivities—a multi-layered display. Spectators could gaze at the
celebrities, who in turn observed the Chinese participants, as all took
part in the activities. The large numbers of people overall only heightened the spectacle. Anna May Wong's prominence at these festivities emphasized her participation as both a Chinese American and a Hollywood
movie star. While most of the "Hollywood stars" sat on flatbed trucks
and were driven through the festival two nights in a row, Wong had her
own booth on the corner of Fergusson Alley and North Los Angeles

Street, where she autographed photographs of herself.[133] Exemplifying
the conflation of consumerism, femininity, and China in American China
relief efforts, Anna May Wong participated with other Chinese American
women in fashion shows—often serving as the celebrity attraction.
Wong served as mistress of ceremonies for a New York fashion show in
1940, of which the centerpiece was the "pageant of Beautiful Women . . .
opening with a parade of beautiful ancient Chinese robes, worn by eight
lovely Chinese girls; this was followed by Fourteen American women,
chosen from the ranks of society's loveliest, who modeled modern
evening gowns . . . all inspired by traditional Chinese dress, but skillfully
adapting Chinese color combinations, motifs and patterns to suit the
American face and figure."[134] Wong and other Chinese Americans thus
perpetuated an aesthetic that evoked American orientalism in the process
of raising public awareness and funds for new, modern China.

## Questionable Citizenship

Despite the rise of more positive American attitudes toward China during these years, Anna May Wong, her family, and other Chinese Americans continued to confront American prejudice based on their Chinese
heritage, including the burden of proving their right to belong in the
United States. When in 1938 Wong's father and siblings returned to the
United States after four years of living abroad in China, Sam Wong was
required to prove his status as an American citizen because he did not
have possession of a reentry certificate that certified his American
birthright. During the initial hearing Wong guaranteed that her father
would not become a public charge in the United States. The three board
members noted that "The demeanor of all [the witnesses] before the
Board was excellent" and unanimously recommended that United States
citizenship "be conceded." [135] A routine cross-reference of the Wong
family's files, however, revealed discrepancies that resulted in an additional hearing. It turned out that in Wong's interview for a reentry certificate for a 1924 movie being filmed outside the continental United
States she gave a different story of her father's place of origin and
brought into question her father's claim to American citizenship. In tran-
scripts of the interview with Sam Wong, the immigration inspector
asked, "Your daughter Anna May made a statement in Seattle, Washington, on June 2, 1924, to the effect that you and your wife, her mother,
were both born in China. Why do you suppose she would make a statement of that kind?" Thus Wong's testimony as a Chinese American could

be used against her father even as her celebrity status as an actor—referred to by various immigration inspectors throughout the reports—could aid his case.

The telling of the family's history before immigration inspectors asserted their status as Americans and simultaneously emphasized their marginal roles since they had to testify and continually prove the right to enter their homeland. (See figure 8, Wong's required certificate of citizenship.)The dichotomy of American opinions toward China and Chinese in the United States, then, was a constant even as sympathy for China grew as Japan's invasion of that nation continued into the late 1930s.

As this incident demonstrates, increased participation and recognition did not necessarily lead to increased acceptance for Chinese in America. Moreover, efforts of Wong and other Chinese Americans on behalf of China fed the widespread opinion that Chinese were not American. The context, however, dramatically changed when Japan bombed Pearl Harbor on December 7, 1941, and the United States entered the war. The wartime alliance between the United States and China gave Chinese Americans an unprecedented opportunity to participate in American civic culture *as* Chinese Americans.[136]

A UNITED FRONT

After December 1941, China and the United States officially had a common national enemy. Within this international context, the vision of the United States as a national community underwent significant change: it became a community whose multiple ethnic groups likewise held the common national ideology of democracy. For minorities and for Euro-Americans alike it was a striking shift. Along with other racial minority and ethnic communities, now Chinese Americans could enact the mutual unity and patriotism that the federal government sought to cultivate among "Americans all." Unlike the choices she faced in portraying Chinese onscreen through the late 1930s, Anna May Wong could participate in activities as both a Chinese and an American and not be publicly dissected as either one or the other.

As a result, Wong's commitment to China was most fully expressed in the extent of her Americanized activities within American civic organizations.[137] She volunteered as an air raid warden and participated in various parades and pageants. Her prolific fund-raising activities on behalf of United China Relief and individual organizations interested in China, and her involvement in the United Service Organization's entertainment of the troops, were full expressions of her Chinese American identity during the war.

## Performing China

As an actor whose appearance authenticated an imagined Asian locale, and whose public personality developed around her Chinese heritage, Anna May Wong lent legitimacy to fund-raisers for China. She had participated in UCR fund-raisers in Oregon, Arizona, Massachusetts, Wisconsin, and Michigan. When a UCR chapter was founded in San Diego, its chairman Edward LeRoy Moore wrote to the Los Angeles branch, "Could you send us some of your stars, say Anna May Wong, and a few others" for its fund-raising events.[138] When the OWI prepared a radio show called "Talks to China," to be broadcast to Chinese audiences abroad, a list of Chinese-speaking personalities was drawn up. At the top of the list was Anna May Wong.[139] During a China Society benefit for UCR in Los Angeles she showed the film of prewar China from her trip as well, while the China City Players presented *Mulan*.[140] These public appearances further reinforced Wong's Chinese-ness, even as she offered would-be patrons an encounter with "China."

Wong's close association with China at once enhanced her ability to raise funds for China relief and diminished its effectiveness. Because she had participated in China relief long before studios added war relief duties to their stars' obligations, an economy of personality caused her frequent appearances and familiarity with Hollywood to lessen rather than heighten interest. Whenever a glamorous and feminine Chinese national arrived in town on a China relief mission, Wong's Chinese American status paled. Miss Lee Ya-Ching, an aviatrix touted as China's "Amelia Earhart," attracted great publicity in the States as a symbol of "the modern Chinese woman" during her national barnstorming tour. The consul T. K. Chang, in charge of raising funds in Los Angeles and Hollywood, recognized her fresh appeal. "Hollywood fell hard for her. . . . Chang and others tell me that Miss Lee can wrap Hollywood around her finger as no other Chinese has ever been able to do. . . . Her serial tour brought in United States $10,000 and [Chinese] $20,000 net. . . . Miss Lee gets all kinds of invitation to the homes of the rich social butterflies, Social Register and others whom others of us can't touch. She accepted an invitation with one playboy and got a $1,000 check out of him for China relief. She accepted an invitation to cocktails with another and got a $5,000 check! Now she's looking forward for a champagne invite. That ought to be worth $10, 000, eh?"[141] Dating in the name of national pride proved lucrative with a young, glamorous Chinese woman who posed with football players and screen actors alike. Nationalist Chinese officials protested the exoticized and sexualized portrayal of Chinese women onscreen, but they were more than happy when this young Chinese woman parlayed "dates" into cash.

Wong's public image—refracting popular ideas of Asian women—indirectly shaped the appearance of other Chinese and Chinese American women in war time fund-raising. The feminization of China relief fund-raising events displayed the dominant perception of China as feminine, unique, and exotic. United China Relief offered lectures on Chinese modern women through its speakers' bureau and simultaneously tried to meet local chapters' demands for a Chinese girl in a silk gown to help pass out programs or collect donations. Fund-raising events literally sold China's cause, and fund-raisers actively sought Chinese American women to "represent" or at least model, "China."

## Consuming China

The decorative use of women runs as a thread from past to present depictions of Chinese women throughout American popular culture. As objects of display, actively selling "China" as a "gift idea" to donors, they survived the move from China as mysterious entity to China as a heroic friend. By the end of April 1942 UCR had enlisted for its efforts "two dozen of the top flight sales executives of most of the big business corporations in America" and reported of this team, "They have been doing a grand job during the last two or three months selling China to the American people instead of their usual products of automobiles, tires, electrical supplies, and other commercial products."[142] Thanks to the latest "scientific methods" of publicity, China was becoming a trend in itself, a fashion that could occupy Americans' minds and adorn their bodies. China as made in America was produced for literal consumption: United China Relief featured its own "Mayling Teas."

Clearly, Chinese women could embody national ideals and sell things at the same time. During the 1942 China Week in New York, for example, C. Scott Fletcher reported on the sale of flowers from rickshaws. The donated flowers would be sold "at the most important spots in New York on July 7, 8, and 9. The rickshaws will be manned by Chinese. The flowers sold by attractive Chinese girls."[143] Chinese men were not active participants but props. Jules Field of Twentieth Century Fox's newsreel department also sought "a group of photogenic Chinese girls in Chinese attire for a rally in Duffy Square" of women representing the United Nations, a request that was conveyed to the YWCA's Chinese girls' club.[144] Femininity made ethnicity more accessible to potential consumers. Surveys conducted by Robert Park's Chicago School noted that Chinese businesses often hired Asian American women for sale positions and had them dress in Chinese attire to interact with the America public.[145]

These events did not provide mainstream Americans with a more realistic view of China and the Chinese. Because fund-raisers relied on entertainment and marketing in order to raise awareness and money, they often perpetuated and relied on stereotypes. Fashion shows and beauty pageants combined women's consumerism, high culture, and China relief (see figure 9). "Fashions for Democracy," one such show at the eighteenth annual Women's National Exposition of Arts and Industries held at the Grand Central Palace in New York, featured "America, Britain and China united on the fashion front to raise funds for war torn China." Publicity photographs for a May 1941 UCR fashion luncheon on the roof of the Hotel Pierre featured debutantes modeling Chinese-influenced designs. Bonwit Teller's outfit worn by one young woman featured "a jade green one-piece silk shantung daytime dress with 'V' neck, featuring the new low front, with buttons down the front and worn with a white pique coolie hat, white gloves and matching shoes." The debutante wore makeup to make her eyes look more narrow, and her hair was arranged in short bangs across her forehead, Anna May Wong style. Several models also used eye makeup to appear Asian, with lines drawn upward from the edges of their eyes and sharp lines drawn downward for the eyebrows. Other "Chinese" fashions included the "coolie" or "singsong girl" looks. Another socialite modeled a pink and black linen suit from Saks Fifth Avenue. "Shown with a matching coolie coat and coolie hat and flexible heavy wooden shoes with straw tops suggest the tilted shoes of the ancient Chinese."[146]

Attempts to market China as an emerging nation-state did not mesh easily with marketing's reliance on easily grasped symbols of enduring and derogatory stereotypes of China. Hence the stereotypical coolie hat was reworked into new styles without losing its essential form, and old stereotypes of China were reworked into the latest trend, that of familiarity and friendship. China was similar but different, and attempts to mitigate this tension merged stereotypical images of old China with the political rhetoric of new China. Similarly, Anna May Wong continued to be marketed to American audiences as an easily identifiable symbol of "Chinese-ness."

## The Lady from Chungking

Wong acted in only two films during World War II, both set in China. Publicity releases noted that the Chinese American actor pledged her salaries from these films to United China Relief. The first, *Bombs over Burma* (1942), was a lackluster production whose quality reflected its two-week shooting schedule.[147] The second film, *The Lady from Chungking* (1943), however, is noteworthy for its focus on Chinese resistance and for a significant departure from previous depictions of Chinese women in American-made films. Reviews by *Variety* and the *Hollywood Reporter* praised Wong's performance but noted the confusing plot.[148]

*The Lady from Chungking* almost completely reversed the predominant narrative of a Hollywood war film set in China, in which an American civilian or soldier witnesses the atrocities of the Japanese soldiers in China and ends up heroically saving Chinese civilians from the Japanese soldiers—often dying in the process as a martyr to freedom. The protagonist of *Lady from Chungking*, Madame Kwan Mei, is a legendary fighter of noble birth who leads the rebels against the Japanese army. While major Hollywood studies relied on Chinese American actors to portray villainous Japanese, this small-budget film instead cast white Euro-American actors as the Japanese enemy soldiers. Chinese Americans portrayed the Chinese guerrillas, many of whom are executed by the Japanese when they refuse to betray their compatriots. Two American characters, Flying Tigers, are imprisoned and thus incapacitated for most of the film. Only with the aid of the Chinese guerrillas are they able to survive and escape. The guerrillas' first priority is notedly not to free the Americans, although this becomes an additional goal. As Kwan Mei reminds them, "our main objective is to prevent a Japanese drive westward to Chungking." The focus is on China's survival, not America's heroism.[149]

The story's ending is particularly remarkable. Japanese soldiers execute Wong's character, Kwan Mei, as she begins to speak about "new China." Her lifeless body falls to the ground, but not in romantic self-sacrifice, as Alan Ladd dies in *China* (1943) or Gene Tierney in *China Girl* that same year. Her character is a defiant martyr to fascism and not to forbidden, interracial love.[150] Again breaking the pattern of her previous deaths, Wong pronounces the film's final words. Madame Kwan

Mei has spoken of the "spirit of China" throughout the film and, as leader of the Chinese guerrillas, has embodied that spirit in action. Now her spirit hovers above her body, and she continues her declaration of China's resolve that she began at the beginning of her execution. Her resurrection is not for the sake of the film audience alone. The Japanese soldiers, who had been reluctant to execute a woman but followed orders lest they be shot by their ruthless commander, are now astounded by the sight of her. Some try to shoot her again, but Kwan Mei—Anna May Wong—cannot be touched and her voice cannot be silenced.

Awkwardly superimposed over the image of her lifeless body, Wong passionately affirms that "new China" will not be destroyed, the spirit of the Chinese will fight on. "China's destiny is victory. It will live because civilization will not die. Tyrants, dictators, the murderers of peace, all will be betrayed. Not even ten million deaths will cripple the soul of China. Because the soul of China is of the earth. Our children will see a new China, strong and free. Each time a bullet is fired, a new China is born, a new enemy faces Japan." Delivering these words with conviction, Wong exhibits more emotion in this scene as a martyred Chinese patriot than she had been allowed to in so many of her earlier and equally tragic roles. The courage of her character cannot be denied. That Anna May Wong was able to transcend her onscreen death only in the midst of World War II reflects the limited opportunities Chinese Americans enjoyed as a result of the United States' alliance with China.

Ironically, Wong's film career was already declining at this point. She was well into her thirties, and her personality was so associated with the China of the past that new China required new personalities. In addition to being overexposed, Wong had portrayed predominately Chinese characters who were exotic in a glamorous way. Perhaps not surprisingly, the few actors who seemed to capitalize on this "new China" were Chinese American men—Keye Luke and Benson Fong, for example—who enjoyed increased opportunities as Chinese heroes or Japanese villains.

## Making Way for New China

Wong experienced the prejudice of others who spoke for China, including Pearl S. Buck. In 1941, even though Wong had already devoted much time and effort to raising money for China, Buck characterized somewhat dismissively the materialistic, cosmopolitan Chinese American Ruth Kin as a "slangy Anna May Wong-type" in a radio play she wrote for UCR. Before the show was broadcast on Sept. 3, 1941, the reference to Wong was deleted.

Her declining popularity also was reflected two years later, when David O. Selznick, a producer and head of the Hollywood UCR chapter, organized a pageant at the Hollywood Bowl in April 1943 to celebrate Mayling Soong's final public appearance in Los Angeles and asked Wong to help advertise the event. Yet despite her dedicated participation in China relief fund-raising efforts he did not ask Wong to participate in the pageant honoring Madame Chiang Kai-shek or invite Wong to the far more extravagant film reception afterward. Madame Chiang Kai-shek was the only Chinese female celebrity present. This omission caused a minor scandal within Hollywood.[151]

As might be expected, Rob Wagner in his Beverly Hills magazine *Script* noted the omission of Wong and other Chinese Americans. "[T]here wasn't a single representative of the Chinese colony, except for the consulate staff. In fact a reception planned by the Chinese was marked off the program so that Madame could consult with top film executives before she met the cream of Hollywood society. There has been no more faithful worker for the cause of United China Relief than Anna May Wong. Was she asked to greet Madame at the film reception? She was not."[152] In the same issue, fourteen pages later, Robert's wife, Florence Wagner, added her own critique. "I'd like to report that there wasn't a single bum note—but there was—one. Where was Anna May Wong? Why was she not first in the parade of those glamorous picture girls who received the sainted visitor?" Wong herself tried to be positive about the situation and was quoted by Wagner as saying, "The important thing is that Madame Chiang was heard by so many people and that the spectacle at the Bowl was such a big success."[153] Later Selznick memos indicate that Wong was omitted at the request of a Chinese official, speaking perhaps on behalf of Soong or for himself: telling his assistant to discuss the matter with T. K. Chang, Selznick stated his belief that the consul knew one of Madame Chiang's entourage, who specifically asked him to leave Wong out of the pageant.[154]

The omission from Soong's reception by those in the film industry was clearly a matter of concern for Wong's career, potentially undermining her reputation as a champion of China. Even though Soong's entourage apparently overlooked many other Chinese Americans in their search for new friends among the wealthy and elite of Hollywood, Wong's identification with China was not something the Chinese Nationalist leaders embraced. Wong's generosity notwithstanding, her movie roles represented perceptions of China's past, celluloid images that outweighed her activism. Soong too was critical of Hollywood films' depiction of China and the Chinese. Speaking before Congress, striding across the Wellesley campus in slacks, parrying with the president over aid to China—hers was the new image that had little use for the old.

Hindered by American orientalism in Hollywood plots and casting, Anna May Wong exhibited savvy as well as tenacious perseverance in developing her own image, seeking opportunities for featured roles in film after her initial recognition as a bit player and character actor. As with most women who enjoyed widespread public recognition during the 1920s and early 1930s amid shifting public expectations about womanhood and femininity, fame and celebrity, race, ethnicity and nationality, Wong understood the recurring need to reinvent herself. She ably maintained her film career, making her one of the few actors to make the transition from silent films to talking pictures in the 1930s.

Anna May Wong contributed to the China mystique by humanizing Chinese Americans for American audiences throughout her career. Despite her lackluster and stereotypical roles, Wong became the most visible Chinese American presence in popular culture worldwide in the thirties (in addition to several tours through Europe, she traveled to Australia and New Zealand and planned to travel through South America). From the outset Wong's words and actions exceeded the stereotypes of American orientalism; journalists remarked with amazement about her standard American English with a trace of a British accent and her bobbed hair and flapper fashion. After she introduced American readers to the unexpected modernity of China during her travels, Wong also explained how Chinese perceived the United States—reaching audiences that Pearl Buck may not have reached with her writings. By simply "being Chinese American" during an era when most Americans considered this an impossibility, Wong publicly challenged American orientalism and demonstrated the possibility of the two cultures coexisting to audiences throughout the United States.

Nonetheless, Wong's wartime activities on behalf of China could not outdistance her film personality. That political life was localized, her activities taking place in smaller functions primarily in the Los Angeles region. Effectively translated and transmitted throughout the world, the public image obscured her "private life," which she had sought to keep private.

Although Anna May Wong's choices may appear contradictory, they reveal the strategic fluidity through which Wong engaged American society and negotiated American orientalism, as well as her developing political consciousness. Her choices provided her with visibility and voice that were largely denied other Chinese Americans until the war. In turn, Wong used both to confront and correct distorted images of Chinese Americans in the United States and abroad. By taking American audiences to China with her, Wong helped demystify the image of China she had perpetuated. Even as she opened possibilities for other Chinese American actors, however, her film career declined.

# CHAPTER 4

# Mayling Soong

In 1943 Geraldine Fitch—a former missionary to China—described for her friends the impact of Mayling Soong's visit to the United States. A featured attraction for wartime America,

> Madame Chiang herself—gracious, beautiful, dignified, courageous—was in the star role and no one could "steal the show." She has rightly captivated the hearts of the American people, and I think has accomplished in one visit what centuries of formal friendship between China and America could not do. She has made Americans realize that the Chinese are like us: our differences superficial, our similarities fundamental. Restauranteur [sic] and laundrymen (and none better) the American people knew, but now they know there are the educated, the cultured, the beautiful, the tolerant, the Christian in China as well.[1]

As Fitch describes in her letter, Mayling Soong (Song Meiling)—known to most Americans as Madame Chiang Kai-shek—symbolized the changing relations between the United States and China during the late 1930s through the 1940s. Soong was a symbol not only of China's new womanhood but of new China as well. While nationalism is inherently gendered, Soong's position was unique because for Americans she embodied the traditionally masculine as well as the feminine role of China. Generalissimo Chiang Kai-shek's dependence on his wife to interpret and negotiate betrayed how much weaker than Western nations China was.

Mayling Soong's visit occurred at the height of the United States' emergence as a world leader. As a representative of the new China and hence an embodiment of the China mystique, she demonstrated the power of American values to influence individuals and national communities. Yet for many Americans who regularly consumed productions of American orientalism, Soong's identity as an Americanized Chinese was unexpected. She reflected a much longer history of international travel and cultural exchange.

Indeed, Mayling Soong had experienced American culture before she ever arrived in the United States. Growing up in the cosmopolitan environment of Wuhan, a port city that boasted its own foreign settlements, Soong and her siblings enjoyed the relative privilege of her father's wealth and American connections. Her American education, Christian faith, and the politics of her family further contributed to Soong's knowledge about the United States.

## LEGACIES

Like many other immigrants, Soong's father, Yao-jun Soong (Song Yaoru), sought to attain the American dream of economic success when he left China for the United States. En route, he befriended the ship's captain, Charles Jones, who converted him to Christianity and became his mentor in the United States and among the American Methodist missionary community in both countries. American missionaries arranged for Soong to enroll at Vanderbilt University in Tennessee. His American and Christian connections served him well in China on his return, and he worked with the American missionaries to evangelize to the Chinese. Eventually, he made his fortune publishing Bibles in the Chinese language for American missionaries to distribute. As converted Christians, he and his wife, Kwei Tweng Nyi (Ni Kwei-tseng)—who had studied English, Chinese, and Japanese—maintained American and Chinese affiliations in Shanghai.

The six Soong children were thus exposed to Americans and American culture through their father's experience in the States, the presence of American missionaries in Shanghai, and their parents' involvement in the Christian Methodist Church. The family's hybridity was apparent in the décor of their home—located within the American settlement of Wuhan—which boasted both a "Chinese parlour with redwood furniture, and [a] foreign parlour with a piano." According to the eldest daughter, Ai-ling, the family all slept on "real American" beds, "with foreign mattresses, which the neighbors considered a curiosity." Significantly, the Soongs sent their daughters—Ai-ling, Chingling, and Mayling—to be educated at the McTyeire Home and School in Shanghai, which enjoyed a reputation for schooling Chinese girls in English and in middle-class femininity.[2]

When Soong was born, China was undergoing revolutionary changes that would challenge Western stereotypes of China as unchanging. As Western nations and Japan increasingly forced their interests onto a reluctant but weak Qing (Manchu) government, Chinese officials and intellectuals presented different ideas for reforming China. The Qing government, meanwhile, faced internal dissent and a realignment of leadership, which in turn resulted in a proliferation of political parties and factions. Arguing against stereotypes of Chinese women as passive and subordinate, Liang Chi-ch'ao (Liang Qichao) and several other intellectuals insisted that China's modernization and revitalization as a nation required that China's "new women" be educated and their feet unbound. In the midst of this political ferment, the elder Soong quietly began to support the Revive China Society, which was both anti-Qing (Manchu) and anti-imperialistic and led by the charismatic Sun Yat-sen (Sun Zhongshan).[3]

Charlie Soong's American education as well as his support of Sun Yat-sen's activities—which challenged the imperial court's rule and thus endangered his family—influenced him and his wife to send all six children, including the daughters, to some of the most elite universities in the United States. According to Ai-ling Soong (Song Ailing), the eldest and first child to study abroad, friends of the family expressed surprise when she departed because it "would be much more profitable to keep his daughter at home. . . . And, they opined, she would be much happier this way and get a good husband, which was doubtful if she went abroad and came back with new-fangled foreign ideas."[4] But in light of Charlie Soong's subversive politics and the intellectual climate during China at this time, the decision to send the girls to the United States for an education did not seem all that unusual. According to Soong herself, "By sending their daughters America-ward to school . . . they were but fulfilling their vision of what educated women could contribute toward a strong revitalized modern China."[5] Chinese educated abroad knew how China was perceived by the Western nations and also understood how perceptions of Chinese women as confined to the home, uneducated and unappreciated, contributed to China's image as less civilized and backward.

## Entry Delayed

Even before she left China, Soong learned how the legacy of exclusion played out in U.S. discriminatory immigration policies against Chinese citizens traveling to America. In July 1904 Soong's oldest sister, Ai-ling—the first to leave home to study in the United States—accompanied a Euro-American missionary family to the United States to attend Wesleyan College in Macon, Georgia. When she disembarked in Seattle, Washington, she was detained. The immigration official in Seattle did not believe that Ai-ling was a student, even though she possessed the proper papers that attested to her identity and the purposes of her visit. She was held at the immigration station for two weeks until she could prove to his satisfaction that she possessed a legitimate student visa. As the historian Delber L. McKee observed, "If the regulations were so rigid that even Miss Soong was detained for more than two weeks, the chances for a young Chinese without connections in high places to enter the country and attend a university were exceedingly slight."[6] Charlie Soong sought the aid of American missionaries and businessmen to procure his daughter's release; with their influence and assistance, Ai-ling Soong presented a student certification from Portugal as a Portuguese citizen and was allowed entry as a temporary visitor.[7] Her ability to "pass" as European suggests that the border imposed by racialized national identity was permeable on certain criteria. A well-to-do and well-connected Chinese family could fashion an identity more acceptable to Americans.

Soong must have worried whether she and Chingling (Song Qingling) would face similar problems when they first arrived at the port of Seattle in 1907. But they were not detained (see figure 10). Only nine years old, she accompanied her sister Chingling to Georgia, where they were reunited with Ai-ling, and Chingling began her studies at Wesleyan College.

## Alienation

For the next several years, Soong lived in a cottage with her sisters and received private tutoring; all three interacted with other students, faculty, and members of the local Methodist church. In 1914 she transferred from Wesleyan to Wellesley College in Massachusetts, a small college that, like many all-women's colleges, sought to nurture its female students. Its mission to educate women presumed a commonality among its students. Its students were also all linked by a common social class. As one of only four Chinese students, however, Soong stood out among her classmates and teachers at the woman's college. A faculty member at Wellesley recalled that, although quite popular among the students, Soong "with all her sociability and considerable popularity, [was] a little remote, watching us, questioning, criticizing or liking, feeling herself a bit of an alien."[8]

Soong apparently recognized and felt the alienation of being culturally and racially different from most of her classmates. Her professor, Annie Tuell, regularly referred to her as "My Heathen Chinee," apparently unconcerned how this derogatory term might affect her Christian student.[9] In return, Soong made little effort to accommodate the patronizing attitudes of Americans or to disguise her contempt. One Wellesley faculty member recalled Soong's "disdain for American smugness." Tuell also recalled that Soong "did not love very many of us, or very hard."

Studying in the United States where Chinese were still perceived as less civilized, Chinese students provided each other with security and community. Soong for example apparently socialized with other Chinese students in the Boston area who were studying abroad in the United States. Soong was very close to her older brother, Tseven (Song Ziwen)—better known as T. V.—a Harvard student, and apparently "popular with the Oriental students at Harvard and other colleges throughout the east." In this context, Soong and other Chinese students in the United States shared a distinct identity as Chinese negotiating American culture. Soong herself "felt specially something unnatural in the whole life of Oriental students here (in America), released from Chinese old rules which had kept the sexes separate and at the same time thrown them unnaturally together as young men and women by the fact that [they] are really an alien colony in a big American world."[10]

In addition to negotiating her Chinese identity abroad, Soong encountered the politics of gender within an American context at a time when middle-class Euro-American women were actively involved in civic life and progressive reforms. Certain of these women served as faculty at women's colleges such as Wellesley, dedicated to preparing young women for an active civic life as moral leaders of society. Soong was particularly inspired by the English literature professor Vida Scudder, who was influential in shaping Wellesley's educational mission. According to Patricia Palmieri, Scudder believed that higher education provided women with direction, a purpose. Scudder lamented "how many women of rare capacity have fairly blotted themselves out from a mistaken sense of duty!" and so sought to prepare women to participate actively in public life as professionals. The faculty at Wellesley hoped to replace those middle-class, predominately white women whom Victorian womanhood had consigned to the private sphere with "a generation of highly trained women, whose energies would significantly alter the political and social fabric of the nation." After her graduation, Soong also became better acquainted with Professor Sophie Hart, who echoed these ideals of public activism, calling for "the conduct of life in accordance with the ideals of service." Exposure to both the possibilities of women's civic participation and developments in China shaped Soong's sense of purpose; she stated that on her return to Chinese society she would seek to end the exploitation of landlords, warlords, and imperial powers that plagued her country.[11]

## RETURN TO CHINA

While she lived a quiet life as an undergraduate in Massachusetts, Soong knew of China's internal political conflict and the exploitation of this conflict by Western powers. In addition, Soong recognized that China's political turmoil had significant consequences for her family's well-being. In 1911 political tensions in China erupted. Revolution brought the Qing dynasty to an end on February 12, 1912. Foreign nations carefully observed these events and monitored their investments and, by the end of 1912, "at least seven predatory foreign powers [had] special interests in China."[12]

The end of Qing rule resulted in efforts to form a Chinese republic. In the midst of passionate debates about whether and how China could remain Chinese yet incorporate Western methods, discussions about the role of women in America's civic life paralleled discussions taking place within universities and colleges in China. Political strategists, including Sun Yat-sen and a young, charismatic Communist named Mao Tse-tung (Mao Zedong), also recognized the important contributions of women and the role of gender equality in their revolutionary activities. Ratification of the republican constitution, the document that would shape Chinese politics in the postdynastic era, included debates about women's equality and right to vote. Although the provisional constitution of February 11, 1912, stated that all Chinese and minorities were equal under the law, its final version ignored the topic.[13]

Hopes for a democratic China were short-lived. Soong was in her first year at Wellesley when as provisional president Yuan Shih-k'ai (Yuan

Shikai) took over the newly formed parliament and sought to cement his own authoritarian rule over China. In response Soong's father, mother, and two sisters joined other supporters of Sun Yat-sen's party, the Nationalist Party, or Kuomintang (Guomindong [revolutionary alliance]), in relocating to Tokyo. There, her father and sisters worked with Sun, who attempted to formulate a strategy for the modernization and centralization of China's government. During these years, Soong acquired two brothers-in-law—Sun himself, who married Chingling, and H. H. Kung (Kong Xiangxi), a businessman and Young Men's Christian Association official, who married Ai-ling. Meanwhile chaos in China continued. In 1914 Japan claimed Germany's territory in the northern province of Shantung (Shandong), and in 1915 Yuan was forced to concede extensive rights to Japan. By December military leaders of several provinces seceded from the central government. After Yuan's death in 1916 and assorted failed attempts to grasp central control of the country, power was decentralized among provincial warlords.[14]

In the face of these dramatic changes, Soong foresaw that the family's return to China in 1916 would be challenging. Annie Tuell recalled that Soong "wondered at difficulties ahead when she should return to a world and domestic standards from which she had grown away." Having spent ten years of her life in the United States, Soong was unsure whether she could fully relate to China and Chinese culture. Her immediate concerns had to do with cultural adjustment and gender expectations. Tuell remembered, "As the return to China drew near, she was really fearful that her Chinese was getting very defective."[15]

Although Soong had felt alienated from her American classmates while in the United States, she now confronted the foreignness of her homeland. In October 1917, only a few months after graduating Soong wrote to a classmate, "Your letter made me quite homesick for Wellesley . . . of course you know we *never* appreciate anything until too late."[16] Even though she returned to relatively cosmopolitan Shanghai, China's "backwardness" in comparison to the "Western civilization" she had enjoyed in the United States reportedly shocked her.[17] A classmate and friend of Soong's recalled her "[g]reat need for adjustment" after having lived half of her life up to that point in the United States. The food, clothes, and language were all relatively new to her.[18]

Spoken language is a key signifier of cultural belonging. Having left China at age nine, Soong was more fluent in English and American culture than Chinese language and culture. Soong's parents recognized that her adjustment to China would be facilitated by her ability to speak

Mandarin Chinese fluently. She recalled that, "Both my parents felt that as I had been away from the country for so long I should devote all my time to studying Chinese seriously before undertaking any work." Nonetheless, Soong participated in a variety of activities that reflected her bicultural fluency. In addition to teaching English at the YMCA, Soong founded, with her sister Ai-ling and other upper-class Shanghai women, the McTyeire Society to raise funds for the Shanghai private girls' school and served as president of the American Women's College Club in Shanghai.[19] Fluency in Chinese had political significance for a community attempting to define a national culture distinct from foreign influences, and Soong's fluency in Mandarin was crucial to establish her legitimacy among the Chinese.[20]

As residents of the American settlement of Shanghai, Soong and her family enjoyed greater protection from the conflicts that faced China; nonetheless, the crises in that city and elsewhere in China, including labor strikes in foreign-owned mills and student unrest, were impossible to ignore. Fresh from her American education, Soong learned the language of Chinese nationalism, which the mass circulation of newspapers had intensified after the Bolshevik Revolution of 1917.[21] During this time she served on the Film Censorship Committee of China, which screened all films before they were exhibited in China and censored those with derogatory portrayals of the country.[22]

Events at the conclusion of the First World War further politicized China. President Woodrow Wilson's wartime rhetoric had inspired hopes that China might finally regain control over the northern province of Shandong. At Versailles in late 1918, Chinese were stunned to learn that Western powers had promised Japan territory in Shandong in exchange for Japan's efforts in the war against Germany. Furthermore, the former Chinese premier Tuan Ch'i-ju (Duan Qirui) had negotiated deals allowing Japan's military presence in two more provinces and financial benefits from the railroads within Shandong. Chinese communities worldwide expressed outrage over these secret deals, and at the United States and European countries for allowing them to stand. Young Chinese women students in particular found a 1918 production in China of Ibsen's *A Doll's House* electrifying because they perceived a relationship between their individual emancipation and China's modernization.[23] A series of student protests known as the May Fourth Movement ensued in Peking (Beijing) during 1919. Many significant developments emerged from the May Fourth Movement, including the founding in 1921 of the Chinese Communist Party (CCP) and the Kuomintang's later reorganization. In Shanghai, Chinese also began to demand a voice in the governance of the International Settlement.

*Chinese Nationalism*

During the next decade Soong increasingly participated in the civic culture of Shanghai as a socialite and as a volunteer in reform efforts. Even though she believed in Chinese self-government, Soong's activities indicate that she was more accepting of foreigners than other Chinese. Indeed, many of her civic activities involved American-based Christian organizations such as the aforementioned YWCA and McTyeire schools.

Similar to many other Chinese students returning from their education abroad, Soong "discovered" and embraced the artistic and literary contributions of Chinese culture that her Western education had overlooked. This newfound knowledge reoriented her Eurocentric perspective. Soong ended up contributing "a great deal of writing for the old *Shanghai Gazette* and translating a number of Chinese stories into English," hoping to demonstrate to Westerners the merits of Chinese culture.[24] When Sophie Hart visited Soong in May 1918, she described Soong as "*ardently* aflame with the spirit of nationalism."[25]

Soong's nationalist fervor, however, was expressed in activities that did not fundamentally challenge the status quo. In 1921, for example, Soong served as secretary for a joint commission of American, British, and Chinese women's club to investigate factory conditions.[26] Her work with the commission resulted in recognition from the Shanghai Municipal Council that, with a wholly international membership of six British, two American, and one Japanese, governed the International Settlement in Shanghai—even though many Chinese lived and worked in the settlement. As the historian Nicholas Clifford points out, a minority of wealthy foreigners voted into power a council that made decisions affecting a majority of Chinese who worked in the settlement.[27]

In 1924 the council appointed Soong to the Child Labor Commission—she was the sole Chinese representative among British and American men and women, to investigate child labor practices in Shanghai factories.[28] Soong's appointment to this commission indicates that her activities and her family's reputation had established her among the foreign community. It may have been that the council appointed Soong to mollify the demands of Chinese nationalists for representation in governance; clearly, they were comfortable that she and her family would not demand drastic changes of the foreign-owned factories. Soong clearly relished the opportunity to reform an industry notorious for its abuses of its workers. "I feel like a lost soul there, or would, rather, were it not for the fact that I know a great deal about the subject, having personally inspected factories, etc. And as you see I am in the midst of industrial history in the making in China and am terribly thrilled."[29]

Soong's hopes for China's self-determination would be delayed after a series of events that began with her brother-in-law Sun Yat-sen's death from cancer in March 1925.[30] In April 1925, an insufficient number of ratepayers (those allowed a vote in the Shanghai International Settlement based on property ownership) attended the meeting to approve the recommended changes of the industrial commission on which Soong had served, rendering its attempts useless.[31] (In contrast, the efforts of the Chinese Communist Party to organize workers to agitate for improved conditions fared better and began bearing results in the late 1920s.) Then in May a Chinese workers' strike at a Japanese textile mill erupted in violence when Japanese guards killed one of the workers. At the command of a British officer, the municipal police then fired on the Chinese protesting this action—eleven were killed. These eleven, known as the May Thirtieth Martyrs, inspired further protests throughout China.[32]

At the same time that anger against foreigners increased, fissures within the Kuomintang widened. Sun's death had left the KMT divided over who would be its next leader. One of the contenders was Chiang Kai-shek (Jiang Jieshi). A merchant's son, Chiang Kai-shek had been educated abroad at a Japanese military academy and was acquiring a reputation as a military leader. In 1922 he had switched allegiances from the warlord Chien Chiung-ming (Chen Jiangmong) to support Chien's adversary, Sun Yat-sen.[33] Soon thereafter, Sun put Chiang Kai-shek in charge of founding and directing the National Military Academy, where he nurtured a loyal cadre of highly skilled army officers and rapidly established his reputation in the Kuomintang.

Mill strikes in Shanghai also resulted in violent confrontation between the Communists and Chiang Kai-shek's KMT faction. Striking workers, invigorated by Communist efforts, brought Shanghai to a halt for two days in February 1926. Chinese business interests affected by these strikes and fearing increasing Communist influence offered financial support to Chiang Kai-shek by the end of 1926. Compounding tensions, his Nationalist troops seized the city of Nanjing in March 1927 and in the process wreaked destruction on foreign consulates and killed several foreigners in what was known as the Nanjing Incident (mentioned in chapter 2). Foreigners were evacuated, under the protection of United States and British troops in the city and gunboats offshore.[34] That same month over 600,000 workers participated in another strike in the Chinese sector of Shanghai.

Chiang Kai-shek had appeared to offer the possibility of negotiation between the strikers and the industrialists in Shanghai. But on April 12 an antiunion group joined the National Revolutionary Army under his command to attack union headquarters throughout the city. Chiang Kai-shek enforced his policies in Shanghai with police power, coercing financial support by blackmailing business interests and working in close cooperation with his former organized crime colleagues, the notorious Green Gang, to establish control over Shanghai. In the process of "maintaining order," Chiang Kai-shek also intended to eradicate the Communists. While Shanghai was under his control, at least five thousand persons with leftist, Communist, or liberal KMT connections were murdered.[35]

Perceiving that nationalism offered an opportunity for them to wrest power over China from the conservative KMT faction—leaving in place the hierarchical structure of power from which they could profit even more—elites within KMT's liberal faction condemned Chiang Kai-shek and his brutal, authoritarian style of leadership. Soong's sister Chingling also opposed China's rule, but Soong's specific nationalism intersected with her family's interest in maintaining their class status and enriching their personal fortunes.

At some point during these years, perhaps while visiting one of her sisters in Beijing or Guangdong—Chingling and Sun had moved to Guangdong in 1919—she met Chiang Kai-shek. Whether encouraged by her family's political interests or propinquity, Soong's acquaintance with the general developed into a personal relationship. Their common background included an education abroad, merchant parents, an intense nationalism, a deep resentment of foreign imperialism, and a conviction that the Chinese could be shaped into a modern, vital nation, even if force were required. Undoubtedly there were political considerations on both sides as well: Soong's family could profit from Chiang Kai-shek's rise to power and, by marrying Soong, the ambitious general could claim Sun Yat-sen as his brother-in-law. Ai-ling's husband, H. H. Kung, already a wealthy industrialist, had a financial stake in opposing the Communists. Only Chingling appears to have reacted strongly against her future brother-in-law's actions in Shanghai. In late 1926 Chiang Kai-shek traveled to Japan to ask Soong's mother's permission to wed her daughter.[36] In December 1927 the two married. Both of their weddings—one traditional Chinese and one Christian—reflected the influences of American and Chinese culture (see figure 11). The secretary of the YMCA performed the Christian ceremony before 1,000 guests, a ceremony that was covered in all of the local press and constituted one of the year's major social events.[37] A traditional Chinese ceremony followed in a hotel. Ching-ling refused to attend the wedding of her sister to the man who had betrayed her late husband's ideals. T. V., Soong's older brother, was appointed by Chiang Kai-shek in 1928 to manage the finances of the Nationalist government.

## THE CREATION OF MADAME CHIANG KAI-SHEK

The marriage of Chiang Kai-shek to Mayling Soong was a political event in China and internationally; American officials in the U.S. Department of State's Far Eastern Division noted the nuptials with interest. Internationally, Soong was well qualified for her role as the wife of China's leader. Her profession of Christianity and her active participation in her husband's government both seemed to indicate the modernization and westernization of China. As a result, opportunities for collaboration between the Nationalist government and American mission organizations developed as Soong attracted the goodwill or at least interest of many Americans who witnessed the emergence of a new China.

Working together in what appeared to be companionate bliss, the Chiangs began to alter the image of China. While Chiang Kai-shek solidified his political power as leader of Nationalist China, Soong increasingly involved American social and Christian organizations in addressing the material needs of China. According to the historian Jonathan Spence, American programs such as the YMCA had been viewed with antiforeigner suspicion until 1927, the same year the couple married. Soong, who had worked with some of the foreign-sponsored reform organizations since her return from the United States, facilitated the collaboration between the aims of her husband's government and the resources and expertise of American social organizations. Among the government's primary areas of concern were the poverty and disease ravaging peasants in the rural areas.[38] These partnerships had the added benefit of presenting her husband's government in a more benevolent, progressive light after the notorious Nanjing Incident.

Concerted efforts to work with Christian organizations increased when foreign powers declined to intervene, even under international conventions, after Japan occupied Manchuria on September 18, 1931.[39] Already emerging patterns were starkly apparent: Chiang Kai-shek would focus most of his efforts on destroying Chinese Communists and other opponents of his regime rather than attacking the Japanese invaders; Japan would continue its aggressive incursions into China and the dominant European powers and the United States would neither help nor interfere. With little aid forthcoming from foreign nations, the Nationalist government looked to individual foreigners for aid and assistance. Among the most able and ready to offer their expertise were missionary organizations eager to increase their influence in the government and among the people. By 1933, feeling "Spirit led," Mayling Soong had enlisted the aid of missionaries and Christian churches in the reconstruction of China.

The Chiangs were not shy about publicizing their cooperation with various mission organizations. The missionary William Richard Johnson was invited to a special meeting where Fox Movietone filmed Soong translating a short speech by her husband, as well as the responses of two missionaries, "for circulation the world over." Johnson wrote home to his supporters in November 1933 about "[t]he General's wife . . . who takes her Christianity seriously." Stating that he could "more than fill this letter with stories of her activities and helpfulness in Christian work," Johnson offered several examples: Mayling Soong had formed a women's club to care for wounded foreign and Chinese soldiers; she proposed a committee of Protestant mission to evangelize in major governmental hospitals; finally, she sought to involve churches in developing the rural areas ravaged by flood, famine, and war.[40] Soong perceived that Christianity and nationalism could coexist to their mutual benefit in improving China's international status.

### National Housekeeping

The figure of an active and powerful Mayling Soong accomplished much good for China's public image abroad. As "first lady" of a new China (and indeed the first wife of a Chinese leader who was so publicly involved in her husband's regime), Soong embodied the nation's potential for modernization. She began to institute American-style, middle-class reforms, and her husband's dictatorial power allowed her to institute these reforms without having to generate a wide base of support and activism among the Chinese. Soong's reforms, particularly her mandate that Chinese women participate in nation-building, received positive coverage in many American newspapers. Theodore White, an American

journalist who wrote about China for *Time* magazine, stated: "in propaganda work abroad, especially in America, the influence of Madame
Chiang is supreme."[41] Owen Lattimore, an American who advised
Chiang Kai-shek during the 1930s, concurred in this assessment, "[Gen-
eralissimo] Chiang was able to make good use of her because of her
standing in the United States."[42] The American media's positive coverage of Soong's activities helped counter any news of the generalissimo's
dictatorial leadership.

Soong's reforms reflected the American progressive tradition in which
she had been instructed at Wellesley, emphasizing education, hygiene, efficiency and behavior. Soong's development of educational institutions
for the orphans of China's war of resistance against Japan demonstrates
the influence of her own education. Expressing her belief in the power of
education to instill national character among the younger generation, she
began two schools in Nanjing for the children of Nationalist soldiers
who had been killed (see figure 12). Just as Wellesley instilled civic responsibility in its students, these students were taught "to live as citizens
of a community."[43] She explained, "These children, I thought, would be
the most valuable material if they were molded right as they all had revolutionary blood in their veins."[44]

Soong envisioned the modern schools as models for all of China. One
observer described the campuses as "an up-to-date American college. . .
right in the heart of China." Even so, the children were reportedly not
allowed to visit their families for fear that "poor surroundings and bad
manners might be detrimental to their characters."[45] If true, this concern
demonstrates how Soong perceived her American education, as well as
her perceptions of China when she returned. While undoubtedly a fer-
vent nationalist who continued to embrace Chinese culture and traditions, Soong nonetheless embraced American-style residential campuses
that inculcated a combination of progressive American notions of social
responsibility and health, American critiques of China's backwardness,
and Chinese nationalist notions of pride, loyalty, and ethnocentrism.

A background of privilege focused her reforms. One critic complained that "the trouble was that Madame placed spiritual values
above material values." This partially reflected her own experience, or
lack thereof.[46] Soong's programs ultimately tended to focus on internal
transformation, as opposed to structural change such as reducing
poverty, as the means to "revive" China.

This was the case when Soong extended her concern to the military
establishment, where she sought to provide moral activities for officers.

"I saw so many of the young officers without homes and without wholesome companionships or amusement after office hours that I began to realize that here was a need which should be attended to somehow." Thus she instigated the Officers' Moral Endeavor Association, conceived of as "a sort of Whampoa club."[47] Officers could meet in a brand-new building, where they were not allowed to drink or smoke but could attend talks about virtuous living.[48] Soong occasionally led the singing of hymns on Sundays. These developments were not always appreciated. Soong recalled in 1934 "all the trouble I had . . . with those who criticized me in saying that I was trying to YMCA the government."[49] The combination of social reform, Christianity, and a strong American presence it represented was perhaps not too far off the mark.

Because Soong's reforms paralleled Western critiques of China they often, as a result, literally reformed China according to Western perceptions. Responding to European and American stereotypes of the Chinese as lacking in manners and civility, Soong considered establishing protocols of behavior for Chinese bureaucrats. She recommended to the generalissimo that rules of behavior be set for receiving foreign visitors, because "she often felt angry at seeing the ways in which members of [the Chinese] government at inner parties behaved—tapping glasses with forks and knives or fooling at table."[50] Like other Chinese intellectuals, she recognized that Western perceptions were colored by prejudice, and the importance of appearances and behavior to command the respect of foreign diplomats and improve China's international status.[51]

### An American Witness

The desire to gain powerful allies in Europe and the United States motivated and legitimized many of Soong's activities in her husband's government. Although the U.S. government maintained its isolationist stance, Soong appealed to American organizations and individual Americans already involved in China, especially missionary organizations. Owen Lattimore recalled in his memoirs that, "Madame Chiang very quickly realized the political usefulness of showing off their Christianity to get the support of U.S. voters."[52]

Her work with Christian missionaries had already ensured that the Nationalist government would be dear to the heart of evangelical American Christians—she was practically described as an American missionary herself when her husband converted to Christianity in 1929.[53] Some

Americans even seemed to believe that Soong, being Americanized, was the true political leader of China.

Soong's combination of spirituality, which affirmed American norms of womanhood and political authority, did not bother observers in the United States who in other contexts may have been troubled by an independent and strong woman leader. Since American women's participation in politics and polity was increasingly linked to modernity, Soong's activities suggested a modernizing China open to women's activism, Christian values, and American influence. The situation of China warranted this dramatic reversal of gender roles.

To American observers, Soong's activities—implementing social reforms that reflected American spiritual and educational values, encouraging Chinese women to take active civic roles during wartime, and serving prominently as her husband's confidante in political matters—reflected well on the generalissimo's stature. It appeared to the general public that her husband, who worked side by side with his wife, was a progressive leader, guiding China quickly into a modern and civilized nation. By contributing to her husband's stature before American and European publics and their governments, helping gain Western acceptance of her husband's leadership, Soong indirectly contributed to Chiang Kai-shek's authority within China as well.

Her image was both produced for American consumption and intended to appear American-made. Its true impact was not on China but on American attitudes toward China. Soong's public confession of her Christian faith, for example, did not change any national policy in China. Yet it provoked a profound shift in China's international image, especially in the United States. In 1934 the editors of *Forum* magazine asked her and several other notable women to provide their thoughts on faith. Soong contributed "What My Religion Means to Me." When approached by *Forum* editors to write the article, Soong nearly turned it down. But her friend Geraldine Fitch, herself a missionary and the wife of YMCA secretary in China George Fitch, convinced her that such a testimony could have material value in developing aid and sympathy for China in the United States.[54] Thus persuaded, Soong discussed different memories and thoughts about her faith with Fitch, who liberally "organized" Soong's recollections into a narrative of conversion palatable to American churchgoers.

Had Fitch's contribution been publicly known, it would have diminished the impact of Soong's testimony. Herself a product of American

culture and trained in evangelism, Fitch had a clear idea of what constituted a "vital personal witness." Fitch had her own designs; she hoped
that Soong's article would be "a tremendously effective personal testimony" for American readers and evidence of the missionary enterprise's
effectiveness in China at a time when the church was losing ground to
modern secularism. This essay surprised the editors, who had assumed
Soong was Buddhist.[55] It also surprised her reading audience.

As was common to the genre of testimonials and conversion accounts,
readers followed Soong's spiritual journey as the wife of General Chiang
Kai-shek and their roles in leading China. "During these years of my
married life, I have gone through three phases as related to my religion."
The first sets the stage for conversion. A series of trials—her mother's
death, upheaval in China—constituted the catalyst to her spiritual
reawakening. "First, there was a tremendous enthusiasm and patriotism—a passionate desire to do something for my country. . . . With my
husband I would work ceaselessly to make China strong. I had the best
of intentions. But something was lacking . . . I was depending on self."

In the second phase, Soong realizes that she is not fulfilling her wifely
role. "Then came the second phase. . . . I realized that spiritually I was
failing my husband. . . . I began to see that what I was doing to help, for
the sake of the country, was only a substitute for what he needed. . . .
Out of that, and the feeling of human inadequacy, I was driven back to
mother's God." According to Fitch, Soong's first and foremost role is not
to lead the country but to support her husband spiritually. She realizes
that, "It seemed to be up to me to help the General spiritually, and in
helping him I grew spiritually myself." In addition to highlighting the development of her own faith, Soong's testimony reinforces women's place
within the domestic sphere as spiritual leaders to provide the moral support for their husbands as they provide leadership in the public sphere.

Having recognized a lack both in her individual efforts on behalf of
China and in her marriage to the leader of China, the testimony merges
Soong's Christianity and nationalism. At this climatic moment Soong realizes that God's destiny for her is to nurture her husband spiritually as
they work together to transform China. "Thus I entered the third period,
where I wanted to do, not my will, but God's. . . . I feel that God has
given me a work to do for China." Soong's version of manifest destiny
gives her the resolve to continue both the spiritual and political battles
before her. "This is no small task. In fact, China's problems in some ways
are greater today than ever before. But despondency and despair are not
mine today. I look to Him who is able to do all things, even more than

we ask or think." The testimony closes with the confidence of faith and clearly suggests that the Chiangs are God's chosen leaders of China. "At this time of writing, I am with my husband in the heart of the bandit area. Constantly exposed to dangers, I am unafraid. I know that nothing can happen either to the General or to me till our work is done. After that, what does it matter?"[56]

As Geraldine Fitch had predicted, this testimony had tremendous impact on Soong's popularity with Americans and contributed to increased positive interest in China. Soong's discussion about Christianity challenged one of the basic tenets of American orientalism, that the Chinese were heathen and immoral and thus unlike Americans. This article played a major role in the transformation of Mayling Soong into a symbol of the unique, special relationship that Americans believed existed between the United States and China.

"What My Religion Means to Me" also presented an equally gendered account of China's national transformation, from ardent nationalism to strength and leadership even beyond its borders—where Christianity was read as democracy, and God's will somehow involved the participation of the United States. Soong's testimony inspired fervor among Americans not simply about Christian faith but about the transformative powers of American ideology. Her witness affirmed the presence of American missionaries and businessmen in China, abetted by U.S. diplomatic and military presence. It further testified to the widening international U.S. influence, linked to the assumption that American international governance after World War II was necessary to maintain a civilized and orderly world. It offered assurance that, despite indications that the generalissimo was more dictatorial than democratic, China might be the answer to the United States' desire to develop Asian countries as future markets and young democracies. Finally, Soong's witness affirmed her ability to communicate with Americans in a social, political, and spiritual language they could understand.

### The Xian Incident

As a product of both Chinese and American cultures, Soong found herself in the position of translating American culture and goals to a Chinese context, and then, in turn, reaffirming the power of the same culture and ideologies back to Americans through the reflection of their impact on her *and* China. By this time, Soong was accustomed to being produced in multiple ways to meet the expectations of multiple audiences. As the generalissimo's wife, she increasingly came to symbolize China's national identity, especially to American eyes. Soong's identity and image would become a collaborative creation of her husband's Chinese Nationalist interests and pro-Chinese American interests.

Mayling Soong received greater international attention after December 1936, when the generalissimo's associate Chang Hsueh-liang (Chen Jiangmong)—known as the Young Marshal—held him hostage in Sian (Xian). The dramatic event captured international interest in a way that previous attempts in raising international support had failed, and it secured her husband's position at home and abroad as China's leader. According to widely circulated accounts Soong, her brother T. V. Soong, and the generalissimo's advisor W. H. Donald flew to Xian. After negotiating with Chang, they secured the generalissimo's release.[57] The reality, however, was more complicated. Chang, a trusted ally of the generalissimo, sought to end his single-minded focus on wiping out the Chinese Communist Party, which was only dividing China against itself in the face of Japan's aggression. Chang and Chou En-lai of the CCP helped negotiate an end to the hostilities between the two parties. It suspended China's internal political conflict for a time, and Chiang Kai-shek emerged as leader of the united front against Japan.

After Xian, the Chiangs enjoyed international interest. In the United States, The *New York Times* featured on its front page excerpts from the generalissimo's diary, supposedly written while he was held hostage, alongside his wife's account and increased his international visibility and accessibility—particularly as he discussed God's comfort while being held hostage and recalled his earlier conversion to Christianity. After their writings about Xian appeared in the *New York Times,* readers deluged the paper asking whether these would appear in book form. Combined, they were published as *Sian: A Coup d'État / A Fortnight in Sian* that same year. Publicizing Soong's role in converting the generalissimo to Christianity enhanced Soong's spiritual as well as political leadership and captured the hearts of Americans, who wondered how much of their own spirit had inspired this woman's actions. Above all, Soong's image as an active and independent woman reflected positively on China's political transformation.[58]

Frequent appearances in newsreels or in *Life* and *Time* boosted the Chiangs' popularity as a power couple. In his publications Henry Luce literally produced positive images of China as a young democracy, with Soong as its guide.[59] Luce's romance with China paralleled that of other "old China hands"—first- or second-generation Americans who had been stationed in China as missionaries, diplomats, or businessmen. Unlike Pearl Buck, who viewed Nationalist China, the Chiangs, and Christian missions with a critical eye, many other China hands willingly and hopefully believed they had contributed to the mentoring relationship the United States enjoyed with China.

After Luce placed the Chiangs on the cover of *Time* as "Man and Woman of the Year" in 1937, Colonel Theodore Roosevelt, Jr., an editor at Doubleday Publishing, quickly secured a contract with Soong to write about her experiences. He gloated to an associate that Doubleday had benefited by the American surge of interest in the Chiangs. "Not only does everyone read about them every day in the newspaper, but this issue of LIFE shows the way they have captivated the public interest. I haven't a doubt that [our] book will be a ready seller." He explained its appeal to an American audience. "Remember, it is the only book in English ever written by Madame Chiang, indeed the only book in English written by anyone who is shaping destinies of the 400,000,000 people who compose China."[60]

The "400 million people" who had haunted so many American imaginations now appeared more benign under the leadership of an English-speaking, American-educated, affluent Chinese woman. The growing visibility of the Chiangs after 1936 and MGM's humane depiction of Chinese in *The Good Earth* (1937) created a popular market for information about China. The abundance of information about Mayling Soong who, it seemed, could bridge the communication gap between the two nations, further intensified interest in this new China. Roosevelt noted that China was now popular with the American public. "I saw in Book Notes last week that numbers of publishing houses were rushing everything that had to do with China."[61]

### Dictating Change

As an American celebrity and as a woman, Soong faced repeated challenges to her authority and legitimacy from within China. There she represented a treacherous body—accused variously of not being womanly, Chinese, or American enough. The multiple interpretations of her governmental roles reveal how different audiences interpreted her identity as an American-educated Chinese woman and hence perceived China.

When Soong held actual positions of authority within her husband's regime, China's progress toward modernity and democracy seemed to eclipse even the modernity of Western nations. In 1936 Generalissimo

Chiang Kai-shek appointed his wife secretary general of aeronautical affairs, a position she held until 1938. Her visible and official role in the Chinese Nationalist government was hailed by some Americans as evidence of the influence the United States now had on China. Other Americans viewed it as evidence of the cooperation and trust that existed between the couple, companions in love and leadership. Whether she in fact wielded so much power is difficult to determine, but the appearance of her sharing power with the generalissimo in a companionate marriage did much to contradict claims that he might be yet another Oriental warlord simply relying on martial law to maintain his power.[62]

Many Chinese did wonder at the appointment and several Chinese military leaders greatly questioned her capabilities as well as her husband's judgment. U.S. Consul Willys Peck alluded to discomfort in the Chinese Nationalist army and government over Soong's growing influence in a personal letter to Stanley K. Hornbeck, the chief of the Far Eastern Division. Peck observed that "Chinese officialdom, especially the military clique, has long been restive under the necessity of gaining Madame Chiang's approval for any proposal presented to her husband and it is said that lately Madame Chiang has gone to the length of taking an actual official post."[63] Soong may have exhibited a political astuteness in her understanding of U.S. society, but her attempts to gain American sympathy did not endear her to Chinese nationalists.

Desire to restructure China's bureaucracy into an efficient, modern system based on American and European models gained her many critics in China. One manifestation of her baleful Western influence was that she held so much power as a woman.[64] Theodore White described Chiang Kai-shek in terms of "spheres of influence." The first sphere consisted of the army, the second of Soong and her social projects.[65] Nationalist Army officers expressed resistance to the foreign influences they perceived in the guise of the general's wife. As Soong herself recognized, her Christian faith and Western upbringing provoked resentment of her as a foreigner and as a threat to their own influence on her husband.

Soong's reform efforts did not go uncriticized by some foreign observers either, although at first these voices of dissent were suppressed. White, a journalist for *Time* magazine, made such observations about Soong in a report as early as June 1940. Concisely announcing "China is a dictatorship," White's critical assessment of China's politics was not published at the time because of the U.S. government's attempts to maintain a strong image of China in the press and the pro-Soong sympathies of White's editor at *Time*, Henry Luce. According to White, the disparate values of family wealth and prestige, Chinese nationalism, and American reforms compromised Soong's ability to effect significant change. Her efforts to improve life for Chinese stopped short of anything that might disturb the structures of power so beneficial to her family and other elites or undermine the military force essential to her husband's control over the government.

In his report, White complimented Soong's dignity and tireless work for China, noting that "her American background is evident in an effort to achieve in the affairs she directs herself American efficiency and American methods." He also noted that she was "the only liberalizing element in Chiang Kai-shek's life," and especially influential in China's international propaganda.[66] But her actual work, White added, "seemed to be directed to an attack on the externalia of Chinese life, rather than an attack on its root-faults.

> The New Life Movement, which is the projection of her image, would make of the Chinese a drawing-room American, preferably a Methodist. It frowns upon smoking, drinking, spitting in the streets, unbuttoned collars, slipshod attire, lavish expenditures, dancing. But it makes no effort to delve down into the depths of the misery of the Chinese people and organize them so to change the structure of their government as "shall be most fitting for life, liberty and the pursuit of happiness." The Kuomintang is nominally a "revolutionary party"; but there is none of the flaming revolutionary in the Madame. Hers is a warm, human sympathy for orphans, widows, homeless, wounded; and much as a "good" American-clubswoman she devotes her energies to movements to the same ends.[67]

White's comments, while insightful, also suggest that he was faulting Soong and American clubwomen for the social limitations their gender imposed. This critique is double-edged—it belittles American middle-class women and their ineffectual volunteer efforts in American society, and it extends to Soong, who in emulating them trivializes her position as the wife of China's leader. By focusing solely on her gender and not on the influences of Chinese politics, White seems to assume along with his fellow Americans that Soong wielded more power within her husband's regime than she actually did and that American women affected United States society and politics less than they did.

### An American Viewpoint

For their part, middle-class American women made Mayling Soong theirs, particularly women who sought to show that they were as capable as men, albeit in different spheres. One newspaper columnist observed that in Soong, "Los Angeles club women have found a new inspiration urging them to greater effort in their self-appointed war tasks . . . they have a feeling of kinship toward this woman who expresses the finest of all womankind." Numerous women's groups affiliated with the Federation of Women's Clubs wrote to the State Department requesting materials on China throughout the midthirties and early forties.[68] Some Americans assumed that Soong was "a symbol of Modern China," because she "had an American education and spoke English brilliantly" whereas the generalissimo "did not even speak English," some even concluded that "she must be the real brains of Chiang Kaishek's government."[69]

Many Americans beheld in Soong the capabilities of American women to transform society. The apparent success of her programs in China— her reforms on hygiene, manners, education, and spirit—could be viewed as a legacy of American ideals. Clare Boothe Luce explained to the radio show host Rita Rite Soong's "American viewpoint."

> she took back to China with her, all the best she had learned from our country: the ideas of political freedom, of social service, and above all of equality between the sexes—and with her husband's aid, she applied them to China, and made them work. In China today . . . Madame Chiang has, with her American viewpoint put the Chinese woman today on an equal [footing] with men in government, and in politics.[70]

Soong's perceived success in China and her location in the genealogy of the American feminist movement affirmed the legacy of the now less than vigorous women's movement in America. Dr. Helen C. White, president of the American Association of University Women, and professor of English literature at the University of Wisconsin, declared that Soong "appropriated in her American education the ideals of educated American womanhood to a degree that would put most American women who have enjoyed the same privileges to shame. . . . We American women, therefore, behold in her the realization of some of our highest ideals and the fulfilment of many of our most cherished aspirations."[71]

Soong, it seemed, had succeeded in maintaining and expanding the feminine sphere of influence in Chinese society while negotiating politically with men and literally helping run the country. She had somehow kept her unique femininity while proving her capabilities. Some Americans helped her achieve this feat, in print at least. When Clare Boothe Luce wrote "Victory Is a Woman" for *Woman's Home Companion* in

November 1943, her progressive drafts indicate a concerted attempt to feminize Soong, with Luce inserting the adjective "womanly" and emphasizing Soong's maternal role to Chinese orphans.[72]

Praise for China's modernization coincided with the National Woman's Party's attempts to raise support for the Equal Rights Amendment. A factor that piqued the party's interest in China was that the first draft of the republican constitution, in 1912, seemed to include equal rights for men and women. The NWP had fought for a similar constitutional amendment from the 1920s. By calling the American public's attention to women's roles in China, the NWP hoped to call congressional and public attention to the gender inequality of women in the United States. This strategy, of course, implied that American women should have equality because the United States was "more modern" than China.

As executive secretary of the NWP, Mildred Palmer similarly employed depictions of gender equality in China, popularized by Buck among others, to indicate that Americans had been misled about the existence of gender equality in the United States. She strikingly reversed the "yellow peril" argument of the nineteenth century that warned of Asiatics racially weakening the national body and justified the exclusion of Asian immigrants. "American readers, knowing how servile has become the position of women in continental Europe and recognizing that oceans are no barrier to such contagion, will take warning. Many American men will ask themselves whether true national unity can be attained and permanently maintained on a basis of legal inequality."[73]

Regardless of where they stood on the Equal Rights Amendment, many women appeared to be fascinated by the seemingly rapid transformation of Chinese women's lives from bound feet to educated and active social reform. Instead of an Asiatic threat based on race, there now existed a European threat based on regressive gender roles that could weaken American nationalism. The only remedy to this potential corruption was an amendment that would guarantee the equality of women in the United States. China hence occupied a relatively paradoxical location for some American women. On the one hand, to many it evoked images of foot binding, devalued daughters, and archaic patriarchal tradition. Yet on the other, here was a Chinese woman who seemed to be equal in stature to her husband, the leader of the Chinese nation, and they foresaw the increasing role of women in the government and society.

We Chinese Women

In discussing how to publicize China's modernization, Chinese officials noted, "To increase the effectiveness of our propaganda, we must constantly be aware of, and bear in mind, the feelings and reactions in the U.S.A. . . . perhaps more than in any other country."[74] They chose women as one topic of emphasis. A catalog of literature and services available from the Chinese News Service, a New York-based branch of the Chinese government, consciously appealed to American women with human-interest news. In addition to a monthly bulletin, *China at War,* and news from Chongqing, the news service also issued "Special Features" that included one- to two-page discussions of human interest on "women, children, war heroes, etc." as well as "summaries of such war activities as that of the women."[75] Several articles emphasized how modern Chinese women demonstrated China's progress. Titles of special pamphlets and books included *Women's Place in Chinese History,* and a volume of Madame Chiang's writings, *We Chinese Women.*

The Chiangs' public embrace of Christianity, the image of the married couple as companions in the fight for China's liberation and modernization, and the way in which Soong defied all expectations of how Chinese women were expected to behave, persuaded many Americans that China was changing and becoming more like the United States ideologically. From the late 1930s through the mid 1940s, the American public seemed infatuated with China and with Generalissimo and Madame Chiang, who symbolized new China. This romanticization of new China—the China mystique—however, was also somewhat paternalistic on the part of the American public, at least those who viewed themselves as part of a modern, civilized, and Christian nation. During the late 1930s most Americans believed that the their country's role was to "protect" China from other nations. In 1939 Buck expressed her horror that a China relief poster used the motto Save China, because it conveyed American superiority and paternalism. Although this motto was changed to China Shall Have Our Help, the implication that China was subordinate and that the United States would rescue China continued throughout the war.

Different segments of the U.S. national community already began incorporating Mayling Soong into their own imagined global community, unified by American ideals. She represented the cultural transcendence of Christianity, the possibilities of modern womanhood, and the influence of American education and social values. Together these ideals suggested progress and modernity, an evolving sense of civilization from the ancient civilization of China to the young and vibrant modern democracy of the United States. The person of Soong represented this linear development from her childhood and education in the United States to her influence on her husband and on the Chinese people. Thus Soong was not simply a witness of the Christian faith, but a witness to the power of the American worldview (see figure 13).

## CELEBRATING THE CHINA MYSTIQUE

When Mayling Soong visited the United States in 1943, the China mystique was at its height. Major newspapers throughout the nation covered Soong's activities, statements, and wardrobe, as she spent February through March traveling across the United States. Lauded as a Chinese woman with an American outlook and mentality, Soong was the most evolved symbol of the United States' influence throughout the world. The various and sometimes competing demands Americans had of Soong throughout her visit reveal how race, gender, and nation fundamentally structure the culture of international diplomacy, including the roles that women play within this culture.[76] Her attempts to negotiate these demands also reflect Americans' changing views of China and celebrity during the 1940s.

Soong's visit to the United States in 1943, for example, reflects the different expectations Americans had of her as a representative of China and a unique American celebrity. In 1941, as chair of the China Emergency Relief Committee, Pearl Buck wrote a letter to Eleanor Roosevelt asking the first lady if she could invite Madame Chiang to visit the United States. Buck, conscious that this request could appear patronizing or even exploitative, suggested that Soong's visit could demonstrate the goodwill and concern that Americans had for China. Roosevelt was unable to issue such an invitation because her status as first lady would imply an official White House invitation.

After the United States entered the war, however, some of the president's advisors suggested that inviting Soong to visit the country could serve multiple purposes. With China and the United States now sharing a front against Japan, the U.S. federal government faced an imperative to educate Americans about the United States-China wartime alliance and how to think about China. One of the White House's goals in encouraging her visit to the United States was to present a united front in the Pacific theater and to further Americans' awareness about international affairs. Additionally, her visit could counter Japan's efforts to undermine the Allied war effort by suggesting that the war was about race, and that Japan was the best leader to overturn European and American influence in Asia. In a letter to the president, Archibald MacLeish, director of the Office of Facts and Figures, suggested Soong's visit,

> because of the obvious good it would accomplish in counteracting the intensive Tokyo propaganda that Japan is fighting for the cause of all races against the white race—particularly, the Anglo-Saxon race. This propaganda has had some effect on the Chinese; it has had more effect on the Filipinos, Malaysians, and the peoples of India. It even reaches, as you doubtless know, our own Negroes.[77]

As this letter indicates, some in the administration, blurring the distinction between nonwhite and non-American, assumed that Mayling Soong could speak out on American race relations from the authentic standpoint of being an ethnic minority. Pearl Buck was already actively addressing this very topic in her speeches and essays. Perhaps Soong's embodiment of racial difference and her representation of China might be more effective than Buck or other Euro-Americans; she might counteract the malicious propaganda and turn Asians and African Americans' attention to cooperation between the races, additionally emphasizing that the war was about more than just the Axis powers' defeat.

In 1942 an opportunity for the Roosevelts to invite Soong to visit the United States arose when she was reportedly in an auto accident and needed medical treatment. Hence the first lady wrote her, "I have discussed the matter with my husband and we both feel that a visit with us at the White House would not only enable us to get to know you better and secure a better appreciation of China's problems, but would also, in large measure, serve the ends of publicity."[78] Because of her position as first lady and the assumption that as a wife she would share and express her husband's interests, and because she was communicating with the wife of China's leader, Roosevelt's communication was clearly a matter of national interest and diplomacy. Its careful wording drew parallels between Soong's physical well-being and the welfare of China. Soong would enjoy access to advanced health treatment and to those who shaped America's attitudes and determined policy. This letter and additional diplomatic encouragement persuaded Chiang Kai-shek that his wife's visit to the United States could be useful; by November 1942 a presidential advisor was arranging for her arrival and medical care in the States.

On November 27, 1942, the president's press secretary issued a press release that Madame Chiang had entered Columbia's health center to receive treatment for an unspecified medical ailment. After her release, Soong would be a guest of the president and first lady at the White House. Intense media coverage and the unifying theme of winning the war against Japan stirred up an almost frenzied interest in Soong and her speaking engagements. Journalists impatiently awaited Soong's first public appearance in the United States at Union Station in Washington, D.C., where she would be received by First Lady Eleanor Roosevelt.[79]

*China's "First Lady"*

From the late 1930s through the Second World War, Soong was celebrated as the epitome of modern womanhood with a considerable amount of leverage within the global public sphere. The expectations of her as a national representative of China offer further insight into the gendering of national identities and, indirectly, of foreign policy.

Mayling Soong's active role in garnering favorable public and diplomatic attention for her husband and China was similar to that of her American counterpart, Eleanor Roosevelt, who had already mastered the art of media relations. As wives of the leaders of their countries, with easy access to domestic and international media, both women published their opinions in newspapers and books. For over a year Soong's speeches advocating women's public roles as moral housekeepers and mothers of the nation appeared in English-language Chinese newspapers. As the writer of a nationally syndicated column, *My Day,* Roosevelt maintained for the most part her identity as a wife, mother, and private citizen (although she never wavered publicly from positions staked by her husband's administration). Unlike Roosevelt, Soong wrote increasingly for international, and particularly American, circulation; her husband's authority ensured that her opinions carried weight. In *My Day* Roosevelt informally communicated events and issues of national interest to a domestic audience. Her commentary on Soong's visit as both first lady and private citizen thus was crucial to establish Soong's legitimacy as a representative of Chiang Kai-shek and China. (See figure 14, a photo taken at the White House.)

Roosevelt herself described Soong's relationship with the national community in terms of a female's role in companionate marriage: "I think any woman in this period must have a special feeling for this very beautiful, very charming, very gentle woman who has still managed to live through such years of hardship and share so completely with her countrymen, that not only does her husband consider her his partner but the people consider her their representative." The perception that Soong was an American daughter further complicated her role as a representative of new China. Although Soong may have seemed unusually liberated for a Chinese woman, Americans could and did just as easily claim her success as their own.[80]

Soong's fluency in English, her attractive femininity, and her American popularity thus were valuable tools in promoting to Americans the alliance between the Chinese Nationalist government and their own. At the same time, the unusual situation in which Soong participated directly as part of the generalissimo's inner circle lent itself to assumptions among some American and British diplomats that Chiang Kai-shek could not be an effective leader if he depended so much on his American-educated wife. The generalissimo's inability to speak or understand fluent English worked to his disadvantage in international relations. Thus, much as Roosevelt did, Soong spoke for her husband. She stated that a meeting between FDR and her husband would be a mistake, because his not speaking English "would make him look unbecoming" and leave him no room to maneuver verbally with a translator. (Apparently, such awkward and embarrassing situations had already occurred when he received foreign representatives.)[81] Hence, foreign diplomats to China had actually spoken with Soong and heard her voice China's needs and strategy, although uncertainty existed as to whether she was conveying her views or the generalissimo's.[82]

### Speaking to the American People

The exigencies of war—China's alliance with the United States, the generalissimo's necessary presence in China to lead the army's defense against Japan, and the pressure on the administration to educate the American public as what to its role in the war might be—allowed Soong access to platforms that might otherwise have been denied her based on her race, nationality, and gender.[83] She was thus invited to address both the House and Senate, and her popular appeal ensured that her words would be circulated among the American general public.

Soong's nationally broadcast speech before the House of Representatives was her first public statement as a foreign dignitary and returning American daughter. She began her speech by noting that in "speaking to Congress, I am literally speaking to the American people."[84] She borrowed the president's strategy of circumventing Congress and appealing directly to the public. She praised the country's celebrated and diverse immigrant heritage, themes that Buck and others had remarked on in the spirit of cultural pluralism, and themes now promoted by the U.S. government itself. Soong called the United States "the incubator of democratic principles" and described the unified diversity she witnessed at air bases

> [among] first-generation Germans, Italians, Frenchmen, Poles, Czechoslova-
> kians and other nationals. Some of them had accents so thick. . . . But there
> they were—all Americans. . . . No suspicion or rivalry existed between
> them. This increased my belief that devotion to common principles elimi-
> nates differences in race and that identity of ideals is the strongest possible
> solvent of racial dissimilarities.[85]

By emphasizing American principles of equality and their role in forging unity worldwide as a result of the war, Soong stated what Americans wanted to hear: that shared democratic principles could likewise tran- scend national borders as China and the United States worked together to ensure the freedom of Asian nations. While she particularly praised the cooperation between the United States and China against Japan, Soong still sharply critiqued the administration's wartime policy. Given the close ties between the two nations and their shared enmity with Japan, she argued, Japan was a greater threat to democracy than Ger- many and geographically represented a greater threat to the United States. Noting that China had been fighting Japan since the late 1930s, she questioned why China continued fight with little assistance while the United States engaged a "Hitler First" strategy in Europe.

Soong's speech surprised some with her focus on substantive issues as opposed to formal niceties. Although she received great praise from newspapers and the public for her speech, the Chinese ambassador to Britain, Wellington Koo, noted in his diary "that the White House was puzzled because not for once did any of the speeches mention the [pres- ident]" and that Soong's references to the American public's desire to focus on the war against Japan "was particularly distasteful" to the White House.[86] She surprised White House officials who had assumed that her visit would strengthen Franklin Roosevelt's public standing by demonstrating his commitment to diversity and to defeating Japan, which had directly attacked the United States, and that she would par- ticipate accordingly to reflect Roosevelt's global leadership.

Even though she was the guest of the president and first lady, Soong welcomed discussions with politicians who supported China's efforts against Japan but not necessarily FDR's leadership. As Koo noted in his diary entry of May 26, 1943, "Joe Kennedy, Mr. J. Forley, Wendell Willkie had seen her several times. They are all opposed to the Pres. politically. Mr. Hoover was about to call too. The Pres. had been evidently uneasy and Mrs. R had suggested that it might be more comfortable for her to live in Hyde Park." Soong herself told Koo that she was careful not to show her speeches to the president or Mrs. Roosevelt, even though "they intimated their wish to go over them before delivery."[87] Soong was not willing to allow anyone to use either her popularity or China without gaining something in return.

Popular American stereotypes about Chinese mysteriousness and deceitfulness also had their part in impressions of Soong within the White House. In one letter Roosevelt noted that her secretary, Tommy (Malvina Thompson), appeared to dislike Soong, "but I think it's because she feels an oriental is inscrutable!" She added that some of her female White House staff also distrusted Soong out of racial prejudice.[88] American diplomats as well were not immune to racist assumptions about Chinese. Accustomed to dealing with other males, some of these officials attributed their unease to what they perceived to be her conscious use of femininity and stereotypical Oriental deceit. In his diary the secretary of war, Henry L. Stimson, recorded his remark to a Department of State official who was to meet with Soong at the White House. "I cautioned him not to be vamped by her and to watch out sharply for what she said, and told him how at my similar interview with her a couple of weeks ago she had been very charming and beguiling and commented on the beauty of my hands."[89] This allusion to vamping—which evokes Anna May Wong's many roles—demonstrates how long-held popular perceptions of Chinese females shaded some diplomats' responses to Soong.

*Feminine Politics*

Despite the obstacles of American orientalism, Soong's intrusion into the male-dominated arena of diplomacy marked her unusual position as both foreign dignitary and celebrity, as evidenced in media coverage about her visit. Features about Madame Chiang appeared on the front page of newspapers and editorials as well as in the style and fashion sections. Magazine editors asked the OWI's Features Department to set up a conference where their representatives could meet China's first lady, an unusual request because magazines did not focus on current news events as did newspapers. Yet as Bess Furman of the Features Department noted, "Mme. Chiang Kai-shek commands universal interest."[90] The magazine conference with Soong attracted publications including *Woman's Home Companion, Charm, Glamour, Cosmopolitan, Parents Life, American, This Week, The Rotarian,* and the *Saturday Evening Post.* Soong's full-color fashion layout for *Vogue* magazine demonstrates the overlapping of her "American" and "Chinese" identities. She was featured wearing designer fashions for the accompanying story, thus simultaneously advertising designer fashion and new China.[91]

Soong's blurred roles as an informal diplomat and international celebrity further demonstrate how the rhetoric of wartime activism extended traditional boundaries for white middle-class women. For example, when Soong was a "special guest" at Eleanor Roosevelt's press conference for female reporters, she was asked about the ERA and her role in advocating equal rights for women in China's government. In response to a question posed about women's role in the peace process, Soong bluntly declared, "I do not mean this as a dig, but statesmen the world over so far have failed to keep peace, to maintain peace. Women never have had a chance at peace conferences to see what they can do. Well, why not give women a chance." Her response was incorporated into NWP goals: Soong "advocated" the Equal Rights Amendment and was quoted as saying, "I have never known brains to have [a] sex." The commentator continued, "With such a warrior and stateswoman advocating it, why oppose it?" and voiced a popular opinion that Mayling Soong and other women be included in the negotiations for peace after the war ended. Roosevelt immediately prompted before another reporter could follow up, "No one has asked Mme. C. about her orphanages."[92]

Although Soong's statements about women's equality and role in world diplomacy were challenging, they still adhered to popular maternalist assumptions about women. While her empowered image as China's first lady leading new China into modernity caught the imagination of self-identified feminists, Soong's image as China's mother figure caring for orphans and others displaced by the war found appreciative audiences from women's service associations across a spectrum of liberal, conservative, urban, rural, religious and secular affiliations. During her visit in 1943, several American women's organizations raised funds for China and informed their members about China. The American Federation of Soroptomist Clubs created a committee on Chinese contacts in March to nurture the members' friendship and knowledge of China through educational and social programs and, as a service project, to raise funds for the student nurses of China. By November 1943 more than 100 clubs (out of a total of 173) associated with the Soroptomists had held "more than 100 educational and social program meetings . . . [dedicated] to deepening our Friendship with China through mutual understanding." That same month the group passed a resolution favoring repeal of Chinese exclusion.[93] Beginning in February 1943 the Associated Women of the American Farm Bureau Federation also raised funds for the medical care of women and children in China. Yet another organization that raised over $22,000 in 1943 for Soong's work with war orphans from January 1943 onward was the Order of the Eastern Star, a rural women's organization that was particularly conservative.[94] Thus Soong's femininity, articulated in her status as first lady and mother to China's war orphans, appealed to women across regional and political lines.

Similarly, many Americans viewed her Christianity as yet another example of her American heritage. Soong's Christian faith enhanced the feminine aspects of her serving her husband and nation, as well as her virtue. In March 21, 1943, right after her successful debut in Washington, D.C., Reverend Ralph W. Sockman claimed that the basis of America's reception for Soong was "the bond of fellowship which Christian missionaries have been weaving between China and America during the last century."[95] During her American visit, Soong's article for *Forum*, "What My Religion Means to Me," was reissued at least three times by church-affiliated organizations in pamphlet form. The World Service Department of the Canadian Council of YMCAs published the article as *My Religion*. In 1943 the International Committee of the YMCA reprinted the generalissimo's testimony, "I Bear My Witness"; a short summary, "The Soong Family"; and "I Confess My Faith" (a reprint of "What My Religion Means to Me"), all under the title *We Believe*.

## White Supremacy and the China Mystique

Walter White, an author and the secretary of the NAACP, had anticipated Soong's visit as a particularly significant occasion to consider China's place in international affairs and the analogous position of minorities in American society. White proposed a panel discussion "to focus attention of Americans on the global nature of the question of skin color and 'white supremacy' both as a factor in winning the war and in winning the peace." He and other Americans asserted that China's war was not simply about defeating Japan but also about being taken seriously and putting racial stereotypes and prejudice to rest. Hence, White hoped,

Soong's unique status as a Chinese representative and American celebrity would provide the impetus for all Americans to confront issues of racial prejudice within American society as well as worldwide. Intimating her own concerns about race relations, Roosevelt forwarded White's letter to Soong during her White House stay. Even though the issue might detract from her purpose to raise support for China, White, other African Americans, and left intellectuals including Richard J. Walsh and Pearl S. Buck believed Soong could use her popularity to discuss racism.[96]

But Soong did not publicly address racial tensions in the United States—abiding by the diplomatic understanding that countries avoid critiquing each other's nationalist myths—and American officials did not publicly acknowledge her husband's authoritarian practices. This complicit silence diminished the possibility of Soong's developing a broader base of support among Americans and increased her reliance on institutions intent on maintaining the status quo, in race relations as in Sino-American relations.

Her silence acknowledged the subordinate position of China and her own advocacy. In courting American political favor she could not alienate Congress, the president, or businesses, which possessed the power to aid China. Her fulfillment of American assumptions about true womanhood—American education, Southern accent, Christian reforms, and affluent background—did not challenge whiteness as a fundamental organizing principle of the United States and the national community.

Debate over race relations would undermine affirmations of cultural, social, or political affinity between the two countries and affirm Japan's critique of the international system of whiteness that informed American foreign policy and subjugated the nations of Africa and Asia. Such open critique was expected from the enemy, not from an ally. While Soong clearly knew about American racial prejudice as well as Chinese racism, the China mystique represented the only viable possibility of achieving concrete results from her visit.

## American Popularity

As an embodiment of new China, Soong grew more and more popular as she made her way across the American landscape, enabling Americans to actually see and hear this woman about whom they had heard so much. "The American public . . . demands personal symbols," Ida Pruitt wrote from China to a friend during this time, and "the Generalissimo and Madame are the symbols of fighting China." Furthermore, she added, the publicity generated by Soong, "has really made . . . the Generalissimo's position more human and understandable to the American public."[97] One indication of her celebrity was that (with the State Department's prompting) her speech at Madison Square Garden preempted an already scheduled boxing match for March 2. As Walter Winchell noted, "she was more important than any boxing match. . . . More important? She's the best scrapper the Garden ever had."[98] For those who were not fortunate enough to see Soong in person, newsreels, newspapers or radio provided access. Her net effect was magnified by the many representations of her image, words, and actions that circulated throughout the United States. (See figure 15, one photo taken at Wellesley.)

To show their support for the national wartime effort, communities sought to participate in the cross-country pageantry as well as the efforts to aid Madame Chiang's new China. Interest in this "first lady of the world" crossed ethnic, class and regional lines. Attempts to persuade Madame Chiang to appear in communities throughout the United States manifested regional boosterism, a sort of "nationalist localism." "Millions in the great expanses of American territory between" her scheduled stops of Chicago, San Francisco and Los Angeles were "eager to see the American-educated First Lady of China, and a great part of her last day's stay in New York, it was indicated by members of her secretariat, was devoted to decisions concerning the flood of invitations which had poured in upon her from all parts of the country." People gathered at her hotel, "anxious to catch a glimpse of her" on the way to the railroad station. Her press conference in Los Angeles was described by one participant as "undoubtedly the largest ever held in Los Angeles . . . attended by more than 100 representatives of wire service, the metropolitan press, and African, Indian and Chinese papers." By the time she departed from the United States, one fan wrote to the White House suggesting "Madame Chiang Kai-shek be appointed the first President of the United Nations," and several more suggested she be a global representative for world peace to the United Nations.[99]

Americans perceived in Mayling Soong the relevance and affirmation of American values in an international context. Stanley K. Hornbeck, of the Department of State's Far Eastern Division, remarked, "What the American public most wants to hear and will most enjoy from Madame Chiang is . . . a narrative regarding modern China and modern America and relations between the two—with, perhaps, broad statements about the war and the peace-to-be thrown in."[100] Hornbeck's observations of the American public during the Second World War were par-

Mayling Soong                                        141

ticularly astute. In a time of increased national consciousness heightened by international conflict, pageantry offers one of the primary means to affirm unity through celebrating core values of the national community and of the world community as well. As a result, Soong during her tour rendered local events national events and national events international.

## DECOMPOSING THE GOOD EARTH

Mayling Soong's speaking tour of the United States officially ended in Los Angeles at the Hollywood Bowl on April 4, 1943. It began with "China: A Symphonic Narrative," a spectacular pageant developed by the Hollywood producer David O. Selznick to convey China's history through music, acting, and narration.[101] In its sweep, the overdetermined historical display of modern China in America's imagination evoked *The Good Earth* and reflected the influence Pearl Buck had on American images of China. Anna May Wong was conspicuously absent, but the drama offered up her legacy of orientalized femininity and glamorous ethnicity as Hollywood stars and Chinese American women paraded onstage. Its celebration of celebrity, reliance on feminine glamour, and casting of ethnicity as nationality enacted social definitions of gender, race, and nation.

"China" relied on the best talent Selznick could pull together. Harry Kronman worked with Selznick on the script. Herbert Stothart, who had composed the score for MGM's *Good Earth* in 1937, composed the symphonic score as well as the "Madame Chiang March." The 120-piece Los Angeles Philharmonic Orchestra and the combined "Los Angeles Choruses" performed the score in the background as the work unfolded. William Dieterle (who had directed an Oscar-winning film about Emile Zola) directed the entire twenty-minute production that combined "Oriental pageantry and military formality" and contextualized for the American audience Madame's historical significance.[102]

### China's History, American Style

The pageant throughout emphasized the symbolic unity between the United States and China. "Go West! Go to the West!" The voice of Generalissimo Chiang Kai-shek, supplied by the actor Edward G. Robinson, rang out from the Santa Monica Hills and over the audience: "My people in the coastal regions . . . Go to the West!" Evoking the westward expansion of the United States and the agrarian wisdom of Jefferson, "the Voice"—as named in the script—articulated the overlapping of fictional and factual narratives, combining the romanticized vision of ambitious American pioneers trekking westward with the overwhelming yet equally romanticized vision of hundreds of victimized Chinese fleeing the Japanese invaders.

The ensuing westward trek of millions of Chinese from the famine, flood, and destruction was enacted by as many local Chinese as the producers could recruit. Their westward movement became the metaphor for the entire narrative as China drew closer to the "West," figuratively and culturally. The score corresponded with the action, modulating from high-pitched atonal strings and clanging gongs to a more familiar orchestration of a martial nature. The contrast provided by the music and the action made the point even more clearly: old China was giving way to a new China, one more educated, industrialized, democratic and Americanized. According to the *Daily News*, the production was "Hollywood at its peak of colorful achievement."

> Scores of Chinese moppets in colorful costumes moved back and forth across the stage as Walter Huston told the story of China. Coolies carried their loads of vegetables, villagers worked at their age old crafts and peace ruled the land.
> *Then came the Japanese,* to stab China in the back. There was movement on a grand scale. A simulated bombing attack scattered the villagers, screaming in terror. The movement continued—to the west, to build a new China.
> Even nature conspired to aid in the spectacle, for at China's darkest hour, as related by narrator Huston, the sun went behind the clouds, to emerge just as China emerged in her new strength with the Generalissimo Chiang Kai-Shek, through the voice of Edward G. Robinson, crying encouragement to the land.
> Even as the spirit of New China surged through the performers, Madame Chiang arose and walked to the podium as though she might have been a part of the pageant. There was no break as she began speaking.

For five reels of precious film stock—in short supply during the war—Soong stood at the podium and described in detail China's resistance against Japan's imperialism. Fully aware that the audience had come to celebrate not only China but itself as a national community, she nonetheless emphasized that China had kept fighting without outside help and had provided "time to the democracies to prepare their defenses." The greatest applause came when she acknowledged "the foresight and statesmanship of President Roosevelt when . . . (applause) [he] took decisive measures to enable America to become the arsenal of democracy."[103]

The pageant also emphasized the role of women as both objects of consumption and as symbols of national pride and character. When festivities began Soong sat with a group of glamorous stars, including Ingrid Bergman, Barbara Stanwyck, Rosalind Russell, Deanna Durbin, Ginger Rogers, and Loretta Young. Spencer Tracy, who had played leading man to many of them, further emphasized their femininity when he, opened the pageant with the following tribute to yet another famous female on display, Madame Chiang:

> China gives us, for this precious hour, a great and gallant guest, a woman, slim and fragile as a woman is, with all a woman's immemorial strength. These two small hands, a woman's hands, have swept the cobwebs from a nation's past. These hands have lit dark corners in its homes, have built its schools, cared for its young and nursed its war-made wounds. These hands, a woman's hands, have helped to shape a nation's destiny. This heart, a woman's heart, whispers a simple woman's hope and all the world must pause and hear. And yet, one does not speak of Madame Chiang Kai-Shek unless one speaks of China too, of China's yesterday which was her heritage, China's tomorrow which is her life.[104]

Tracy's scripted introduction emphasized Soong's womanhood and femininity. The two sentences that did not address her womanhood focused instead on woman's activities as traditionally centered on nurture and healing. The introduction then reinscribed her femininity on the national identity of "China."

By overdetermining gender—simultaneously embodying and disembodying Soong—the introduction contains her challenge to the gender hierarchy of United States and Chinese nationalism. It equates Soong's influence in China and traditional social roles ascribed to women in the United States. Her startling command of American public discourse on China has less to do with taking an active role in China (and United States) politics than with mobilizing China's women within accepted parameters of feminine behavior—nurture, reform, and education.

Although the pageant's focus on Soong as a woman may make her more accessible to the American public, the excessive focus on her gender also erases markers of class and racial difference. Nowhere within the narrative is she referred to as "Chinese." Crediting her with almost single-handedly ushering China into the present effectively obscures the intellectual and political responses of Chinese men and women to Western imperialism over hundreds of years and ignores the costs of Chiang Kai-shek's coerced modernization to the Chinese populace.[105] Reading Soong's life as the history of China—her past as heritage and her life as the future—effectively rewrites China's history within the period of U.S. involvement in China.

### An American Mindset

The spectacular pageantry at the Hollywood Bowl illustrates the wartime blurring of entertainment and news coverage of the war. Entertainment took precedence over the narrative itself, which provided a more palatable but less factual portrayal of the events leading to China's renewal. This particular American narrative suggested that Chinese lived off the "good earth" in pastoral peace until the vicious Japanese attacked, conveniently overlooking the Western powers' acquisitive role in China and the internal factions within China that contributed to the poor living conditions for Chinese.[106] Chiang Kai-shek was represented as an Americanizing force, calling his people to the West, but the generalissimo himself was far from Americanized. The narrative itself served as a metaphor for Sino-American relations, a product of fictional license engaged in by both the Chinese and the American governments and numerous Americans: Japan was not the only country to take advantage of China, China was not at this point a united nation, Chiang Kai-shek was not a Jefferson, nor for that matter was Sun Yat-sen a Chinese George Washington.

Madame Chiang, the ultimate symbol of a modern and Americanized China, provided the central motif. The syndicated newspaper columnist Louella Parsons explained the pageant's concept: "the idea is to take the lucky people who will be present . . . right to China with, of course, the gracious First Lady of that country as the key note around whom the colorful idea pivots."[107] Continually in search of ways to "sell China," Selznick perceived Soong to be the ideal product for mainstream American consumption. "[S]he is the one dramatic figure around which something important could be done," he later noted, "and she represents the only showmanship that can be put to use in this country."[108] A new, improved China had arrived in America and was accessible and comprehensible to the American public in the person of Mayling Soong.

The pageant relied on the fascination of many Americans with Soong in order to stake America's claim on China. The American media identified her as one of their own, a product of an American education and hence endowed with an American mind—an affirmation of the American way in Christianity, thought, and behavior. The extent to which Americans perceived Soong to be "like them" was indicated when a group of congressmen inquired of the Bureau of Immigration and Naturalization about the possibility of providing honorary U.S. citizenship to Mayling Soong—this in spite of the fact that Chinese immigrants were *not* allowed to become naturalized citizens, and that Chinese were largely excluded from immigrating to the United States at this time.[109]

The media's fond claim of America's influence on Soong's character performed an even greater erasure of class privilege. Americans' need for visible Chinese heroes and unifying symbols of Sino-American unity necessarily ignored the obvious class subtext of Soong's success story. Numerous articles eagerly chronicled the development of Soong's American character but glossed over the privilege her American accent betrayed.[110] Her family's wealth, which had facilitated her transnational identity, might be attributed as much to the conditions resulting from foreign imperialism in China as it was to her father's skillful entrepreneurship.

## GENDER POLITICS AND INTERNATIONAL DIPLOMACY

Soong's desire to negotiate China-United States relations and wartime strategy did not fulfill traditional feminine roles. Although Soong seemed quite comfortable meeting with male legislators, diplomats, and officials during her visit, Roosevelt observed that male officials from her husband's administration were not comfortable with China's first lady. Her combination of power and femininity made them uncomfortable, and they were afraid that they would be manipulated into agreeing to something they had not intended. In a letter to her daughter, Anna, Roosevelt observed that "In a queer way I think the men are afraid of her. She is keen & drives for her point & works to nail them down. They squirm."[111]

### The Politics of Protocol

While her informal role as the wife of China's leader undermined her effectiveness with American officials, Soong attempted to use her popularity with the American people to advance China's wartime interests. Soong undoubtedly enjoyed greater access to diplomatic negotiations than she would have otherwise because she was perceived as a partner in her husband's leadership and because of China's popularity. Within the culture of diplomacy that already devalued her input based on her gender, race, and nationality, Soong's demands were perceived by various officials as the products of feminine unpredictability. On the one hand, she and her entourage demanded protocol befitting rulers and royalty; on the other, perceiving herself as an informal diplomat without official status, Soong raised issues that were not welcome at the negotiating table yet reflected her frustration with the global racial and national inequities China faced.

The differences between Winston Churchill and Mayling Soong's visits to the United States in 1943 highlight the gendered practice of politics. Winston Churchill's April 1943 visit to Washington presented a marked contrast to the fanfare of Soong's—and deliberately so. He met with the president, addressed a joint session of Congress, and assured the American public that the "Hitler first" strategy was sound, and that Japan would be defeated. Jack Stinnett of Oklahoma City queried, "Why, it may be asked, was Churchill's visit so hush-hush, and Madame's so well advertised? Simply because Madame's visit had to do with molding public opinion, while Churchill's had to do with secret conferences over future United Nations war strategy. In the former there was every reason for publicity—in the latter every reason for secrecy."[112]

During Churchill's visit, FDR tried to arrange a meeting between the prime minister and Soong, but protocol proved to be a more formidable obstacle than he expected. Wellington Koo and the British ambassador Lord Halifax worked diligently with high hopes for such a meeting to improve their countries' relations. But determining the location of the meeting, which itself reflected issues of power and status, symbolized the existing tensions between the two nations. The president and first lady sought to ease the impasse by inviting both to lunch at the White House. T. V. Soong recognized that FDR intended to "provide a solution to a delicate problem," and that "the [president's] invitation was more or less a command." When Soong declined the invitation to the White House but accepted Hyde Park as a compromise, Churchill replied that he was too busy to take an additional trip to New York. FDR and Churchill, as well as the Chinese diplomats Koo and her brother T. V., viewed Soong's refusal to travel to the White House as the temperamental machinations of a "diva." Her nephew L. K. Kung expounded to the Chinese ambassador to Britain: "as a Lady, Mme. Chiang should be called on by Churchill; and as a statesman, she could meet him only half way," at Hyde Park. [113] Soong's entourage justified their expectation of Churchill's agreeing to meet her halfway through a protocol of gender—the man paid respects to the woman. Churchill rejected this assumption because statesmanship trumped gentlemanly behavior.

The focus on protocol further illustrates the fundamental male privilege in shaping the political discourse. When Soong was successful in her public performance of power, a traditionally male site, Churchill claimed the private as the site of greater importance and was able to force Soong to negotiate on those terms. The importance of his work kept him immobile in seclusion, whereas her implicitly less significant work made her schedule and location more flexible. Soong thus met the challenge of the initial rules, only to find them abruptly and arbitrarily reversed in Churchill's favor. Significantly, FDR's attempt to arrange this meeting suggests that he did perceive her as representing China, regardless of her ambiguous position. Soong's resorting to traditional forms of gentlemanly and womanly behavior, however, was interpreted as a demonstration of her capriciousness and inability to conduct matters of state.

For Soong, the question of protocol and place was a question of politics: she believed that her symbolic interaction with Great Britain extended beyond China to include other countries that had hitherto been treated as less than equal by European powers. During the negotiations over where to meet Churchill, she passionately denounced British attitudes toward China: "Great Britain must realize that China of today is no longer the China of yesterday and she should not accept the same old, paternal patronizing attitude toward her."[114] Underlying Soong's focus on protocol were her experiences with British colonialism and racism, and her conviction that she represented not only China but colonized Asian and African countries also.

## The Fighter

Tellingly, the glimpses of Soong that reflected her political commitment and passion for China were not those that emphasized protocol or that received the most media coverage. One of her former secretaries, Ilona Ralf Sues, insisted that Soong "was entirely different from the person the Western world pictured her to be. She was no angel of mercy but she was the one and only effective American Ambassador to China." Sues suggested that a "real" Madame Chiang existed behind the image, one who was "not the sentimental Good Samaritan, not the widely publicized pious Bible-quoter, not the bluestocking reformer, but Madame Chiang Kai-shek the Fighter—for a decent government, for an efficient administration, for a modern China."[115]

This Mayling Soong made few public appearances during the
United States visit. When she visited San Francisco, Mayor Angelo
Rossi neglected to invite labor interests, including the International
Longshoremen's and Warehouseman's Union. This union had been the
first to support China's boycott of Japanese goods in 1932 (and allow
Chinese American pickets on the docks), backing a nation that its own
government did not take seriously, and at great economic cost to
members and their families. Although Chiang Kai-shek had worked
with Chinese industrialists to wipe out the unions in Shanghai, Soong
could show her appreciation of an American union that acted inde-
pendently. In the words of one reporter, Soong "took matters into her
own hands. She descended on the Longshoreman's hall and addressed
them as 'fellow workers' for half an hour. After all, it was this union
that had been in hot water for many years because of its refusal to pass
Chinese picket lines and load scrap metal to make bullets to kill the
Chinese."[116] An Associated Press report of Soong's address at this
"suddenly scheduled mass meeting" of AFL-CIO, Maritime Union,
and Railroad brotherhoods presents a different image of the composed and dignified woman most Americans expected. Instead of
obliquely referring to China's heroism, Soong linked China's victory
to U.S. wartime production.

> She spoke in impassioned tones, shouting and almost screaming at times.
> Calling the union men assembled her "fellow" workers because their pro-
> duction was helping China, the elegantly dressed wife of the Chinese gener-
> alissimo cried: 'Do you want to lose this war?'
>     As a voice the answer came: 'No!'
>     'Do you want to increase production?' she asked.
>     'Yes! Yes! Yes!'
>     'Then,' she shouted, 'let all labor cooperate and increase production.'
>     'Production must increase,' she yelled. 'There must be no dissension, no dif-
> ference of opinion among us.'[117]

This image was a far cry from the more highly publicized, feminine, and
demure image of Soong in the press and had as much to do with Americans' molding her image to fit their own expectations of how a woman
and a dignitary should behave. Nonetheless, at times she brushed aside
her determination to remain outside the domestic politics of the United
States. Such was the case at a tea party attended by all of the heads of
Hollywood film studios. During this gathering, the studio executives expected that she would provide them with advice on plots and presentation to show China in a better light. When they asked how they could

help China through their films, Soong answered honestly with passion. One observer wrote, "She spoke of the 'stupidity' of always representing China in the spirit of 'Chin-Chin Chinamen' and the unjustifiable use of the word China men to denigrate Chinese—There was a moment of tension . . . silence & stiffness prevailed in the room filled with some 40 odd people."[118]

## American Memories

While Chinese and American officials dismissed Soong's focus on protocol as an expression of her irrational femininity, her motivation went much deeper. She shared her memories about Americans while a child in China with her husband's advisor Owen Lattimore. "She several times spoke to me very bitterly about her father, who had gone up in the world through working for American missionaries, having always been treated by the Americans as a Chinese of poor origin. He would travel in the interior and visit Chinese Christian communities, distributing religious materials and tracts. When he came back and reported to the missionaries in Shanghai, he would have to stand in front of the white people who were sitting. They never invited him to sit down . . . he was treated more like a servant than a colleague. She thought that the American attitude to herself also had always been: 'Oh yes, she is clever of course, but after all she is only a Chinese.' She felt that the American attitude was racist and condescending, and she bitterly resented it. That was why, whenever she visited the United States, she insisted on top ceremonial protocol."[119]

Even with top protocol, however, Soong felt great pressure to prove her legitimacy to Americans and other Westerners. Her lectures became increasingly, absurdly, weighed down with obscure words as if to establish her intelligence and ability, her right to be heard. On June 16, 1943, she spoke before a joint session of the Canadian Parliament on "Democracy versus Ochlocracy," and a reporter struggled to record her words: "Ochlocracy . . . is but the inchoate roccoco [sic] of mob rule bred on febrile emotions and unrestraint."[120]

Thus, while Soong recognized the necessity of U.S. aid, and in several ways sought to institute reforms in China modeled on her American experience, she simultaneously perceived, as Buck did, the relationship between racial prejudice and imperialism. Unlike Buck, who as a white American could critique the United States and European imperialism more freely, Soong could only indirectly demand the respect that was not given to her father as a Chinese citizen. Soong thus was speaking not only on behalf of Nationalist China to the American public but against the racism and imperialism she had experienced throughout her life. Her anti-imperialism also extended beyond China's borders to other Asian countries that had been subject to colonization. (Not surprisingly, her critique of the violence of Western imperialism did not extend to a critique of her husband's oppressive government and abuse of power or of the ways in which family members profited from exploiting their positions as well.)

Based on her own knowledge of the prejudice Chinese encountered in the United States, Soong urged officials to repeal Chinese exclusion laws. Immediately after Soong's February 1943 appearance in Congress, Representative Martin J. Kennedy introduced his bill to repeal Chinese exclusion: "We welcome you also, as a daughter is welcomed by her foster-mother, to the land where you received an American education. . . . I take this auspicious occasion, in your gracious presence, as an indication of my unbounded admiration of a nation's courage which has amazed the world, to introduce this day a bill to grant to the Chinese rights of entry to the United States and rights of citizenship."[121] Over the next month several editorials in favor of repeal mentioned Soong by name, and some even proposed repeal specifically as a tribute to her. Toward the end of her stay in the United States, Soong herself noted the opportune moment to press for repeal. While meeting in New York, "she told [the Chinese ambassador] Dr. Wei to press for the passage of the Kennedy bill to remove the restrictions on Ch[inese] immigration on the [C]hinese Exclusion Act and said it was the time to do it as the wave of sympathy for China, as a result of the visit, was at its height."[122]

## The Politics of Celebrity

Throughout her visit to the United States, Soong negotiated the tension between the American public's sense of owning her image and her desire to represent China with dignity. The 1940s witnessed a significant shift in the tension between elitism and egalitarianism embodied by celebrities. As Joshua Gamson explains it, celebrities were perceived to be "public servants," and "the public was increasingly credited with *control* of celebrity."[123] A range of interests had always read Soong's celebrity in a variety of ways. The *Chicago Defender,* a black publication, viewed her as a representative of an emerging non-Western world power and proclaimed Soong's visit as a sign of progress for nonwhite

populations throughout the world. Feminists celebrated Soong as an example of the role women should play in international politics as peace-
makers, reading into her womanhood their expectations of themselves.
Some Americans saw Soong as an American success story, representing
individual merit and accomplishment. Others saw her as a Chinese
woman embodying the potential for democracy to inspire change
throughout the world. Christian leaders and missionaries cited her as an
example of Christianity's powerful and potential legacy. Americans in
general interpreted Soong's visit to the United States as a personal quest
for American aid. Aware of many of these views, Soong tried to avoid
other people's attempts to capitalize on her name or presence.[124] The
Hollywood Bowl pageantry illuminates the balancing act Soong performed during her 1943 visit.

Like Pearl S. Buck and Anna May Wong, then, Mayling Soong navi-
gated a gendered landscape of power and authority that limited the extent to which women could wield public influence. Soong continually negotiated the tension of her position in the United States: the popularity
and fame she enjoyed in the United States, based partly on her feminine
glamour and unique personality, threatened to undermine the serious intent of her visit. To initiate any extended discussion of issues such as
global race relations and Western imperialism could jeopardize her popularity with the American public, whose support and interest were critical to her and China's influence in the United States. In many ways,
Soong sought to transcend the gendered division of labor in diplomacy.
Her gender automatically provided her with a popular audience, but the
respect and attention she sought for China were reserved for statesmen,
not their wives.

In bringing China to the United States, Soong faced an entirely different and unfamiliar context of political and cultural politics. In China
her American popularity and connections had served her well. She engaged in constant strategizing and political intrigue—involving her conflicts with the Chinese military traditionalists and even her siblings—to
maintain her position within the generalissimo's inner circle of advisers.
And within the United States, Soong now had to manage her popular
image and celebrity. For the American public, her celebrity appearance
was the end result of her visit. Her audience in China, however, was
waiting to see if she could transform her popularity into political influence on U.S. foreign policy. Soong's visit to the United States vastly increased her visibility and recognition as well as her vulnerability. In the
United States, she had little political and emotional support on which to

draw. China relief organizations tended to be more interested in her ability to produce public support and funds for China than in any specific policy. Soong, as a visitor, had no choice but to wield her influence and negotiations openly. Although she spoke before Congress and met with the Committee on Foreign Affairs, she held no official bargaining power. She then took her attempts to negotiate power in favor of her husband's regime to the public sphere.

The Chinese officials who organized Soong's tour did not understand the dynamic nature of celebrity in the United States: celebrity based on public fascination does not automatically accord public power but can actually erode it. The 200 percent increase in donations to China relief organizations during her tour in 1943 contributed to Americans' sense of ownership of Soong's personal actions, but not to her empowerment in American politics.[125] When she was considering a trip to the United States in October 1942, her friend Geraldine Fitch offered her an American's advice. Recognizing the public's short attention span, she suggested, "Come . . . for *two weeks only* . . . with all the fanfare . . . and then—*disappear completely.*"[126] By the 1940s, the increased marketing of celebrities and figureheads, according to Gamson, made the celebrity image less persuasive, the audience less inclined to accept the image alone: "The distrust of public fronts was undercut by the promise of the private life exposed."[127] Critics said that Soong's tour had dragged on too long, had lost its personality, and had become a vanity production. As her public image lost its intrigue, her private life increasingly overshadowed her public image.

When she attempted to limit those readings that celebrated America through her coming to visit the United States, Soong's actions, as well as her failing marriage, inspired further readings that focused on her legitimacy as a national representative. During her stay in the United States, rumors began circulating among diplomatic circles that Chiang Kai-shek's second wife had moved back to Chongqing and was residing with the general; other rumors circulated that the son's pregnant lover was actually the pregnant lover of the generalissimo.[128]

Americans' ideals of appropriate behavior for a diplomatic representative of China also called into question her authority to speak for the Chinese. Many columnists pointed out the contradiction between Soong's extravagant receptions with champagne and caviar and her pleas for the starving Chinese. The White House, Wellesley, and UCR received letters complaining about this. As one China supporter described it, "She was . . . accused of snobbishness and arrogance and a prima donna temperament. Even her sex life and her financial integrity were smeared in a widespread rumor-mongering campaign."[129] The American press and politicians criticized Soong for being either too feminine—less rational, politically naive, and lacking understanding about military matters—or not feminine enough because she allowed her marriage to fall apart.

Gossip about Soong's not having children further undermined her status as "China's first lady." Public speculation about her possible refusal to have children raised questions about her femininity. This, in addition to reports of uncivil behavior, had political and personal consequences. Politically, questions of whether her behavior was fitting for a "first lady" undermined her effectiveness in pressing China's case. Soong appeared to have also lost power within her husband's inner circle to her brother T. V. and others, along with the generalissimo's confidence. Her health progressively worsened as she made her way west. By the time she reached Los Angeles, she was severely ill and newspapers reported that she had a nervous breakdown. The generalissimo was furious with the reports circulating about her in the United States and demanded that she return to Chongqing immediately. Although Soong returned to Chongqing in late October 1943, she and her sister Madame Kung departed soon after for Brazil, lending fuel to the speculation about her marriage to the generalissimo.

When Soong had first arrived in the United States, she hoped that a successful visit would solidify her status within her husband's government. As Madame Chiang Kai-shek, her personal life in China was inevitably politicized because of her American popularity. "It was always the same thing: the United States was the barometer—when America helped, Madame was on top; when America failed China, she was under fire."[130] Thus the political ramifications of her tour were equally personal. She expressed as much when she confided to Harry Hopkins, the president's special assistant, "the President must not let me down with the Generalissimo."[131] Yet U.S. officials saw her as a woman with little more than propaganda value for their own purposes; they did not seem to realize that Soong might also wield significant influence with Chiang Kai-shek, and their lack of support weakened her credibility with her husband and made her vulnerable to the criticism from other forces within the KMT.

Soong's gender, race, class, religion, and the assurance that *she would return to China* generated her positive reception by many Americans. She had been able to capture Americans' imaginations as Madame Chiang Kai-shek by symbolizing what Americans needed and wanted to understand—that China and the United States held similar goals in the post-war world, and that Chinese and Americans could communicate. Her participation in affirming the two countries' wartime alliance further contributed to the image of cooperation that American officials sought. But her attempts to transform that popularity into political leverage to effect institutional change faltered. Her negotiations as a Chinese woman seeking to alter U.S. policy toward China and Chinese in America over-reached her status as a woman and a Chinese within the United State's culture of diplomacy.

Soong's tour marked the culmination of the China mystique. But it also revealed the China mystique for what it was—American orientalism expeditiously rearranged to fit the needs of the United States during a par-ticularly dramatic transformation from isolationist, 100 percent Ameri-canism into an internationalist nation that valued cultural pluralism.

# CHAPTER 5

# Transforming American National Identity— The China Mystique

Orientalism assumes that the cultures of the West and Orient are in diametric opposition. American orientalism from the turn of the century through the 1920s projects similarly distorted images of Chinese as primitive, slavish, exotic, manipulative, and amoral while American nationalism views its own population as modern, free, civilized, and trustworthy. Regardless of ideological borders people moved back and forth between the two nations. As the family histories of Pearl Buck, Anna May Wong, and Mayling Soong indicate, interaction between the United States and China has always relied on individuals—missionaries, immigrants, and diplomats—to link the two cultures. The formation of American mission boards, restrictive U.S. immigration laws, and U.S. treaties with China to monitor their movement institutionalized assumptions that informed American orientalism and nationalism.

Thus as a child Pearl Sydenstricker Buck knew China better than she knew the United States. Her presence in China resulted from the imperialism of Western powers in China, which had forced the Chinese government to make accessible its ports as well as its people to foreign commerce and missions. Her mother's longing for "home" and her father's desire to nurture a human legacy in China indelibly shaped Buck's understanding of the United States. The internal decline of the Qing dynasty and the intrusion of acquisitive Western nations encouraged many Chinese males to seek out better economic opportunities elsewhere, including the United States. Anna May Wong knew China as a nostalgic memory of the Chinese American community in which she grew up and as the exotic portrayals of China in Hollywood films. The weight of racial prejudice in the United States reinforced her identification with China as the homeland, a location and community where she and other Chinese Americans might find acceptance. Mayling Soong, in contrast, grew up in a China adjusting to the changes wrought by Western imperialism. Her father's American education presented the United States as place of opportunity, and his work with missionaries demonstrated the ethnocentric arrogance of Americans toward the Chinese. Soong herself engaged American society and its attitudes about China through her American education, and later as a representative of China's interests during the war.

In negotiating the relationship between China and the United States, all three women experienced its contradictions. All three enjoyed certain advantages through travel and their participation in American popular culture; they also confronted the limitations of gender, race, ethnicity, and nationality in their own lives.

ADVANTAGES

*Travel*

Through travel each woman gained access to greater social mobility to confound the assumptions of American orientalism. Pearl Buck's experience at Randolph-Macon Woman's College as the marginalized daughter of missionaries shaped her views of the United States. She was able to use her experience of "authentic China" in writing her first two novels, *East Wind, West Wind* and *The Good Earth*. She did not recognize that she owed her success in the United States to her privilege in China, even though she recognized the imperialism of missions and the arrogance of foreigners. Mayling Soong remembered her father's humiliation by foreign missionaries when she was a child in China. Traveling from a prominent position in China based on class to a marginal one in the United States based on ethnicity, she observed many of her Wellesley classmates from a distance—yet on returning home, Soong realized how alienated she had become from Chinese culture. Paradoxically, after marrying Chiang Kai-shek, she appeared to enjoy less power in China than in the United States, where to many her gender, nationality, and leadership marked her American-ness. Anna May Wong, in contrast, gained more recognition and freedom to recreate herself in Europe than in the United States or China, where she faced dual marginalization because of her ethnicity and gender. Hence she fashioned a dual identity by fulfilling gendered expectations as both a Chinese and an American in order to travel to China, the country on which her celebrity had been built.

This "in between-ness" allowed each woman to claim multiple affiliations and allegiances. As atypical American "immigrants," international mobility gave Wong, Buck, and Soong the chance to escape their immediate limitations. Reversing the immigration patterns of her ancestors, Wong ventured beyond the borders of United States in search of employment. Both Buck and Soong traveled between the United States and China, their departures structured by changing relations between the two countries. Trans-Pacific travelers, all three women complicate contemporary studies of Western women travelers to "non-Western" regions, reflecting the same power differential between geopolitical locations in more complex ways.

*Popular Culture*

By participating in the production of popular images of China for American consumption all three overcame the limitations of their gender to gain public visibility.[1] Both Wong and Buck found in representing China access to economic success and social mobility in American society. Wong attracted the interest of Hollywood through her looks and her willingness to act out Hollywood's exoticized fantasies of the barely clad, culturally repressed Chinese female. In challenging assumptions about Chinese and Chinese American feminine behavior as she embodied images of the Orient, she gained an international audience and enjoyed social mobility that was not the norm for Chinese American women. The hypersexual vamp had nothing in common with O-lan, the Chinese female Buck introduced to her readers—a docile and passive, hardworking woman who put aside her own desires—and in the process of reshaping American perceptions of China, went from isolated, missionary wife to popular critic and celebrity. Although her father's wealth had given Soong an affluent lifestyle, her image transcended those Wong and Buck had presented for American consumption. Her feminine attractiveness contributed to her popularity and visibility as a symbol for China, but her education, English, and Christianity had a dramatic impact on the way many Americans perceived and represented China during the late 1930s.

The process of becoming celebrities and their relative success in shaping the production of their own images hinged on class status, racial identity, and educational level—which shaped their access to those who had the power to produce culture. Buck married the man who published her book and made her American dream come true. In addition, her husband's connections with the liberal intelligentsia provided Buck entrée to contemporary discussions about American national identity, class and racial tensions in the United States, and other intellectual developments.[2] Because her husband was her publisher and publicist, Buck enjoyed more editorial control over her public image than Wong or Soong and more readily maintained her identification with China.

Soong likewise, with her family's political lineage and wealth, entered into a profitable marriage. In her position as first lady of China and the wife of a virtual dictator, her image was the responsibility of the China News Agency and other government propaganda offices. She also gained the support of Henry Luce, whose editorial control over *Time* and *Life* magazines shaped Americans' knowledge about China. Thus distant from her American audience she appeared saintlike in her devotion to China's orphans, her ministrations to wounded soldiers, and her provision of spiritual sustenance to her husband. Then the visit to the United States placed the Chinese officials in charge of publicizing Soong's image into an entirely different context where the American press had unedited access.

In marked contrast to both Buck and Soong, Wong's liminal Chinese American identity made the hypervisibility of her body and participation in stereotypical portrayals of China her prime access to control of her image. Given these limits, however, Wong was able to develop and nurture positive relationships with many in the film industry. The respect Wong enjoyed among the press also is evident in the film critics' consistent support of her acting despite the poor overall quality of many of her films and in journalists' inclusion of her thoughtful social commentary in their articles. The way in which Wong continually created a space of reinvention for herself through travel—particularly through her adept positioning within the political context of the development of the British film industry–allowed the public glimpses of the Chinese American behind the Oriental image.

## LIMITATIONS

Buck, Wong, and Soong all enjoyed greater visibility because of their participation in American popular culture as interpreters of China. Their experiences abroad—in China, the United States, and Europe—allowed them to negotiate the limitations posed by the social locations into which they were born, and to recreate themselves by emphasizing different aspects of their identities to best suit the cultural, social, and political demands of their immediate circumstances. At the same time, affiliation with the United States and China also proved a burden, because American orientalism's either/or distinction constrained each woman's expression of her individual identity. Celebrations of cosmopolitan transnationalism during the 1930s and 1940s notwithstanding, their experiences suggest that the conditions of transnationalism could just as easily prove the conditions for marginality—particularly when limitations of gender, race, and nation come into play.

## Gender

In response to the rigid ideologies represented by American orientalism and American nationalism, the three women made sense of their particular identities within the cultural and social context where they were located at key points in their lives. For example, Anna May Wong grew up as a member of the Chinese American community, which was socially and economically marginalized based on its racial identity and national affiliation. She also grew up consuming popular images of Chinese culture as more patriarchal than the United States, and of Chinese women as thus less free and educated than either Chinese men or Euro-American women. These images, along with the popularized language of assimilation, shaped her perception of herself as an American Chinese woman who was breaking with Chinese traditions by being independent, attending school, and wanting to have a career. Becoming American for Wong also translated into consuming American popular and material culture, fashioning herself in the latest flapper style.[3]

When Pearl Buck married, she faced the overdetermined role of true womanhood as a missionary wife. Within the missionary community, men made the decisions. However, they depended on the women to minister to multiple generations through Chinese mothers and their children, and to maintain their home and care for their children. In addition, missionary wives filled the maternalist role of nurturing and serving both the missionary community and the Chinese community where they were stationed. As Buck described her mother's experience on the mission field, missionary wives often had to suppress their own desires in order to fulfill these expectations of service to God, their husband, the church, the missionary community, and the Chinese community. The family's terror during the Nanjing Incident of 1927 and the mission board's reaction brought home to her how insignificant individual lives could be to institutions like militaries, churches, and nations. Almost in protest, she determined to create a space for her individual self-expression through writing.[4]

Even as the Western powers dismissed China as irrelevant to their global interests in the 1930s, and after her husband became leader of the KMT, Mayling Soong channeled her passion for China and her knowledge of American missions into programs that attracted the interest of private American nonprofit organizations located in China. Her intimate understanding of these organizations and their leadership facilitated the application of foreign knowledge, expertise, and funds to produce limited, material improvements in certain regions in China. Simultaneously, exposed to the Chinese concept of "new women" as well as the American applications of true womanhood and progressivism, Soong made herself a visible presence in her husband's government. She performed China's modern womanhood for an international audience and thus gained legitimacy and recognition for the Chinese Nationalist government. Soong smartly inverted American orientalist assumptions about China by emphasizing the role of Chinese women as actively involved in the national community.

*Race*

The varying degrees to which each woman was able to use her celebrity as a platform from which to address contemporary political and social issues, moreover, reflected her ability to enact *whiteness,* a racial ideology that values white culture and normalizes its dominance over non-white cultures. Whiteness, so fundamental to American social relationships and international relations, constituted the foundation of American popular culture during this time (and even today) because it defined the consuming audience and shaped what was produced for consumption. Anna May Wong's ongoing role on and off screen was to portray the desirability of whiteness. Tiger Lily, Annabelle Wu, and Princess Taou Yuen all wanted a taste of the forbidden whiteness as represented in romantic love for a white man; Wong's personal desire, as projected in articles that accompanied her films, was to be accepted into white society. Had she been white, her activities for China relief during the late 1930s and the war would have ensured her recognition by Madame Chiang Kai-shek and thus a seat with the other actors at the Hollywood Bowl.

Pearl Buck enjoyed significant advantages from being white. Even though she was perceived as heretical by the Protestant mission board, divorced her missionary husband, and claimed to be Chinese, her embodiment of whiteness allowed her to maintain her respectable public image and celebrity (similar behavior by Wong or Soong would have provoked a very different reaction because their racialized identities undermined their claims to womanhood). Her racial identity allowed her the unusual status of being considered an authority about China—a position normally reserved for males. The racial logic of gender and race, however, suggests that because Buck publicly claimed a Chinese identity—a claim that would diminish a Euro-American male's social status and undermine his credibility—she occupied a unique niche in American society. Furthermore, her identity as a Euro-American woman made Buck more trustworthy than the two others, not only because of her presumed disinterest but because of her embodiment of white femininity that was inherently more virtuous than Chinese femininity.

In many ways Mayling Soong too benefited from the system of whiteness because her social location allowed her access to several of its attributes. Her education from childhood through college at English-speaking private schools for women reflected her family's wealth and status. She received an education in American upper-middle-class values, language, and behavior. Additionally, she was a Methodist Christian who demonstrated a commitment to service in her community. When she achieved global prominence, moreover, the American congressmen's attempts to grant her U.S. citizenship suggest that middle-class femininity might trump racial origin. At the height of her popularity, Soong clearly challenged stereotypical Chinese femininity.

Although all three women were able to negotiate whiteness and even benefit from it, however, whiteness fundamentally devalued Chinese culture and restricted Chinese Americans from full participation in the American polity. The system of whiteness helped determine who enjoyed the power to define the Orient, even as whiteness defines the American national identity. As a result, the benefits the three women received from representing China were nonetheless limited by their perceived "Chineseness."

## Nation and Ethnicity

Although each woman attempted to construct her own identity beyond the limitations of cultural expectations based on her social location,

Pearl Buck enjoyed greater success than Anna May Wong or Mayling Soong. Wong initially appeared in the press a fully Americanized flapper, eschewing her Chinese heritage. Within five years, however, when she went abroad to Europe, she gained fame as one of the world's "best dressed women" and for ushering in Oriental chic on the continent. Buck initially represented herself as a stranger to the United States. Yet, as she criticized racial prejudice against blacks during the war, she often referred to her Southern heritage to establish her American identity. Soong at first dreaded returning to a China she barely knew after her graduation from Wellesley College. But within a few years, former classmates described her as an ardent Chinese nationalist. How each woman produced herself and was herself produced invites further analysis of why specific aspects of identity were emphasized over others in particular contexts, at particular points of time.

With different cultural and socioeconomic backgrounds, each woman experienced differently what it meant to be Chinese, American, Chinese American, a celebrity, and a woman, and each positioned herself accordingly. Although Buck, for example, would in no way be considered Chinese American today, her claims of authority on China and Chinese Americans were not contested when she made them. How did Buck qualify as more "authentically" Chinese than an American-born person of Chinese descent like Wong? Wong knew very little about China through experience and only visited China once. In contrast, Buck grew up in China, was fluent in Chinese, and was knowledgeable about Chinese culture. If Wong had little cultural knowledge of China yet full knowledge of American prejudice against Chinese, did this make her Chinese American? If there is a spectrum of Chinese American identity, would Buck qualify for a place somewhere on it? These discrepancies—of ethnicity, cultural experience, and racial identity—highlight specific historical circumstances in Americans' perceptions of China and Chinese, the value placed on experience as knowledge, and the complexities of ethnic identity during this era.

The association of these particular women with China and the United States raises questions about Chinese American identity itself and the coordinates that map it. Each of these women with different national histories arguably claimed, or was claimed, to be Chinese American, on the basis of language, descent, location, and, most of all, experience. The possibility for all three women from diverse backgrounds to claim a Chinese American identity in American society and culture challenges the meaning of "Chinese American." Buck defined herself as culturally Chinese and American to circumvent the limitations of her gender and to critique missions and the church which dominated women and Chinese simultaneously. Thus, she claimed "Chinese American" status to finesse the social dynamics of power. Wong was an American citizen, yet she appears to have relied on her Chinese and feminine identities both as a way to circumvent the economic oppression of Chinese Americans. Referring to China as the homeland may also have provided a sense of security; she could imagine a place where she belonged, even if she never actually lived or visited there. Both Wong and Buck maintained the fluidity of their identities as a means of protection and security. Soong and Buck lived for many years in each other's country. Buck's claims to Chinese American identity would seem to justify Soong's claims to Chinese American identity as well. American perceptions of Soong as a Chinese American benefited to a very limited extent the Chinese government and Chinese Americans. For Soong, however, claims that she was American rendered her vulnerable to cultural acquisition by American society and linked her standing in China to her ability to achieve strategic gains in the United States.

## THE CHINA MYSTIQUE

The assumption by some Americans that Soong was more American than Chinese in her femininity complicates the relationship between gender, race, and nation. Both American nationalism and Chinese nationalism relied on women to communicate and embody nationhood. Thus the censure of Wong during her visit to Nanjing illustrates how her portrayals of Chinese prostitutes and murderers intersected with her own Chinese heritage to promote negative views of Chinese culture and society. This configuration of gender, race, and nationality had informed American rejections of Chinese immigrants as unable to assimilate decades earlier. Soong and Chiang Kai-shek represented the same dynamic in their marriage: perceived by virtue of an American education to be a modern influence on her Chinese husband, she demonstrated his civilized and reasonable nature. Soong's activities supposedly reflected changes in Chinese society that would allow women's participation; even though Chinese women's activism as early as the 1912 constitutional debates was apparent to the international community and of interest to American suffragists, more Americans accepted the type of reform work she engaged as a legitimate and lasting change.

During the 1930s the cultural chasm between China and the United

States began to narrow. Through Buck's writings, many Americans came to perceive Chinese as human individuals facing similar struggles and sharing similar desires for family, sustenance, and love. Her speeches and essays drew on her own experiences and presented Americans with a very different perspective of China and the United States. Soong demonstrated in her testimony the passion for China she and her husband shared, and how they worked side by side to change China. In her books about Chinese women, she related the changes occurring in Chinese society. Wong's travelogue from China brought along American readers to experience with her the unexpected industrialization and modernity of Shanghai and the ways in which American culture already influenced urban life. On her return, she also lobbied for more positive portrayals of Chinese and starred in two films that featured a Chinese American female protagonist. Soong, Buck, and Wong's public negotiations of their complex identities and their roles in shaping popular perceptions about China combined to prepare Americans for a radical change in American orientalism. Hence interested Americans had several opportunities to get beyond the stereotypes.

*The China Mystique and World War II*

Throughout the age of American expansion—from the late nineteenth century to 1919—American orientalism informed the triangular diplomatic relationship between China, Japan, and the United States. The U.S. government focused primarily on cultivating its relationship with Japan, perceived to be the more powerful and modern nation, in order to solidify its military and economic presence in the region. China, which was neither powerful nor an ally, became the recipient of Asian prejudice and racist hostility. However, with the United States in isolation once more after World War I, the U.S. government hovered between the Asian countries in its desire to remain neutral. The China mystique emerged fully when Japan declared war on the United States and the United States entered World War II. The continual fear that China might betray the United States and form an Asiatic alliance with Japan was a motivating factor for the United States to cultivate the China mystique among Americans, regardless of the reality of Chiang Kai-shek's oppressive government.

The transformation of China from alien to ally represented an immense undertaking in reshaping American perceptions of China on the part of the U.S. government. Nationalist China had already been advertising itself along with other nations since the late 1920s, when the development of advertising as a science and industry likewise became a tool for nations to establish their international identities. As products for popular consumption, nationalism likewise depended on women to communicate a nation's progress, freedom, and modernity. Soong, for example, had a small secretarial staff to compose letters to her Wellesley classmates about her work with the general in rural China, intending that these letters be circulated to others. During the 1930s, as the war with Japan intensified, the Nationalist government increased its publications about China's struggle, the mobilization of women for war, and need for international support. However, many of these publications were circulated among a self-selected readership that already supported China.

The shift to a more positive perception of China thus occurred with a shift in American nationalism from an inward, isolationist focus on what made the United States a unified nation to an external, international focus. When the U.S. government entered the war, then, it mobilized the producers of popular culture to educate Americans about the necessity of American participation in the war, and the postwar role of the United States in maintaining the peace. In 1942 the Office of War Information set up bureaus that focused on magazine articles, comic strips, radio, and production of feature or documentary films and newsreels. Images of the United States as a beacon of light, a global policeman, and a leader in world democracy helped Americans envision this new form of nationalism. This same propaganda effort also sought to educate Americans about their new allies: Great Britain, Russia, and China. The OWI's nationwide coordination of popular culture and public information facilitated the distribution of the Allied nations' propaganda in addition to developing its own and helped develop cooperation between their governments and American media.

Despite an alliance with China, however, American fear and revulsion toward all Asians persisted. The U.S. government's previous neutrality and apathy toward Asia in general had allowed racial hatred to focus on visible physical differences. The racist epithets "yellow" and "Jap" were wielded indiscriminately against persons of Chinese, Korean, or Japanese ancestry. The primary challenge for American officials was to reeducate Americans—including those who produced popular culture—about new China when American orientalism was so embedded in the American national identity. Wartime alliances now required Americans to differentiate among "Asiatics" on the basis of national identity. The American public had to be reeducated in its prejudices. Both American and Chinese governments constructed walls of rhetoric to contain the potential divisiveness of race, emphasizing the two nations' common values—a love of democracy and freedom, a desire for peace, and most of all, an all-consuming hatred of the Japanese. This change of affections was displayed in the pageantry of America's spectatorship of war beginning in the 1930s. Mayling Soong's heroics in China, Anna May Wong's more positive portrayals of Chinese heroines in the movies, and Pearl Buck's humane portrayals of the Chinese as a peace-loving, democratic, people, already had contributed to this shift.[5] During the 1940s all three women also helped stage China for American consumption, to portray the ravages of violence—in words, action, and expression—for Americans in the comfort of movie theaters or their own homes.

As a result of coordinated government and private efforts in the United States, China benefited from a surge of popularity with the American public. The groundwork that Buck had accomplished in presenting Chinese as sympathetic individuals proved invaluable to the efforts to educate Americans about China. She effectively used China as an example of the need for Americans to accept cultural diversity in the United States and to embrace internationalism abroad. Similarly, the image of Soong as an Americanized Chinese circulated to a broader national audience, an example of how Chinese people were beginning to evolve into a more democratic and modern nation. However, although increased cooperation between the United States and China resulted in more positive Chinese roles after 1941, Wong's career did not noticeably benefit. Actors of white European descent, including Gene Tierney and Katharine Hepburn, still played modern Chinese females in feature films.

## The China Mystique and a New Nationalism

Intense American national interest in Mayling Soong as the embodiment of the China mystique united diverse perspectives and interpretations, and reflected how Americans saw themselves. Like Pearl Buck on her return to the United States, Soong was the outsider, and through her eyes Americans might survey the sum of themselves and their country's landscape. Americans' interest in Soong was as much—if not more—focused inward on their own national community as on the country she represented.

The China mystique articulated new forms of American orientalism and American nationalism in an internationalist perspective. China represented a young democracy, taking steps toward the West and following the model of the United States. Just as American orientalism had been inspired by Manifest Destiny and had reached its height with the expansion of the American empire, the China mystique reinterpreted the United States' relationship with China, and more generally with Asia and the world. Some American officials and policymakers extended this vision to assume that China's political development would result in economic development as well; as Henry Luce envisioned for his new American century, China represented a vast market for the thriving American economy. Others, including some of the Chinese Nationalists, assumed that China would be the cornerstone of a new Asian sphere of American democratic influence.

During the late 1930s and through the war Anna May Wong juggled American orientalism and the China mystique, paradoxically reversing roles from her earlier career. She embodied orientalized femininity to raise money for China relief and enacted the modern, heroic Chinese leader of Chinese guerrillas in *Lady from Chungking*. For her and for other Chinese Americans who dressed up in Chinese fashions for the patriotic parades, fund-raisers, and Soong's visit, the war allowed a blurring of allegiances to China and the United States.

Soong's feminine embodiment of China and lack of leverage in foreign policy also reflected the limitations of the China mystique. While her visit helped unify Americans who viewed her as spectacle and consumed China as the latest trend, the China mystique kept up the fundamental power dynamic of American orientalism, in which a dominant United States directed, consumed, and provided, in frustratingly familiar form. Soong's attempts to resist the appropriation of China for American nationalism and to refocus the Allied war strategy toward Japan resulted in a backlash that targeted her personally at the end of her American visit. Rumors about her husband's infidelity, her lack of children, and her prima donna air questioned her femininity and suggested that she was actually a "dragon lady"—an overly aggressive and dominant Oriental female.

By the latter half of the war, as Soong's popularity waned along with her attempts to represent China as an equal to other international powers, China's image had changed little with the American public. Even though images of China evolved from ancient, despotic, and alien to modern, democratic, and familiar, most Euro-Americans continued to view new China and the Chinese as reliant on the United States. A wartime study of American attitudes toward national and racial stereotypes was conducted by social scientists at Columbia University as the

National Stereotypes Research Project. One report on attitudes toward countries considered as postwar problems drew on papers written by American subjects about other nations at the end of war. Twenty-four of these papers were about China. According to the summary, "some considered [Chinese] educable adults while others treated [them] as trusting children. All [agreed] that they were courageous, peace-loving, backward and uncivilized needing the United States and or the United Nations [aid] in developing their educational possibilities, sanitary conditions and religious training. At all times they were spoken about as inferiors to be treated kindly whether as heathen; THE WORTHY POOR; stupid, industrious children or retarded adults with latent possibilities."[6] Furthermore, the report noted, Americans' attitudes toward China were utilitarian: "China can be useful as an ally if there is a future war, in trade and as a bulwark in the Far East." Finally, a sense of international responsibility also manifested itself: the U.S. "owed" China for the lack of wartime support it had provided, as well as for the sale of raw materials to Japan. In contrast to attitudes toward China, the Americans viewed France, Finland, and Great Britain as equal to the United States.

The swiftness with which the China mystique reverted to negative forms of orientalism likewise demonstrates that rather than replace American orientalism, it simply rearranged those forms in a more positive light for political and social expediency to meet the demands of America's new international identity.

## Chinese Americans and the China Mystique

Yet to dismiss the China mystique as propaganda without political effect overlooks the impact it had on Chinese Americans and undermines its service to Buck, Wong, and Soong as they engaged the politics of nationalism, gender, and race. A look at the ways in which some Chinese Americans experienced the transformation of American orientalism to the China mystique reveals the changes that did take place, partly because of these three women's activities.

For the Chinese American community, Pearl Buck's *The Good Earth* represented a change in American attitudes toward China. The filming of Buck's novel in the late 1930s also provided an opportunity for Chinese Americans throughout California to become more visible by participating in the representation of China. The impact of Buck's novel and film combined was manifest in a special *Good Earth* edition of the *Chinese Digest*, the nationally distributed Chinese American newspaper (see figure 16). Buck's activism on behalf of Chinese Americans continued, but not in her fiction. She and her husband, Richard J. Walsh, used *Asia* magazine to editorialize on the racial prejudice Americans directed toward Chinese Americans.

Anna May Wong also appeared in the pages of the *Chinese Press* as a dignitary for the 1939 World's Fair and Golden Gate International Exposition exhibit of a Chinese village or on behalf of yet another China relief fund-raiser. (See figure 17, taken at a similar event in 1941.) Although her presence seemed overshadowed by Buck and Soong during the 1940s, Wong's experiences reflect why the China mystique mattered. The prewar discourse of American orientalism made sharp distinctions between Chinese and American. Its ideological polarization of China and the United States fragmented the identities of Wong and other Chinese Americans, dividing or silencing them in American society. The China mystique, however, promoted the similarities between China and the United States.

Thus many Chinese Americans eagerly and publicly claimed American patriotism and civic participation for themselves. For those Chinese Americans who participated in the activities welcoming Mayling Soong to southern California (some chose not to; because of their Communist affiliation others were excluded; Wong's participation was marginal), the Hollywood Bowl pageant was also a celebration of America. A special "Welcome Madame Chiang Kai-shek!" edition of the *Chinese Press* provided various Chinese communities throughout California the opportunity not only to welcome Soong but to express their unique role in their own communities (see figure 18). These claims to America and a regional history illustrate that some Chinese saw no contradiction between their American identities and Chinese affiliation. As Bessie Loo, one Chinese American participant, recalled, "The event brought Chinese prestige way up," and she "felt very proud to be Chinese. [She] felt herself to be very Chinese, yet she felt herself as an American."[7] The American celebration of China, especially during Soong's 1943 visit, allowed Chinese Americans to be fully Chinese and American simultaneously without having to explain or define their actions.

Even so, most Euro-Americans continued to perceive Chinese Americans as foreigners during the war; they were still Chinese. The National Stereotypes Research Project included a wartime survey on national and minority stereotypes conducted among high school students in Ohio, and faculty, students and staff at Vassar College throughout 1942 and 1943. The results illuminate the perceived distinction between China as a nation versus the Chinese as a race: "where the nationalities listed are rated presumably as foreigners in their own countries the Chinese draw the 'most friendly' rating . . . whether rated as 'country' or as 'people.'" But *as a minority group within the United States* Chinese ranked among the lowest five of the eighteen groups: in ascending order these were Japanese, blacks, Communists, Chinese, and Mexicans.[8]

Although the China mystique did not change widespread perceptions of Chinese Americans, it nonetheless provided an opportunity for Chinese Americans to gain naturalized citizenship through the repeal of Chinese exclusion. When Representative Kennedy's bill for repeal, dedicated to Madame Chiang, was introduced in the session, Buck and her husband mobilized to support the bill. In 1943 Walsh organized and chaired the Citizens' League for the Repeal of Chinese Exclusion to lobby congressmen. This group and Buck's testimony at the hearings contributed to the passage of repeal to improve international relations with China and counter Japanese propaganda. Tellingly he, among others, advised Chinese Americans to be silent on repeal for fear that this would hurt the bill.

But Chinese American communities mobilized to write letters and phone their representatives and senators. The successful repeal legislation replaced the exclusion laws with an annual quota of 105 Chinese eligible for American citizenship. Some Chinese Americans urged Chinese immigrants to flood the Immigration and Naturalization Service with applications for citizenship. The point was less to gain citizenship than to demonstrate the widespread desire to become an American. The increased fluency in the symbols of nationalism and belonging on the part of Chinese Americans occurred during the transformation of China's image and brought concrete changes. These changes, however small, allowed Chinese Americans to define themselves as active participants in American civic culture. As Buck had suggested in her speeches and letters to African Americans, in itself this act of self-definition is an expression of claiming America.

POWER

The experiences of Pearl Buck, Anna May Wong, and Mayling Soong demonstrate that self-definition in opposition to the identities structured by the community is a conscious strategy; it does not occur by happenstance. Naming and defining are specific expressions of power. The feminist scholar Carolyn Heilbrun calls power "the ability to take one's place in whatever discourse is essential to action and the right to have one's part matter." Because the American public so identified all three women with China, each one's voice and actions mattered—albeit differently— within the discourse of the China mystique. On the one hand, their speaking for China allowed many Americans to "cover over the fact of the ignorance that they [were] allowed to possess, into a kind of homogenization" of China.[9] On the other hand, their resisting the attempts of their communities and of American popular culture to define them challenged any single interpretation of China or the United States. As has been repeatedly demonstrated in histories of marginalized communities, each woman developed a fluid contingent identity, negotiating community demands while attempting to maintain her individuality. Each woman strategically emphasized different aspects of her identity at different times within the identity imposed on her by producers of popular and political culture. Accustomed to repositioning herself to the best possible advantage within specific contexts, each woman was able to respond to the changing demands of nationalism during the war. In the process of constructing their own identities during the 1930s and 1940s in relation to China and the United States, Pearl S. Buck, Anna May Wong, and Mayling Soong each shaped Americans' more positive perceptions of China. In the process, they also contributed to the ways in which Americans defined themselves as a national community.

# Notes

## 1. GENDERING AMERICAN ORIENTALISM

1. J. Lossing Buck's *Chinese Farm Economy* was published in 1930 by University of Chicago Press and "has remained permanently influential." Peter Conn, *Pearl S. Buck: A Cultural Biography* (New York: Cambridge University Press, 1996), 114–15.

2. The United States was only of several destinations for Chinese males who migrated from China.

3. David Alexander, *Imperialism and Idealism: American Diplomats in China, 1861–1898* (Bloomington: Indiana University Press, 1985), 4.

4. See for example, Gina Marchetti, *Romance and the "Yellow Peril": Race, Sex, and Discursive Strategies in Hollywood Fiction* (Berkeley: University of California Press, 1993); Susan Jeffords, *The Remasculinization of America: Gender and the Vietnam War* (Bloomington: Indiana University Press, 1989); and Robert G. Lee, *Orientals: Asian Americans in Popular Culture* (Philadelphia: Temple University Press, 1999).

5. Two notable exceptions are Traise Yamamoto's *Masking Selves, Masking Subjects: Japanese American Women, Identity, and the Body* (Berkeley: University of California Press, 1999); and Caroline Chung Simpson, *An Absent Presence: Japanese Americans in Postwar American Culture, 1945–1960* (Durham, NC: Duke University Press, 2001). Yamamoto's introduction provides an insightful reading of the gendered relations between Japan and the United States. Although most of her analysis is based on late twentieth-century texts, Yamamoto locates the origins of the Japanese American female subjectivity to the late 1930s and especially the war years. Similarly, Chung Simpson focuses on the postwar Japanese American absence, but her work—particularly her analysis of Iva Toguri d'Aquino (accused of being "Tokyo Rose")—is an important examination of the effects of the wartime gendering of U.S.-Japan relations.

6. Lisa Lowe, *Critical Terrains: French and British Orientalisms* (Ithaca: Cornell University Press, 1992); Ali Behdad, *Belated Travelers: Orientalism in the Age of Colonial Dissolution* (Durham, NC: Duke University Press, 1994); Anne McClintock, *Imperial Leather: Race, Gender and Sexuality in the Colonial Contest* (New York: Routledge, 1995).

7. Ella Shohat and Robert Stam, *Unthinking Eurocentrism: Multiculturalism and the Media* (New York: Routledge, 1994).

8. John Kuo-Wei Tchen, *New York before Chinatown: Orientalism and the Shaping of American Culture 1776–1882* (Baltimore, MD: Johns Hopkins University Press, 1999).

9. Mari Yoshihara, *Embracing the East: White Women and American Orientalism* (New York: Oxford University Press, 2003).

10. Ibid.

11. Some of the most provocative works regarding Asian Americans as orientalizing subjects include Judy Tzu-Chun Wu, *Doctor Mom Chung of the Fair-haired Bastards* (Berkeley: University of California Press, 2005), Leslie Bow, *Betrayal and Other Acts of Subversion: Feminism, Sexual Politics, Asian American Women's Literature* (Princeton: Princeton University Press, 2001); and Rachel Lee, *The Americas of Asian American Literature* (Princeton: Princeton University Press, 1999).

12. Gary Y. Okihiro, *Margins and Mainstreams: Asians in American History and Culture* (Baltimore, MD: Johns Hopkins University Press, 1994).

13. Tchen, *New York before Chinatown.*

14. Stuart Creighton Miller documents the saturation of American culture and politics with images of Chinese in *The Unwelcome Immigrant: The American Image of the Chinese, 1785–1882* (Berkeley: University of California Press, 1969).

15. Miller, *Unwelcome Immigrant;* and Harold R. Isaacs, *Images of Asia: American Views of China and India* (New York: Capricorn Books, 1962).

16. Michael H. Hunt, *Ideology and Foreign Policy* (New Haven: Yale University Press, 1987), 16.

17. Amy Kaplan, "A 'Manifest Domesticity,' " *American Literature* 70 (1998): 581–606.

18. James C. Thomson, Jr., Peter W. Stanley, and John Curtis Perry, *Sentimental Imperialists* (San Francisco: Harper and Row, 1981), 47.

19. Alexander, *Imperialism and Idealism,* 44.

20. Sucheng Chan, *Asian Americans: An Interpretive History* (New York: Twayne, 1991), 5–8.

21. Sucheng Chan, "European and Asian Immigration into the United States in Comparative Perspective, 1820s to 1920s," in *Immigration Reconsidered: History, Sociology, and Politics,* ed. Virginia Yans-McLaughlin (New York: Oxford University Press, 1990), 44.

22. George Anthony Peffer, "Forbidden Families: Emigration Experiences of Chinese Women under the Page Law," *Journal of American Ethnic History* 6 (1986): 28–46; and Sucheng Chan, "The Exclusion of Chinese Women, 1870–1943," in *Entry Denied: Exclusion and the Chinese Community in America, 1882–1943,* ed. Sucheng Chan (Philadelphia: Temple University Press, 1994), 58–75. There were several cases from the 1870s onward where Chinese

women were sent back to China because they could not convince immigration authorities that they were wives or students.

23. Jennifer P. Ting, "The Power of Sexuality," *Journal of Asian American Studies* 1, no. 1 (February 1998): 65–82.

24. Jane Hunter, *The Gospel of Gentility: American Women Missionaries in Turn-of-the-Century China* (New Haven: Yale University Press, 1984), 7.

25. Ibid., 31.

26. Patricia Neils, introduction to *United States Attitudes and Policies Toward China: The Impact of American Missionaries,* ed. John C. Brewer and Patricia Neils (New York: M. E. Sharpe, 1990), 10.

## 2. PEARL SYDENSTRICKER BUCK

1. Patricia Hill, *The World Their Household: The American Woman's Foreign Movement and Cultural Transformation, 1870–1920* (Ann Arbor: University of Michigan Press, 1985); and Hunter, *Gospel of Gentility.*

2. See for example Peggy Pascoe, *Relations of Rescue: The Search for Female Moral Authority in the American West, 1874–1939* (New York: Oxford University Press, 1990); George Sanchez, " 'Go After the Women': Americanization and the Mexican Immigrant Woman, 1915–1929," in *Unequal Sisters: A Multicultural Reader in U.S. Women's History,* ed. Ellen Carol DuBois and Vicki L. Ruiz, 2nd ed. (New York: Routledge, 1990), 250–63; and Linda Gordon, *Heroes of Their Own Lives: The Politics and History of Family Violence, 1880–1960* (New York: Viking, 1988).

3. Arthur M. Schlesinger, Jr., "The Missionary Enterprise and Imperialism," in *The Missionary Enterprise in China and America* (see note 13), 354–55.

4. Pearl S. Buck, *My Several Worlds* (New York: John Day, 1954), 6.

5. Pearl S. Buck, *American Argument with Eslanda Goode Robeson (*New York: John Day, 1949), 6.

6. Thomson, Stanley, and Perry, *Sentimental Imperialists,* 47.

7. Ibid.

8. Buck, *American Argument,* 7–8.

9. PSB to Roger Sherman Greene, 13 Jan 1940, 1–2, PSB: bMS Am 1864 (732), correspondence to and from Roger Sherman Greene and the American Committee for Non-Participation in Japanese Aggression, Roger Sherman Greene Papers, Department of Manuscripts, Houghton Library, Harvard University, Cambridge, MA.

10. Schlesinger concluded that the missionary enterprise could not be called imperialist in terms of economic models but functioned as cultural imperialism: missionaries taught and spread the notion of Western cultural superiority. Schlesinger, "Missionary Enterprise," 336–73. The authors of *Sentimental Imperialists* counter with the notion that if the missionaries were imperialists at all, they acted out of benevolence to assist China, not conscious arrogance or superiority.

11. Renato Rosaldo, *Culture and Truth: The Remaking of Social Analysis* (Boston: Beacon, 1989), 67–70.

12. PSB to Emma Edmunds White, 29 Aug 1918, Kuling, China, 1, Emma Edmunds White Collection, Special Collections, Lipscomb Library, Randolph-Macon Woman's College, Lynchburg, VA (hereafter cited as Edmunds White Collection).

13. John K. Fairbank, introduction to *The Missionary Enterprise in China and America*, ed. *John K. Fairbank* (Cambridge, MA: Harvard University Press, 1974), 3.

14. Thomson, Stanley, and Perry, *Sentimental Imperialists*, 56.

15. PSB to Edmunds White, 29 Aug 1918.

16. PSB to Mrs. Buck, 8 Apr 1918, copy of letter, 3, box 13: Letters—PSB to Buck family, 1918, Nora B. Stirling Collection, Special Collections, Lipscomb Library, Randolph-Macon Woman's College, Lynchburg, VA (hereafter cited as Stirling Collection).

17. PSB to Mrs. Coffin, 12 Dec 1918, Nanhsuchou, China, copy of letter, 2, box 13, Stirling Collection.

18. Ibid.

19. See Kathleen L. Lodwick, "Hainan for the Homefolk: Images of the Island in the Missionary and Secular Presses," in *United States Attitudes and Policies Toward China* (see chapter 1 note 26), 97–110. Lodwick discusses reports from the mission field and notes, "Often there were articles about the plight of women" (106).

20. PSB to Mrs. Coffin, 12 Dec 1918, 4.

21. PSB to "Home-people," 14 Oct 1917, Nanhsuchou, China, copy of letter, 1, box 13, Stirling Collection.

22. PSB to Mrs. Coffin, 12 Dec 1918, 4 (emphasis added). Except as noted here, all emphasis in quoted passages is original.

23. Sanchez, "Go After the Women."

24. Thomson, Stanley, and Perry, *Sentimental Imperialists*, 53.

25. Cynthia Enloe points out that focusing on the treatment of women as a cultural difference can allow indigenous nationalist movements to dismiss feminism as a foreign influence. See Cynthia Enloe, *Bananas, Beaches, and Bases: Making Feminist Sense of International Politics* (Berkeley: University of California Press, 1990), 60.

26. Pearl S. Buck, *Fighting Angel* (New York: John Day, 1936), 190.

27. Ibid., 189.

28. Pearl S. Buck, *The Exile* (New York: John Day, 1936), 284.

29. Neils, introduction, 12.

30. Thomson, Stanley, and Perry, *Sentimental Imperialists*, 55. The high point of Protestant missions in China would be 1925. With only 200 living in China in 1870, the number of missionaries (including wives, who were "assistant missionaries") quintupled to 1,000 at the turn of the century, and quintupled again to 5,000 in 1925 before declining to around 3,000 by 1930 and thereafter.

31. Shirley Stone Garrett, "Why They Stayed: American Church Politics and Chinese Nationalism in the Twenties," in *The Missionary Enterprise in China and America*, 286–67, 304–6; and Neils, introduction, 12.

32. Neils, introduction, 13; Paul A. Varg, "The Missionary Response to the Nationalist Revolution," in *The Missionary Enterprise in China and America*; Schlesinger, "Missionary Enterprise," 316 and 354–55; and Thomson, Stanley, and Perry, *Sentimental Imperialists*, 50.

33. These influences are visible in a report on Christian education in China, where the author states "Jesus' prayer for unity and human solidarity will be answered, not by the egotistic, classical ideal in education, but by the altruistic, so-

cial ideal." See James B. Webster, *Christian Education and the National Consciousness in China* (New York: E. P. Dutton, 1920), 100.

34. PSB to in-laws, 1927, 2–3, box 13, Stirling Collection. Years after the incident, Buck refused to verify reports that rather than be taken away, she held ready a loaded revolver to kill her children and herself. David Malcolmson to PSB, 30 Jan 1945, Potomac, IL, box 199, folder 15, John Day Archives, Manuscripts Division, Department of Rare Books and Special Collections, Princeton University Library, Princeton (hereafter cited as John Day Archives).

35. PSB to Lewis Stiles Gannett, 15 Jun 1927, Unzen, Japan, 1, bMS Am 1888 (150), letters 1927–1935, Lewis Stiles Gannett Papers, Department of Manuscripts, Houghton Library, Harvard University, Camabridge, MA.

36. Cornelia Spencer, *The Exile's Daughter* (New York: Coward-McCann, 1944), 46.

37. PSB to Emma Edmunds White, 4 Jan 1928, Shanghai, China, Edmunds White Collection.

38. Ibid.

39. Garrett, "Why They Stayed," 284, 303. The justification for a continued missionary presence in China employed the rhetoric of America's responsibility to China by damning the Communists as the instigators of antiforeign violence and raising expectations of Chiang Kai-shek and the right-wing faction of the Kuomintang as protectors of the foreign missions, and presenting China as a country following in the moral and civilized steps of its American mentors.

40. Ibid., 290–91, 293, 300, 308–9.

41. Richard J. Walsh to David Lloyd, Paget Literary Agency, 17 Sep 1929, box 21, folder 8, John Day Archives.

42. PSB to Earl Newsom, John Day Co., 24 Feb 1931, Nanking, box 36, folder 9, John Day Archives.

43. PSB to Richard J. Walsh, 26 Jan 1931, box 36, folder 9, John Day Archives.

44. PSB to Emma Edmunds White, 27 Jan [1931], Nanking, 2, Edmunds White Collection.

45. PSB to Richard J. Walsh, 22 Jul 1931, Nanking, box 36, folder 3, John Day Archives. *The Good Earth* first appeared in China as a magazine serial in January 1932. Although there also were many strongly critical reviews of her work that pointed out errors of fact and questioned the ability of a foreigner to truly represent Chinese life, Buck did not send those. Liu Haiping states that from the publication of *East Wind, West Wind* until her departure from China in 1934, "at least fifty articles on Buck and her novels appeared in Chinese periodicals or as prefaces to Chinese translations of her works" and most were positive. Also according to Liu, many reviews pointed out errors of fact and the resemblance of her writings to the Chinese classics yet praised Buck for her ability to present the Chinese sympathetically. Liu Haiping, "Pearl Buck's Reception in China Reconsidered," in *The Several Worlds of Pearl Buck*, 56.

46. Conn, *Pearl S. Buck*, 123.

47. "*The Good Earth* Is Coming!" John Day advertisement, 4, box 2, David Lloyd Agency Files, Manuscripts Division, Department of Rare Books and Special Collections, Princeton University Library, Princeton (hereafter cited as David Lloyd Agency Files).

48. bell hooks, *Black Looks: Race and Representation* (Boston: South End Press, 1992), 21–40.

49. Richard de Cordova, "The Emergence of the Star System in America," in *Stardom: Industry of Desire,* ed. Christine Gledhill (New York: Routledge, 1991), 24–25.

50. The beginning of a 1941 book, "Growing Up in China," an intended "parallel volume to *The Exile*," appears to have been lost. This manuscript was to be "the story of her childhood, and covers none of her adult experiences." See Richard J. Walsh to David Lloyd, memorandum, 5 May 1941, box 3, folder 6, David Lloyd Agency Files.

51. Warren I. Susman, *Culture as History* (New York: Pantheon Books, 1973).

52. Dorothy Canfield Fisher to Critchell Remington, 24 Jan 1931, Arlington, VT, copy of letter, box 5, folder 12, Stirling Collection.

53. Years later, in conversations with Theodore Harris, Buck denied having anything to do with the filming of *The Good Earth* (her correspondence in MGM files demonstrates otherwise). Theodore E. Harris, *Pearl S. Buck: A Biography by Theodore E. Harris in Consultation with Pearl S. Buck* (New York: John Day, 1969).

54. Chinese exclusion laws still in place heavily restricted Chinese entry into the United States. Information on "Good Earth" from Mr. Lee, 28 Sept 1933, 3, folder 2, MGM Studio Collection, *The Good Earth,* Cinema-Television Archives, University of Southern California, Los Angeles (hereafter cited as MGM Studio Collection).

55. Casting notes for screen tests on 12 Dec 1935, folder 10, MGM Studio Collection. The casting notes for Keye Luke's screen test allowed that Luke "[d]eserved serious consideration—a slight possibility," because he was an established Chinese American actor but had "become stereotyped for playing in Charlie Chan pictures," in which he portrayed the assimilated and Americanized Number One Son.

56. *Film Daily,* 3 Feb 1937, *The Good Earth* MGM 1936, MPAA Production Code administrative files, Margaret Herrick Library, Academy of Motion Pictures Arts and Sciences, Beverly Hills (hereafter cited as Herrick Library).

57. *"The Good Earth" Souvenir Program,* MGM Studios, Culver City, CA, 1937, MGM Studio Collection.

58. Gary Dean Best, *The Nickel and Dime Decade* (Westport, CT: Praeger, 1993), 6–8.

59. Helen Foster Snow, who wrote about China under the pseudonym Nym Wales, greatly contributed to Nora Stirling's analysis of Buck with her own recollections of meeting Buck in China in the 1930s and their conversations. Snow asserted, "PEARL BUCK UNIVERSALIZED THE CHINESE PEASANT for the first time." See Snow's letter to Stirling, 5 Oct 1976, box 11: Snow, Stirling Collection.

60. Patricia Raub, *Yesterday's Stories: Popular Women's Novels of the Twenties and Thirties* (Westport, CT: Greenwood Press, 1994), 86.

61. Ibid., 59–62.

62. Ernestine Stodelle, *Deep Song: The Dance Story of Martha Graham* (New York: Schirmer Books, 1984), 96–97.

63. Barbara Morgan, *Martha Graham, Sixteen Dances in Photographs* (New York: Duell, Sloan and Pearce, 1941), 12.

64. Nora B. Stirling, *Pearl Buck, a Woman in Conflict* (Piscatawny, NJ: New Century, 1983), 134.

65. Walsh is cited in ibid., 133.

66. Pearl S. Buck, "Race Relations and Race Pride," *Opportunity, Journal of Negro Life,* Jan 1933, 1, 2; reprinted from her December 11 address in Harlem. Carter was the editor of this journal.

67. Pearl S. Buck, "Is There a Case for Foreign Missions?," John Day Pamphlet Series, 18 (New York, 1932), 7, 14.

68. Buck's statements that she did not believe in original sin were of doctrinal concern.

69. PSB to Rev. Dr. Cleland McAfee, 21 Apr 1933, New York City, box 79, folder 2, John Day Archives.

70. Cleland B. McAfee to Richard J. Walsh, 18 May 1933, ibid.

71. Lossing Buck later married a Chinese woman. Rubie Walsh relocated to an apartment and never remarried.

72. Conn makes this observation in *Pearl S. Buck,* 163. He also compares Buck to the male protagonists of Malcolm Cowley's *Exile's Return: A Literary Odyssey of the 1920s* (1951; reprint, New York: Penguin Books, 1976)

73. Pearl S. Buck, "Relief—For the American Conscience," in *What America Means to Me* (New York: John Day, 1943), 92. This essay was first published in the *New York Times Magazine,* 10 Jan 1943.

74. Pearl S. Buck, "On Discovering America," *Survey Graphic* 26, no. 6 (Jun 1937): 315.

75. Pearl S. Buck, "China Faces the Future," in *What America Means to Me,* 84; reprinted from her 13 Oct 1942 lecture for the New School for Social Research, New York.

76. PSB to William Lyon Phelps, 14 Apr 1939, New York, Za Phelps Collection, Yale Collection of American Literature, Beinecke Rare Book and Manuscript Library, Yale University, New Haven.

77. David Buck relates Buck's views on China's needing to return to empire in the footnotes of his paper. David D. Buck, "In Search of America," in *The Several Worlds of Pearl S. Buck* (see note 49), 29–43.

78. Buck, "On Discovering America," 313.

79. Ibid., 314.

80. Buck's agent, David Lloyd, received numerous requests for permission to reprint this essay. A few organizations wished to issue it in pamphlet form. Many editors of junior high and high school textbooks on literature wanted to incorporate it as a reading assignment. Nearly all of them commented on how helpful it was to read about her immigrant experience. Box 20, folder 7, David Lloyd Agency Files.

81. See Conn, *Pearl S. Buck.*

82. Buck, "On Discovering America," 355.

83. David A. Hollinger, *In the American Province: Studies in the History and Historiography of Ideas* (Bloomington: Indiana University Press, 1985), 184, 58.

84. Margaret Mead, *And Keep Your Powder Dry: An Anthropologist Looks at America* (New York: William Morrow, 1942), 5, 8, 11.

85. PSB to William Lyon Phelps, 14 Apr 1939, New York.

86. In her essay "On Discovering America," Buck stated: "I came from

China, a land of long homogeneity and of unity, except perhaps for that least important of all, political unity" (313).

87. *This Proud Heart* correspondence, box 133, folder 30, John Day Archives.

88. Nancy F. Cott, *The Grounding of Modern Feminism* (New Haven: Yale University Press, 1987); Pearl S. Buck, "Message to Randolph-Macon," *Alumnae Bulletin,* Sep 1943, 16, Student Archives and clippings files, Special Collections, Lipscomb Library, Randolph-Macon Woman's College, Lynchburg, VA.

89. Pearl S. Buck, "America's Discontented Women," manuscript, 3, box 24, folder 13, David Lloyd Agency Files.

90. The concept of assimilation was popularized by social scientists during the 1930s, a response to anxieties about the United States losing its "American" identity to the influx of foreigners during the 1920s.

91. PSB to David Lloyd, 7 Feb 1939, New York, 2, box 15, folder 5, David Lloyd Agency Files.

92. PSB to Freda Utley, 24 Sep 1940, box 4, Freda Utley Papers, Hoover Institution Archives, Hoover Institution on War, Revolution, and Peace, Stanford. The scholar Buck referred to was Nathaniel Peffer.

93. Pearl S. Buck, "John-John Chinaman," in *The Woman Who Was Changed and Other Stories* (New York: John Day, 1979). This story was commissioned by Henry L. A. Cossit, the editor of *American Magazine,* in 1941 and published in 1942.

94. Pearl S. Buck, "His Own Country," WJZ broadcast transcript *Living Literature,* 3 Sep 1941, 6, box 12, folder 18, David Lloyd Agency Collection.

95. Ibid.

96. Philip Gleason, *Speaking of Diversity: Language and Ethnicity in Twentieth-Century America* (Baltimore, MD: Johns Hopkins University Press, 1992), 262–63.

97. See Robert B. Westbrook, *John Dewey and American Democracy* (Ithaca: Cornell University Press, 1991), 240–62.

98. Ibid., 250.

99. Gleason, *Speaking of Diversity,* 20.

100. Ibid., 62–63.

101. One critic lamented, "[t]o the popular mind, Mrs. Buck's sympathetic understanding of the Chinese peasant makes her an authority on all Chinese matters, an opinion which she fosters by as many articles and speeches as she can manage between books." See "Elsa Maxwell's Party Line—Outside Asia," *New York Post,* 28 Apr 1943, 12. (This column was written at a time when severe criticism of China was being raised in the press.)

102. Isaacs, *Images of Asia.* Buck's continued activism on behalf of China in the late 1930s and early 1940s, as well as her continued production of writings about China, has been chronicled by Peter Conn.

103. Patricia Neils, *China Images in the Life and Times of Henry Luce* (Savage, MD: Rowman and Littlefield, 1990); and T. Christopher Jespersen, *American Images of China, 1931–1949* (Stanford: Stanford University Press, 1996).

104. Susman, *Culture as History.*

105. PSB to Bernhard Knollenberg, 25 Sep 1942, 1–2, Special Collections, Beinecke Rare Book and Manuscript Library, Yale University, New Haven.

106. Pearl S. Buck, "Books About Americans for People in Asia to Read," reprint from *Asia Magazine,* Oct 1942, 1–2, box 3, folder 6, Papers of Paul Jordan Smith, Clark Library Special Collections, University of California at Los Angeles (UCLA).

107. Pearl S. Buck, *Asia and Democracy* (London: Macmillan, 1943), 75, 79.

108. Buck, "On Discovering America," 355.

109. Buck, *Asia and Democracy,* 74. This British edition of *American Unity and Asia* (New York: John Day, 1942) was retitled for a broader, European audience.

110. Pearl S. Buck, "Equality," reprinted in *What America Means to Me,* 22.

111. Richard J. Walsh, memorandum of information by the president of the John Day Company, box 167, folder 37, John Day Archives.

112. Pearl S. Buck, "A Letter to Colored Americans," 28 Feb 1942, reprinted in *Asia and Democracy,* 80, 81.

113. Buck, "Equality," 22.

114. Buck, "Letter to Colored Americans," 84.

115. "Woman of the Year, Miss Pearl S. Buck," *Chicago Defender,* 12 May 1943, 1.

116. Pearl S. Buck, "East Is East, West Is West, —— Can Meet," box 167, folder 43, John Day Archives.

117. PSB, letter to the editor, *New York Herald-Tribune,* 13 Feb 1942, box 57, 1942 PACC, pt. 1, PSB, Institute of Pacific Relations Archives, Rare Book and Manuscript Library, Columbia University, New York (hereafter cited as Institute of Pacific Relations Archives).

118. PSB to F. C. Overbury, 26 Aug 1942, PSB correspondence with Overbury family, file 1, Overbury Collection, Barnard College, Columbia University, New York.

119. "Peoples of the Pacific: 10 Stimulating Evenings Devoted to Our Neighbors in the Pacific Area (Jointly presented with Springfield College and the East West Association)," box 73, folder 19, United Service to China Archives, Public Policy Papers, Department of Rare Books and Special Collections, Princeton University Library, Princeton (hereafter cited as USC Archives).

120. Pearl S. Buck, "Freedom for All," 18 ; reprinted in *Asia Magazine,* May 1942, from the speech on 14 Mar 1942, New York.

121. Ida Pruitt to PSB, 11 Dec 1942, New York, carbon copy, box 89: Important Correspondence, PSB, INDUSCO Archives, Rare Book and Manuscript Library, Columbia University (hereafter cited as INDUSCO Archives).

122. Chester Kerr to Richard J. Walsh, 27 Jul 1942, box 176, folder 20, John Day Archives.

123. Chester Kerr to Clarence B. Boutell, G. P. Putnam's Sons, 20 Jul 1942, box 174, folder 2, John Day Archives.

124. Review of *American Unity and Asia,* *New Leader,* 15 Aug 1942, box 3, Stirling Collection.

125. Shohat and Stam, *Unthinking Eurocentrism,* 224, 226.

126. Bruno Lasker to William H. Lockwood, 27 Dec 1941, 2, Institute of Pacific Relations Archives.

127. Shohat and Stam, *Unthinking Eurocentrism,* 226.

128. PSB to Eleanor Roosevelt (confidential), 22 Mar 1943, 9, copy in

Henry Morgenthau Diary, book 618, 202–16, reel 181, Franklin D. Roosevelt Presidential Library, Hyde Park, New York (hereafter cited as FDR Presidential Library).

129. John W. Dower, *War Without Mercy: Race and Power in the Pacific War* (New York: Pantheon Books, 1987).

130. My thanks to Jennifer Kimie Arguello for helping me formulate this relationship of Pearl Buck's feminism and "Chinese-ness" in conversation.

131. Yet—in Buck's 1949 published conversations with Eslanda Goode Robeson—confronted directly with her own racial and national privilege and with no other margins to which she could retreat culturally or geographically, Buck resorted to her fundamental minority position as a woman. Robeson recalled going into a segregated soda fountain and asking for a drink "with what must have been something like murder in my eyes," and being served. She declared, "There are times when many of us just feel we can't take any more." Buck rejoined, "I know that feeling. Sometimes I feel it because I am a woman. Mine is not a very good country for women." Buck, *American Argument*, 11, 12.

132. Patricia Hill Collins, *Black Feminist Thought: Knowledge, Consciousness, and the Politics of Empowerment* (Boston: Unman Hyman, 1990); and Gloria Anzaldúa, *Borderlands = La Frontera* (San Francisco: Aunt Lute Books, 1999).

133. Chela Sandoval introduced this concept in 1991 as a way to convey women of color's ability to negotiate their multiple subjectivities. Chela Sandoval, "U.S. Third World Feminism: The Theory and Method of Oppositional Consciousness in the Postmodern World," *Genders* 10 (Spring 1991): 1–24.

### 3. ANNA MAY WONG

1. George Anthony Peffer, *If They Don't Bring Their Women Here: Chinese Female Immigration before Exclusion* (Champaign: University of Illinois Press, 1999).

2. On the first account, see press sheets, *Limehouse Blues,* Paramount, 1 Aug 1934–31 Jul 1935, 17, Paramount Pressbook Collection, Herrick Library; and Robert S. Taplinger, director of publicity, "When Were You Born?" 2, publicity materials, Warner Brothers Corporate Archives, Cinema-Television Library, University of Southern California, Los Angeles (hereafter cited as Warner Brothers Archives). And on the earlier account see text discussion about AMW's exit interview in 1924. In a 1928 interview Wong also stated that her parents came from China. E. E. Barrett, "Right from Wong," *Picturegoer,* Sep 1928, 24. Wong often told interviewers how her father's father, Wong Leung Chew, traveled to northern California to prospect for gold in the 1860s and later opened up a store with four other Chinese men in Michigan Bluffs, Placer County (after-hours gambling in the store's back room was shut down in 1901). The scrutiny under which immigrants entered and exited and inconsistencies in Wong's father's story suggest that he may have claimed a fictitious American birthright— as others did (aided by the San Francisco earthquake and fire), in order to circumvent a discriminatory system. On 8 Jul 1901 John R. Dunn, Chinese Inspector in Michigan Bluffs, submitted a report (no. 104) on the Wing Chun Leong Co. there to the Collector's Office at the San Francisco Customs House (National Archives and Records Administration, Pacific Branch, San Bruno, CA)

and enclosed an affidavit signed by James P. Van Eman, Notary Public, with photographs of each member of the firm. My thanks to Neil Thomsen for locating this report.

3. For example, see Erika Lee, "At America's Gates" (Ph.D. diss., University of California, Berkeley, 1998), 397–402; and Madeline Yuan-yin Hsu, *Dreaming of Gold, Dreaming of Home: Transnationalism and Migration between the United States and South China, 1882–1943* (Stanford: Stanford University Press, 2000).

4. The 1880 census records 605 residents of Chinese descent. By 1890 the number had tripled to 1,900. See Lucie Cheng and Suellen Cheng, "Chinese Women of Los Angeles, a Social Historical Survey," in *Linking Our Lives: Chinese American Women of Los Angeles,* ed. Lucie Cheng, et al. (Los Angeles: Chinese Historical Society of Southern California, 1984), 13.

5. Judy Chu and Susie Ling, "Chinese Women at Work," in *Linking Our Lives,* 4.

6. Michel S. La Guerre, *The Global Ethnopolis: Chinatown, Japantown, and Manila Town in American Society* (New York: Palgrave Macmillan, 1999).

7. U.S. Bureau of the Census, "Thirteenth Census of the United States: 1910-Population," 16 Apr 1910, Los Angeles City (part of), District 7, Enumeration District 91, sheet 3B; and "Fourteenth Census of the United States: 1920-Population," 19 Jan 1920, Los Angeles City, Precinct 316, District 8, Enumeration District 215. sheet 20B. The majority of those residing on the block in both 1910 and 1920 censuses could read and write and rented their homes.

8. Sucheta Mazumdar, "In the Family," in *Linking Our Lives,* 37.

9. Robert L. Wagner, "Two Chinese Girls . . . Stenographic Notes of a Recent Broadcast," *Rob Wagner's Script,* 21 Nov 1936, 1, Herrick Library; see also his article, "Better a Laundry and Sincerity," *Rob Wagner's Script,* 34; and "Two Chinese Girls: Stenographic Notes of a Recent Broadcast," box 32, Robert L. Wagner Collection, Clark Library Special Collections, University of California at Los Angeles (hereafter cited as Wagner Collection).

10. Anna May Wong, "The True Life Story of a Chinese Girl," *Pictures,* August 1926, 107–8.

11. Judy Yung, *Unbound Feet: A Social History of Chinese Women in San Francisco* (Berkeley: University of California Press, 1995), 125–26, 128–29. In San Francisco Jade Snow Wong (no relation) was also taunted by a white boy after school; Yung describes Wong's refusal to respond to the teasing as "a defense stance of accommodation that the second generation had been taught to assume when confronted by racial conflict."

12. See Paul A. Varg, *Missionaries, Chinese, and Diplomats: The American Protestant Missionary Movement in China, 1840–1952* (Princeton: Princeton University Press, 1958), 71. According to Varg, missionaries (at home and abroad) accommodated "the rapidly developing humanitarianism of early-twentieth century America."

13. Ibid., 70–71. Varg noted the irony of American sentiments toward missions: "apparently the public had developed such an aversion toward damnation that, while they did not want the Chinese to come to California, neither did they want them to go to hell."

14. Wong, "True Life Story," 108.

15. Anna May Wong, "The Childhood of a Chinese Screen Star," *Pictures,* September 1926, 34.

16. Yung, *Unbound Feet,* 35.

17. Cheng and Chang, "Chinese Women of Los Angeles," 4–5.

18. Gloria H. Chun, "Go West . . . to China: Chinese American Identity in the 1930s," in *Claiming America: Constructing Chinese American Identities during the Exclusion Era,* ed. K. Scott Wong and Sucheng Chan (Philadelphia: Temple University Press, 1998), 173.

19. Wong, "Childhood of a Chinese Screen Star," 72.

20. Suggestions for Screen Treatment "China Seas" by Crosby Garstin Dictated by Rich ——, 1, "China Seas (1 of 9)," MGM Studio Collection.

21. Wong, "Childhood of a Chinese Screen Star," 72; Anna May Wong, "My Film Thrills," *Film Pictorial,* 11 Nov 1933, 6. Transferred back to the California Street School in the fifth grade, Wong wrote that she and her sister had expected teasing but were now included in schoolyard activities.

22. Ronald Haver, Program Notes for *Toll of the Sea* [1922 Technicolor Motion Picture], n.d.; and Douglas S. Wilson, "Program Notes," Toronto Film Society, 3 Oct 1988, season 40, program 1, 1, Film production files, Herrick Library.

23. Wong's later roles were Tiger Lily in *Peter Pan,* then the exotically named Zira in *The Fortieth Door,* and the Eskimo girl Keok in *The Alaskan* (all 1924), and finally a harem girl in a play staged in the film *His Supreme Moment* (1925).

24. Florence Jung, interview by Suellen Cheng, 2 Dec 1979, tape 3A, box 9, Chinese Historical Society of Southern California Joint Oral History Project, Clark Library Special Collections, UCLA.

25. "Anna May Wong Grabs Top Honors," *Hollywood Reporter,* 28 Jul 1931, 3, AMW clippings file, Herrick Library.

26. Robert McElwaine, "Third Beginning," *Modern Screen,* n.d., 41, 80, 11D Research Data, P85–958, reel 20, micro 1054, AMW subject file, United Artists Collection, Division of Archives and Manuscripts, State Historical Society of Wisconsin, Madison (hereafter cited as UA Collection), 41.

27. According to Paramount publicity, she modeled her role on her friend Dr. Margaret Chung, a Chinese American female physician in San Francisco who was active in China relief and war activities. For more about Chung's life and experiences see Judy T. Z. Wu's insightful analysis in her forthcoming *Mom Chung of the Fair-haired Bastards. King of Chinatown* implied a love triangle between the character Dr. Mary Ling, her Chinese American beau, Bob (with the Korean American actor Philip Ahn in a familiar role), and a white Euro-American gangster tiring of his criminal past, played by Akim Tamiroff, an actor of Russian ancestry.

28. Warner Brothers to AMW, letter and contract, 17 Jan 1938, 1–3, Anna May Wong, artist: AMW contract material for *When Were You Born?,* Warner Brothers Archives. Wong's contract for the film paid her $1,750 a week for a minimum three weeks, with the possibility of producing up to six more films within five years. This contract was unique in allowing Warner three different options to procure Wong for additional films. The apparent inspiration for her detective role was Twentieth Century Fox's popular and profitable series of Charlie Chan films, which began developing the roles of Chan's Chinese American sons in 1937.

29. *Film Daily,* 9 Jun 1938, *When Were You Born? 1938* MPAA production code administrative files, Herrick Library.

30. Paramount Press Sheets, "King of Chinatown," 1 Aug 1938, and 31 Jul 1939, Paramount Pictures Collection, Herrick Library.

31. Paramount Pictures, *Dangerous to Know* press kit, 14 Mar 1938, 14, Copyright Registration files, Motion Picture, Broadcasting, and Recorded Sound Division, Library of Congress, Washington DC (hereafter cited as Motion Picture Division).

32. Vincent Sneed notes this as well. See "Love in Vain: Racism and the Film to Anna May Wong," *China Doll* 1, no. 1 (Aug 1991): 1.

33. AMW to Fitzroy K. Davis, 26 May 1937, Exeter, NH, Theatre Arts Collection, New York Public Library (hereafter cited as NYPL Theatre Arts Collection).

34. "Lord Chumley" (scenario), n.d., screenplay by Bertram Millhauser, (scene 24), 9–10, *Forty Winks* (Lord Chumley), Paramount Pictures Collection, Herrick Library.

35. Ibid. (scenes 25, 462), 9–15, 165.

36. Kathy Peiss, *Hope in a Jar: The Making of America's Beauty Culture* (New York: Owl Books, 1999).

37. Clipping, n.d, AMW biographical file, Herrick Library (emphasis added).

38. Richard de Cordova, *Picture Personalities: The Emergence of the Star System in America* (Chicago: University of Illinois Press, 1990), 10. In the absence of archived diaries or letters, we cannot tell whether Wong found the public image projected onto her beneficial or internalized it.

39. As another observer noted, the public accepted Wong "as a 'unique' character among the Asiatic race. But she had been developed by Hollywood." Christine Choy, "Images of Asian-American in Films and Television," in *Ethnic Images in American Films and Television,* ed. Randall M. Miles (Philadelphia: Balch Institute, 1978), 151.

40. Kathryn H. Fuller, *At the Picture Show : Small-town Audiences and the Creation of Movie Fan Culture* (Washington DC: Smithsonian Institution Press, 1996), 151–52.

41. De Cordova, *Picture Personalities,* 10.

42. Mazumdar, "In the Family," 36.

43. Wong, "Childhood of a Chinese Screen Star," 72.

44. Fuller, *At the Picture Show,* 154–59.

45. Geraldine Sartain, "The Tragic Real Life Story of Anna May Wong," n.d. [after 1936], 3, Research Data, 85–958, reel 20, micro 1054, UA Collection.

46. Helen Carlisle, "Velly Muchee Lonely," *Motion Picture Magazine,* March 1928, 41, 94, 101; and Audrey Rivers, "Anna May Wong Sorry She Cannot Be Kissed," *Movie Classic,* Nov 1931, 41, both in Arts Special Collections, UCLA.

47. Rivers, "Sorry She Cannot Be Kissed," 41. California banned marriage between white and nonwhites as early as 1880. Wong was wrong about *Java Head;* she eventually played Taou Yen four years later. But she was also correct: her character kills herself at the film's end under duress from her evil brother-in-law.

48. "Loretta Goes Oriental," *Photoplay Magazine,* March 1932, 71.

49. Hayes would also be director Sol Lesser's first choice to play MCKS in his projected 1943 film for MGM.

50. Bessie Loo, presentation, general meeting of the Chinese Historical Society of Southern California, 6 May 1981, tape 5B, Clark Library Special Collections, UCLA.

51. In *Variety Film Reviews, 1926–29,* vol. 3 (New York: Garland, 1983), 8 May 1929, a reviewer noted that Wong's "stage appearance in London proved that her voice is unsuitable for the talkers."

52. Raymond Ganley, "*The Crimson City,* Okay as Program Fare," *Film Daily,* 1273, *The Crimson City* production files, Herrick Library.

53. Paul Lauren Gordon, *Power and Prejudice: The Politics and Diplomacy of Racial Discrimination* (Boulder, CO: Westview Press, 1996) 647–49.

54. "PARAMOUNT UTILIZES ANNA MAY WONG TO PRODUCE PICTURE TO DISGRACE CHINA," enclosure in Jesse Lasky, Jr., to Jason S. Joy, 14 Jan 1932, with enclosed translation from unidentified Chinese newspaper, *Shanghai Express* (Paramount 1932), MPAA production code administrative files, Herrick Library.

55. Enloe, *Bananas, Beaches, and Bases,* 48, 54.

56. Robert L. Wagner, "Horrible Hollywood," *Rob Wagner's Beverly Hills Script Weekly,* 13 Jul 1935, box 7, Wagner Collection.

57. Helen Callaway, *Gender, Culture, and Empire: European Women in Colonial Nigeria* (Oxford: Macmillan, 1987), 57.

58. Enloe, *Bananas, Beaches, and Bases,* 44; Callaway, *Gender, Culture and Empire,* 63.

59. Letter to Ben Piazza, Casting Dept., MGM Studios, 6 Nov 1933, Culver City, 2, folder 2, MGM Studio Collection.

60. Sidney Skolsky, "Hollywood," 17 Dec 1935, 1935–36 clippings, Sidney Skolsky Collection, Herrick Library. Skolsky, a film industry insider, noted the tension on the set the day of her screen test as Wong, looking "regal in the Chinese garment" and made up for the part, prepared to perform the scene before the camera.

61. McElwaine, "Third Beginning," 41, 80.

62. Albert Lewin, "THE GOOD EARTH-tests," memorandum, 10 Dec 1935, folder 10, MGM Studio Collection.

63. Memorandum, 14 Dec 1935, folder 10, MGM Studio Collection.

64. Regina Crewe, "Frosted Willow," *New York American,* n.d., AMW clippings file, NYPL Theatre Arts Collection.

65. Ruth Vasey, *The World According to Hollywood, 1918–1939* (Madison: University of Wisconsin Press, 1997), 153. Between World Wars I and II, Vasey estimates, 35 percent of the U.S. film studios' gross income came from abroad (7–8).

66. Louise Leung, "East Meets West," *Hollywood Magazine,* Jun 1938, 40 and 55, reprinted in *China Doll* 1, no. 2 (Oct 1991): 2, 40, 55.

67. According to Judy Yung, Jade Snow Wong's *Fifth Chinese Daughter* (1950) was the first autobiographical account of a second-generation Chinese American woman published from 1902–45. Yung, *Unbound Feet,* 12. In 1909 Edith Maude Eaton (as Sui Sin Far) wrote "Leaves from the Mental Portfolio of an Eurasian," in *Mrs. Spring Fragrance and Other Writings,* ed. Amy Ling and Annette White-Parks (Urbana: University of Illinios Press, 1995), 218–30. My thanks to Zhaojian Xhao for providing the reference to Eaton.

68. See for example Sucheng Chan, "Race, Ethnic Culture, and Gender," in *Claiming America,* 149.

69. The demographic consequences for one Chinese community could be quite profound. According to Judy Yung, "The Chinese birthrate in San Francisco was twice as high as the city-wide rate because of cultural values that favored large families and sons as well as the lack of knowledge of birth control among Chinese women." Yung, *Unbound Feet,* 81.

70. Sartain, "Tragic Real Life Story," 3.

71. Wong, "True Life Story," 29, 106. Wong related how her father expected her to help support her half brother in China who was, she claimed, studying to be a scholar. She refused to do so, however, observing (possibly for the audience's sake) that she was perhaps of a more modern mindset. "I believe a man who reaches thirty should support himself." Combined archival and textual sources suggest that relatives in Sunning province arranged Sam Sing Wong's first marriage.

72. According to Sucheta Mazumdar, most Chinese women who had married prior to 1920 had bound feet. Mazumdar, "In the Family," 33–35. If this were the case for Wong's mother, it would make the circumstances of her death even more poignant. She was struck by a speeding car when trying to cross the street in front of her home.

73. The 1910 census lists Lee Gon Toy as being twenty-six years younger than her husband; the 1920 census lists her as being twenty-two years younger.

74. On the changing expectations toward marriage of 1920s American youth, see Paula Fass, *The Damned and the Beautiful: American Youth in the 1920s* (New York: Oxford University Press, 1977).

75. Carlisle, "Velly Muchee Lonely," 94.

76. Sue Fawn Chung, "Fighting for Their American Rights: A History of the Chinese American Citizens Alliance," in *Claiming America,* 11.

77. Chan, "Race, Ethnic Culture," 141.

78. Wong, "Childhood of a Chinese Screen Star," 75.

79. Betty Willis, "Famous Oriental Stars Return to the Screen," *Motion Pictures,* October 1931, 45, Herrick Library. The other "Oriental star" returning to Hollywood was the Japanese national Sessue Hayakawa, who eventually returned to Japan.

80. Rivers, "Sorry She Cannot Be Kissed," 39.

81. Marguerite Tazelaar, "Film Folk in Person," *New York Herald Tribune,* 30 Apr 1933, AMW clippings file, NYPL Theatre Arts Collection.

82. Vivien North, "There's a SECRET ANNA MAY WONG," *Picturegoer Weekly,* 8 Sep 1934, 8.

83. Tazelaar, "Film Folk in Person."

84. Kenneth Green, "British Studio News and Gossip," *Era,* 7 Jun 1933, 18.

85. Doris Mackie, " 'I Protest,' by Anna May Wong in an interview with Doris Mackie," *Film Weekly,* 18 Aug 1933, 11.

86. Nonetheless she surprised audiences with her ability to learn from their cultures. In Britain, Wong responded to criticisms of her American accent by paying for private speech lessons and acquiring an English accent. "When I came back [to the States], I decided to keep my English accent," Wong explained to one interviewer, "because I think it suits me, and I believe it's right to take whatever becomes you and make it part of yourself." Willis, "Famous Oriental Stars Return," 45.

87. Anna May Wong, "When East Meets West," *London Magazine,* May 1929, 484.

88. Barrett, "Right from Wong," 25.

89. E. O. Hoppe, "What Is Beauty?" *Looker-On,* 4 Jun 1929, 18.

90. In the context of an appeal to a cosmopolitan universalism among Europe's film industries in the 1930s, Tim Bergfelder makes a similar argument with a greater focus on the German as well as the British film industry. Tim Bergfelder, "Negotiating Exoticism: Hollywood, Film Europe and the Cultural Reception of Anna May Wong," in *"Film Europe" and "Film America": Cinema, Commerce and Cultural Exchange 1920–1939,* ed. Andrew Higson and Richard Maltby (Exeter, UK: University of Exeter Press, 1999), 302–24.

91. Vasey, *World According to Hollywood,* 40–41.

92. Ibid., 41–42.

93. Vasey, *World According to Hollywood,* 145.

94. "From the Ancient Chinese: 'The Circle of Chalk,' at the New Theatre," *Illustrated London News,* 23 Mar 1929, 475. For comments about her accent, see the review by V.H.F., in *The Newest Plays,* April 1929, 16, about the March 14, 1929 performance at London's New Theatre, which says of Wong, "Her speech was not even American; it was Hollywood. Surely it was a coffin in which Hi-Tang [Wong's role] buried her father, not a 'karf': and I hope it was a child that she bore—not as it sounded, a 'chow.'" The review in *Stage,* 21 Mar 1929, 16, was more blunt: "[H]er speaking voice sounded rather harsh and twangy, and her vocalization also seemed rough and not too tuneful."

95. Marjory Collier, "That Chinese Girl," *Picturegoer,* May 1930, 26.

96. Rivers, "Sorry She Cannot Be Kissed," 39.

97. Willis, "Famous Oriental Stars Return," 90.

98. Rivers, "Sorry She Cannot Be Kissed," 44.

99. "Anna May Wong Returns after Triumph Abroad," 2 Jun 1931, AMW biographical file, Herrick Library. Wong reportedly learned these languages for her first talkie, *Flame of Love,* which was dubbed in German, French, and English.

100. E. Le Berthon, "Anna May Wong Was a Laundryman's Daughter," *Picturegoer Weekly,* 17 Oct 1931, 17.

101. "Phil Lonergin Sends It Hot from Hollywood," *Picturegoer Weekly,* 29 Sep 1934, 19.

102. Wagner, "Two Chinese Girls."

103. North, "There's a SECRET ANNA," 8.

104. John K. Newnham, "Chinese Puzzle," *Film Weekly,* 17 Jun 1939, 19; reprinted in *China Doll* 1, no. 2 (Oct 1991) AMW subject file, Motion Picture Division.

105. Anna May Wong, "Manchuria," *Rob Wagner's Beverly Hills Script,* 16 Jan 1932, 7. In 1932 AMW wrote an essay condemning Japan's invasion of Manchuria in the 1931 Mukden (Shenyang) Incident and subsequent resignation from the League of Nations rather than accede to international pressure for withdrawal from Manchuria. The twenty-seven-year-old Wong incorporated tropes of orientalism throughout her descriptions of both China and Japan and wrote with purplish optimism about China's eventual spiritual triumph over Japan's material and technological progress. Discerning little differentiation between

their populations, she expressed her belief that "the East" was a spiritual alternative to the modernization prevalent in the West.

106. AMW first performed on the theater circuit in England in early June 1933, at the Holburn Empire. She had gold fingernails custom-made for the occasion. According to this report, she had toured for five months after completing her work in Hollywood and before returning to England. W. J. Bishop, "First Vaudeville Appearance in England of Anna May Wong," *Era,* 7 Jun 1933, 15.

107. Noël Coward, "Half-Caste Woman," reprinted in the program, National-Scalan Theatre, Germany, 1–14 Feb 1935, AMW Gift, NYPL Theatre Arts Collection.

108. AMW to Fitzroy K. Davis, 28 Dec 1935, Los Angeles, Special Collections, NYPL Theatre Arts Collection.

109. Leung, "East Meets West," 40.

110. "Anna May Wong Tells of Voyage of 1st Trip to China," 17 May 1936, *New York Herald-Tribune,* sec. 2, pt. 2, pp. 1, 6.

111. Robert L. Wagner, "A Chinese Girl Goes 'Home,'" *Rob Wagner's Script,* 10 Jan 1936, 23, box 8, Wagner Collection.

112. Chun, "Go West," 174–75. Chun relies on immigration statistics but does not explain how she came to this figure, nor how she determined who was Chinese-born.

113. Wagner, "Chinese Girl Goes 'Home,' " 23. Wong believed that "[m]odern China is learning to respect drama," a development facilitated by motion pictures.

114. Wagner, "Two Chinese Girls."

115. "Anna May Wong Tells of Voyage," 1.

116. "Anna May Wong Relates Arrival in Japan, Her First Sight at the Orient," *New York Herald-Tribune,* 24 May 1936, sec. 2, pt. 2, p. 1.

117. "Anna May Recalls Shanghai's Enthusiastic Reception," *New York Herald-Tribune,* 31 May 1936, sec. 2, pt. 2, pp. 2 and 6.

118. Ibid, 6.

119. Ibid.

120. Wagner, "Chinese Girl Goes 'Home,' " 23.

121. *New York Herald-Tribune,* 21 July 1936, AMW clippings file, NYPL Theatre Arts Collection.

122. "Anna May Wong 'Amused' at Chinese Appetite," *New York Herald-Tribune,* 7 Jun 1936, sec. 2, pt. 2, p. 2.

123. Leung, "East Meets West," 40, 55.

124. Ibid., 55.

125. Wagner observed, "it took a trip to far Cathay to make Anna May realize how much more becoming were Chinese clothes on a Chinese girl. That, and the oblique suggestion of Mrs. Wellington Kuo, wife of the famous Chinese ambassador." Robert L. Wagner "A Chinese Girl Comes Home!" *Rob Wagner's Script,* 12 Dec 1936, 11, Herrick Library.

126. Richard A. Oehling, "The Yellow Menace: Asian Images in American Film," in *The Kaleidoscope Lens: How Hollywood Views Ethnic Groups,* ed. Randall M. Miller (n.p.: Jerome S. Ozer, 1980), 182–206. Oehling also pinpoints the shift in American portrayals of Chinese to the mid-1930s (197).

127. Charles Choy Wong, "Los Angeles Chinatown: A Public and Home

Territory," in *The Chinese American Experience: Papers from the Second National Conference on Chinese American Studies (1980)*, ed. Genny Lim (San Francisco: Chinese Historical Society, 1984), 143.

128. Leung, "East Meets West," 40, 55.

129. "Actress to Aid China War Fund," *New York Times,* 22 Jun 1938, AMW clippings file, NYPL Theatre Arts Collection.

130. "N.E.K.," 24 Mar 1938, unidentified newspaper, ibid.

131. "Honor Chinese Star for War Aid," *Brooklyn Daily Eagle,* 2 Oct 1938, ibid.

132. United China Relief recognized the importance of publicity, observing in 1941 that "our publicity department is doing a grand and increasingly effective job of educating America on China. If the European war does not engulf us, America will yet wake up about China and be ready to do a typical American job for China." Arthur Rugh, Occasional Bulletin no. 17, 10 July 1941, 1, box 17, folder 10, USC Archives.

133. Souvenir program and directory, Moon Festival, 8–9 Oct 1938, Los Angeles, AMW Gift, NYPL Theatre Arts Collection.

134. ABMAC [American Bureau of Medical Aid for China] Bulletin, Nov 1940, 4–6, box 144: ABMAC Bulletin 1940, 1944–45, INDUSCO Archives.

135. Record of Board of Special Inquiry hearing, 21 Nov 1938, San Pedro, CA, 7, box 41, file 14036/1459-A, Segregated Chinese files, San Pedro office, RG [Record Group] 85, Immigration and Naturalization Service, National Archives and Records Administration, Pacific Branch, Laguna Niguel, CA.

136. For example, see Yung, *Unbound Feet,* ch. 5.

137. Wong's political affiliation is ambiguous at best. Among her friends were intellectuals and artists, many of them left of the political mainstream. Wagner, her mentor in Hollywood, was known to be affiliated with the Communist Party. Another friend, Paul Robeson, actively participated in party-sponsored activities. Wong did not publicly state her political views.

138. Edward LeRoy Moore to David O. Selznick, 10 Jul 1941, box 1012, folder 5, David O. Selznick Archives, Harry Ransom Humanities Research Center, University of Texas at Austin (hereafter cited as Selznick Archives).

139. S. Joseloff to Philip Lilienthal, telegram, New York, 17 Jul 1943, entry 521, box 3017, RG 208, Office of War Information, National Archives and Records Administration, Suitland MD annex.

140. *(San Francisco) Chinese Press,* 9 May 1941, 4.

141. L. ——, "Report no. 197," 9 Sep 1939, 3, folder 54, George and Geraldine Fitch Papers, Harvard-Yenching Library, Harvard University, Cambridge, MA (hereafter cited as Fitch Papers).

142. B. A. Garside to Peter Rhodes, 9 Apr 1942, box 23, folder 29, USC Archives.

143. "Sale of Fresh Flowers and Rickshaws," interoffice memo to Paul G. Hoffman, 19 Jun 1942, 2, box 6, folder 19, USC Archives.

144. Marian Cadawallader to Helen E. Wong, International Center YWCA, New York, 23 Jun 1942, box 80, folder 1, USC Archives. The club is the Ging Gawk Girls' Club.

145. William C. Smith, *Americans in Process: A Study of Our Citizens of*

*Oriental Ancestry* (Ann Arbor: Edwards Brothers, 1937), 92–93. Judy Yung also refers to Smith's study in relation to Chinese American women. Yung, *Unbound Feet,* 136–37.

146. "Fashions for Democracy," press release, September 1941, box 80, American Bureau for Medical Aid for China Records 1937–79, Rare Book and Manuscript Library, Columbia University, New York (hereafter cited as ABMAC Records).

147. AMW earned a total of $4,000 for the two films. And two aspects distinguish *Bombs over Burma* from the generic war film plot: the villains are German spies, not Japanese; and, as if to underscore that the story is being told from a Chinese perspective in China, for the first few minutes Wong, the schoolchildren, and the other characters speak Mandarin.

148. The OWI reviewer, Norbert Lusk, wrote that the film suffered from a low budget. He added that the acting was "unskilled, with the exception of Anna May Wong whose innate dignity helps or disguised the shortcomings of the others." Norbert Lusk, summary of *Lady of Chungking,* n.d., Office of War Information Evaluation files, Motion Picture Division.

149. Ibid.

150. Ibid. Lusk observed that the tragic ending "lifts a machine-made story of conspirators triumphant into something rather noble."

151. David O. Selznick to Barbara Keon, memorandum, 23 Mar 1943, box 304, folder 12, Selznick Archives. Tension appears to have existed between the Los Angeles and Hollywood Citizens Committees to Welcome Madame Chiang Kai-shek. AMW was active in the Los Angeles committee, led by Mayor Roger Smith; Selznick headed its Hollywood branch (as well as the UCR chapter).

152. Les W., "Sidelights on a Happy Visit," *Rob Wagner's Script,* 17 Apr 1943, 4, box 3819, folder 4, Selznick Archives.

153. Florence Wagner, "Missimo in Hollywood," *Rob Wagner's Script,* 17 Apr 1943, 10, ibid.

154. Frances Inglis to Joseph Steele, memorandum, 21 Apr 1943, box 325, folder 6, Selznick Archives.

## 4. MAYLING SOONG

1. Geraldine Fitch, newsletter to "Friends," 1 Jul 1943, Huletts Landing, NY, box 54, Fitch Papers.

2. Ibid. The school was founded in 1892 by Laura Askew Haygood, the first female Methodist Episcopal missionary sent to China. "Laura Askew Haygood, 1845–1900," Georgia Women of Achievement Ninth Induction Ceremony, Midgeville, GA, 31 Mar 2000, www.gawomen.org/honorees/long/haygoodl_long.htm (accessed 13 Nov 2003).

3. Jonathan D. Spence, *The Search for Modern China* (New York: W. W. Norton, 1990), 228–29; Sun Yat-sen (and Chiang Kai-shek, his future brother-in-law) believed that an authoritarian, predemocracy period might be necessary (365). On arguments for reform, see John Fitzgerald, *Awakening China: Politics, Culture, and Class in the Nationalist Revolution* (Stanford: Stanford University Press, 1996).

4. Ai-leen Wu Chow (secretary to Mme. Kung) to Emily Hahn, 31 Oct 1939,

2, box 6: 1934–53 Soong Sisters, Emily Hahn Papers, Manuscripts Department, Lilly Library, Indiana University Library, Bloomington (hereafter cited as Hahn Papers).

5. Mayling Soong Foundation brochure [1949?], alumnae: Mayling Soong and Her Classmates, Class of 1917 Collection, Wellesley College Archives, Wellesley College, Wellesley, MA (hereafter cited as Class of 1917 Collection).

6. But according to Emily Hahn, the missionary wife died in Yokohama, and Ai-ling, who was entrusted to a Korean missionary, was detained. A teenage Ai-ling later expressed her anger over the incident to President Theodore Roosevelt, who apologized. Emily Hahn, *The Soong Sisters* (Garden City, NY: Doubleday, Doran, 1941), 48–49, 94.

7. Delber L. McKee, *Chinese Exclusion Versus the Open Door Policy, 1900–1906: Clashes over China Policy in the Roosevelt Era* (Detroit : Wayne State University Press, 1977), 94.

8. Typed transcript of recollections from Annie Tuell and Emma Mills about Mayling Soong, 2, Correspondence, Papers of Madame Chiang Kai-shek, Wellesley College Archives, Wellesley, MA (hereafter cited as MCKS Papers).

9. Ibid.

10. Ibid.

11. Patricia Ann Palmieri, *In Adamless Eden: The Community of Women Faculty at Wellesley* (New Haven: Yale University Press, 1995), 151–53, 155; Spence, *Search for Modern China*, 313.

12. Spence, *Search for Modern China*, 275.

13. Ibid., 256. A group of politically active women and men sought an equality clause specifically including men and women, but these attempts were interrupted by political changes and ultimately rejected in August. Kazuko Ono, *Chinese Women in a Century of Revolution, 1850–1950*, ed. Joshua A. Fogel, trans. Kathryn Bernhardt, et al. (Stanford: Stanford University Press, 1989), 81–87. A series of Supreme Court decisions in 1914 established married women's rights in China. Spence, *Search for Modern China*, 285.

14. Spence, *Search for Modern China*, 294, 297, 284–88.

15. Transcript from Tuell and Mills, 2. Her 1941 Wellesley biography states, "Apprehensive of a family-made marriage when she returned home, she became engaged at one time while she was in Wellesley. It was later of course, broken off." Hélène Kazanjian, biographical data sheet (October 1941) on MCKS (Mayling Soong), Office of Publicity, Wellesley College, 3–4, box 3: Biographies of Chinese Ladies, ABMAC Records.

16. Mayling Soong to Helen Esse, 26 Oct 1917, 2, "Correspondence, n.d, 1916–77)," MCKS Papers.

17. Ilona Ralf Sues, *Shark Fins and Millet* (Boston: Little, Brown, 1944), 164. Sues worked as a press secretary for the generalissimo's government and occasionally met with MCKS. However, much of her account about the couple is uncredited to any source and may simply be based on rumors circulating through Shanghai at the time.

18. Helen McKeag's notes for talk on MCKS, card 6, Speeches about Mme. Chiang Kai-shek, MCKS Papers.

19. Untitled document on Soong sisters, 2, box 6: 1934–53 Soong Sisters,

Hahn Papers; its three pages appear to be MCKS's transcribed replies to written questions from Hahn.

20. Hahn, *Soong Sisters,* 105; as quoted in Kazanjian, biographical data, 4.

21. Spence, *Search for Modern China,* 304, 313.

22. Soong to Esse, 26 Oct 1917, 2.

23. Spence, *Search for Modern China,* 293. For the most comprehensive study of Chinese women's activism and changing status during the revolutionary period, see Ono, *Century of Revolution.*

24. Untitled document on Soong sisters, 3.

25. Sophie Chantal Hart to Elisabeth Luce, 22 Apr 1933, 3–4, Mayling Soong and Her Classmates, Class of 1917 Collection.

26. Florence Ayscough, *Chinese Women Yesterday and Today* (Boston: Houghton Mifflin, 1937), 117.

27. Nicholas R. Clifford, *Spoilt Children of Empire: Westerners in Shanghai and the Chinese Revolution of the 1920s* (Hanover, CT: Middlebury College Press, 1991), 21–22. The council was founded in 1854. It relied on twelve advisory committees and twelve departments.

28. Ibid., 101, 111.

29. Mayling Soong to Betty Nicholson, as quoted in *The Rookie,* 1924, 75, Class of 1917 Collection.

30. Fitzgerald, *Awakening China,* 8–9.

31. Clifford, *Spoilt Children of Empire,* 101–2.

32. Spence, *Search for Modern China,* 340–41.

33. Ibid., 334.

34. Ibid., 352.

35. Ibid., 353, 361–62; Brian G. Martin, *The Shanghai Green Gang: Politics and Organized Crime* (Berkeley: University of California Press, 1996), 111 (on Chiang Kai-shek's cooperation with organized crime to suppress the Communists, see 98–112).

36. Wellesley College's updated autobiography of Mayling Soong states that she met Chiang Kai-shek in 1920. General biographical information, MCKS Papers, Kazanjian, biographical data, 5. MCKS's mother assented only after the general agreed to study Christianity and produce proof of a divorce from his first wife, Chen Jieru, who had apparently agreed to it only under extreme pressure. According to other accounts, Green Gang leader Du Yuesheng helped him negotiate the divorce, which financially supported Chen and relocated her to the United States. According to many reports, the general had two common-law wives when he was in Canton with Sun Yat-sen. See Martin, *Shanghai Green Gang,* 144.

37. Hahn, *Soong Sisters,* 134.

38. Spence, Search for Modern China, 382, 386, 368–69.

39. Immanuel Y. Hsu, *The Rise of Modern China* (New York: Oxford University Press, 1970), 646.

40. William Richard Johnson to "Nanchung ites," 26 Nov 1933, 1–2, general correspondence, box 14, folder 243, William Richard Johnson Papers, RG 6, Special Collections, Divinity School Library, Yale University.

41. Theodore H. White, "Politics in China," 1 Jun 1940, 2, box 595, folder 1, subject files, congressional files, Clare Boothe Luce Papers, Manuscript Divi-

sion, Library of Congress (hereafter cited as Luce Papers). On the draft in the Luce collection, "propaganda" is crossed out, and "publicity" written in the margin.

42. Owen Lattimore, "C. Generalissimo and Madam Chiang," 26–27, box 49, folder 8: Working for Chiang Kai-shek, Owen Lattimore Collection, Manuscript Division, Library of Congress.

43. Sues, *Shark Fins and Millet,* 116. According to Sues, Chingling (Mme. Sun Yat-sen) initially suggested these schools; they were disbanded in 1937.

44. Untitled document on Soong sisters, 4.

45. Sues, *Shark Fins and Millet,* 116, 118.

46. Ibid., 166. Yet personal experience does not explain why her sister Chingling grew up in the same circumstances and had a radically different perspective on reforms.

47. Untitled document on Soong sisters, 3.

48. Sues, *Shark Fins and Millet,* 166.

49. MCKS to Geraldine Fitch, 9 Apr 1934, 3, MCKS, letters to, from, Fitch Papers.

50. Wellington Koo, May 26 Wednesday 7:30 dinner with MCKS, *Diary no. 11, May 15–June 1943,* box 216, Wellington Koo Papers and Diaries, Rare Book and Manuscript Library, Columbia University (hereafter cited by diary nos.).

51. Fitzgerald, *Awakening China,* 8–12. MCKS's brother in-law Sun Yat Sen included issues of hygiene and grooming in his 1924 lectures on creating a new image of China.

52. Lattimore, "Generalissimo and Madam Chiang," 26.

53. Chiang Kai-shek was baptized on 23 Oct 1929.

54. Geraldine Fitch to MCKS, 27 Sep 1935, Fitch Papers. She added, comparing MCKS's testimony to "others in the series, Mrs. Roosevelt, Lady Astor, Pearl Buck, Mary Pickford and all, I felt yours was by all odds the most vital personal witness to a real spiritual experience within." The next day the two women spoke, and Fitch wrote up the article in Shanghai while MCKS returned to Nanjing.

55. Geraldine Fitch, "The First Lady of China," notes for speech to Wellesley Club [22 Oct 1938], Pasadena, CA, Fitch Papers; and Fitch to MCKS, 27 Sep. Fitch wrote to MCKS about a dinner she attended when several Americans had remarked on the testimony's "earnestness and obvious sincerity." Fitch added, "It is hard at such times to keep my proud husband from saying that I have been helping you with some writing, including that; but I feel that probably you would prefer to have that kept confidential, as though you were doing your own articles." And in addition to "organizing" MCKS's thoughts, Fitch herself composed the final paragraph and mailed out the article the day before Soong's changes arrived. "Since you asked me to use my discretion, and since it was to be mailed without your seeing it again, I merely hinted at the rehabilitation idea . . . and then ended *strong* [illegible word] the magnitude of the problem; facing them with your husband; but no despondency or despair now; unafraid *because,* etc. I think you will like it, since you liked the directness of the article."

56. Madame Chiang Kai-shek, *My Religion,* pamphlet (Toronto, Ontario: World Service Department of the Canadian National Council of YMCAs, n.d.), 3–5, YMCA of USA Archives, University of Minnesota, St. Paul.

57. Chang was the associate who had withdrawn from Manchuria on the general's orders. By all accounts he and the Chiangs had been extremely close before this incident. Although many Americans believed that MCKS, her brother T. V., and Donald had negotiated the general's release, later historians have noted the role of Communist leader Chou Enlai in his release and in negotiating the Communist-KMT alliance with the general as leader. For example, Hsu focuses on Chou's role, not MCKS's; see *Rise of Modern China*, 661–63.

58. Henry M. Snevily, North American Newspaper Alliance to Col. Theodore Roosevelt, Jr., Doubleday, 16 Apr 1937, box 17, folder 2; *New York Times*, which advertised the nine installments of MCKS's Xian recollections on 15 Apr 1937, 10; and John W. Wheeler to Col. Roosevelt, 23 Apr 1937, box 17, folder 2, all three in Ken McCormick Collection of Doubleday and Company, Manuscript Division, Library of Congress (hereafter cited as McCormick Collection).

59. Christopher Jespersen notes that the *March of Time* newsreels played to an audience of twelve million in the United States alone; by 1941, Luce's periodicals—*Time, Fortune,* and *Life*—had a combined circulation of 3.8 million. T. Christoper Jespersen, *American Images of China, 1931–1949* (Stanford: Stanford University Press, 1996). Patricia Neils, who has studied in depth Luce's fascination with China during the era, observes that *Life* boasted more covers of the general alone or with his wife than of any other individual before or since; see *China Images of Henry Luce*.

60. Col. Theodore Roosevelt to Mr. Downey, memorandum, 16 Aug 1937, box 17, folder 2, McCormick Collection.

61. Ibid.

62. In the late 1930s U.S. officials connected to China noted reports of widespread corruption and coercion within the Nationalist government. Further rumors circulated that MCKS and her eldest sister (Madame Kung) had made fortunes speculating on government bonds, essentially profiting at the expense of the Chinese population. Willys Peck to Stanley K. Hornbeck, 24 Feb 1936, 2–4, box 336, Stanley K. Hornbeck Collection, Hoover Institution Archives, Hoover Institution on War, Revolution and Peace Archives, Stanford (hereafter cited as Hornbeck Collection).

63. Ibid. In February 1936 the couple reportedly experienced marital strife, so much so that the generalissimo's first wife had returned to Nanjing. In a March 1936 letter Peck wrote that Chiang's critics had arranged for the first wife's arrival. Willys Peck to Stanley K. Hornbeck, 19 Mar 1936, 3, box 336, Hornbeck Collection.

64. Sues, *Shark Fins and Millet*, 167–68.

65. White, "Politics in China," 1 Jun 1940.

66. Ibid., 2–3.

67. Although these reports were filed in Luce's congressional files, it is unlikely that White would have given her copies of his reports. I believe she received these from her husband, the publisher of *Time* and White's boss.

68. Hester Scott, "Mme. Chiang Inspired Clubwomen," *Los Angeles Examiner,* 3 Apr 1943, box 3819, folder 3: Publicity Clippings, Selznick Archives. Jespersen also discusses this phenomenon in *American Images of China,* ch. 5. Although club members were determined to learn more about foreign affairs, perhaps *The Good Earth* had spurred their specific interest in Chinese women.

69. Lattimore, "Generalissimo and Madam Chiang," 26.

70. Clare Boothe Luce, "Women March to Victory," interview by Rita Rite, 3:45 PM, Oct 1942, Stamford radio station WSRR, typescript, 3, box 671, folder 12, Luce Papers. Luce compliments the women of Russia and Britain ("full of Mrs. Minivers"). When Rite asks her if all Chinese women's progress is due to MCKS's American upbringing, Luce says no, it is also due to Madame's Christian faith in addition to her American ideals.

71. Helen C. White, "Dedication," *Phi Delta Gamma Journal* 9, no. 1 (May 1944): 2, Articles about MCKS, 1944–1947, MCKS Papers.

72. Clare Boothe Luce, "Victory Is a Woman" (drafts), box 312, folder 7, Luce Papers; and see Mary P. Ryan, *Womanhood in America: From Colonial Times to the Present* (New York: Franklin Watts, 1983).

73. Mildred Palmer, letter to the editor, *Baltimore Sun,* 27 May 1941, box 3, 1921–46, Alma Lutz Papers, Schlesinger Library, Radcliffe College (hereafter cited as Lutz Papers); Palmer based her comments about gender and China on Buck's *Of Men and Women* (New York: John Day, 1941).

74. Victor Hoo, memorandum on the improvement of the publicity service in Chungking, notes of meeting of 26 Jun 1942, 29 Jun 1942, 3–4, box 5: Documents: Memorandum, Victor Hoo Collection, Hoover Institution Archives, Hoover Institution on War, Revolution and Peace Archives, Stanford.

75. Catalog of literature and services available from Chinese News Service, n.d., New York, entry 296, box 1559: China, RG 208, Records of the Office of War Information, National Archives and Records Administration, College Park MD annex.

76. Callaway, *Gender Culture and Empire,* 8–11.

77. Archibald MacLeish, director, to Franklin D. Roosevelt, 19 Feb 1942, Washington DC, 2, Franklin D. Roosevelt Presidential Papers, OF [official file] 150: China, 1941–42, FDR Presidential Library (hereafter cited as FDR Papers). FDR forwarded a copy of this letter to Secretary of State Cordell Hull, who concurred with the potential of a visit to counteract "Tokyo propaganda."

78. Eleanor Roosevelt (ER) to MCKS, 16 Sep 1942, box 3, MCKS subject file, Lauchlin Currie Papers, Hoover Institution Archives, Hoover Institution on War, Revolution and Peace Archives, Stanford.

79. Press release, 27 Nov 1942, OF 150: China, 1941–42, FDR Papers. The White House social entertainment office kept Madame's schedule, which was disseminated through the president's press secretary, Stephen Early. Revisions were made in pencil and included the wry anonymous comment: "By Feb. 16 bulletins will probably be issued every 15 mins." Memorandum for Mr. Woodward, State Department, 15 Feb 1943, 1 PM, chief of social entertainment office, correspondence, 1933–45, FDR Presidential Library.

80. Eleanor Roosevelt, *My Day,* 19 Feb 1943, Washington DC, 1, box 3087: *My Day* column: drafts, speech and article file, ER Papers, FDR Presidential Library.

81. Koo, May 26 Wednesday 7:30 dinner.

82. See for example the communication between the secretary of state and Willys Peck, the Nanjing consul. He and his wife made a social call on MCKS "and in reply to questions she confirmed that an offensive and defensive alliance has recently been proposed to the Chinese government by the Japanese govern-

ment." Willys R. Peck, "Special Dispatch to Secretary of State from Peck no. 16. Confident.," 28 Jan 1935, Nanjing, OF 150, China 1933–38, FDR Papers.

83. Based on comments in Walter White's papers and the *Chicago Defender,* several African Americans understood that MCKS was setting a precedent for persons of non-European descent (even though the president of Libya was received as a guest at the White House, he was not invited to address both houses of Congress).

84. "Speech to Congress," *Life Magazine,* 1 Mar 1943, 26.

85. Ibid.

86. Wellington Koo, March 29 11:30, Washington DC, *Diary no. 10, Mar 6–May 14 1943,* box 215.

87. Koo, May 26 Wednesday 7:30 dinner; and March 26 Friday 11:30 PM, *Diary no. 10.*

88. ER to Anna Roosevelt Boetiger, 28 Feb [1943], Washington DC, 1, box 57, Eleanor Roosevelt correspondence, Anna Roosevelt Halsted Papers, FDR Presidential Library.

89. Henry L. Stimson, Tuesday, 4 May 1943, 3, *Diaries* 43:14 (Microfilm Reel 8), Henry L. Stimson Diaries (microfilm), Manuscript Division, Library of Congress.

90. Bess Furman to Tao Ming Wei, draft of letter, n.d., box 35: Mme. Tao Ming Wei, Papers of Bess Furman, Manuscript Division, Library of Congress.

91. "Mayling Soong Chiang," *Vogue,* 15 Apr 1943, Articles about MCKS (4/1943–5/1943), MCKS Papers.

92. Information bulletin for national and state officers, Equal Rights on Radio: excerpts from Rupert Hughes' NBS broadcast on 10–10:15 from Hollywood, 2 May 1943, box 3, folder 38, Lutz Papers. Perhaps Roosevelt intervened to protect MCKS's image, knowing from personal experience the limits of Americans' tolerance for women's active role in politics. And overtly political questions in turn placed Roosevelt in an awkward position because as first lady she represented the interests of American women as well as the president.

93. Madaline E. Murphy to Nell V. Beeby, *American Journal of Nursing,* 8 Jun 1943, box 1: A-Armstrong, ABMAC Records. The two other appointed members of this committee were Ruth Yap Hoy from Honolulu, and Katherine Lew from Peking.

94. B. A. Garside to Mrs. Charles W. Sewell, Associated Women of the American Farm Bureau Federation, Chicago, 26 Jan 1943, box 70, folder 10; and Garside to Minnie Evans Keyes, 11 Jan 1944, box 73, folder 21, both in USC Archives. Freemasons, Job's Daughters, and Order of the Eastern Star were all related. Although men and women were members of the Eastern Star, women led the effort to raise funds for China.

95. Dr. Ralph W. Sockman, "When Life is Too Short," radio address, 21 Mar 1943, issued by the dept. of national religious radio, no. 25, Sermons 1942–43, no 5–6, Speeches about MCKS, MCKS Papers.

96. Walter White to ER, 5 Dec 1942, 2, ser. 2A, box 168: MCKS, NAACP Papers, Manuscript Division, Library of Congress; White to Roosevelt, 16 Feb 1943, ser. 100, box: 1703: Walter White, personal correspondence 1943, ER Papers, FDR Presidential Library. The African American newspaper *Chicago Defender* has a very interesting, positive interpretation of MCKS's visit and the

backlash she faced at the end of her stay. Their critique of her politics also seems accurate.

97. Ida Pruitt to Walter H. Judd, 7 Apr 1943, 1, box 92: Important Correspondence, INDUSCO Archives.

98. Walter Winchell, *New York Daily Mirror*, 15 Feb 1943, box 3819, folder 3, Selznick Archives.

99. Wellington Koo, 10 April, Saturday, *Diary no. 10*. Lida Livingston, "Queries on War and Peace Answered by Mme. Chiang," *Hollywood Citizen News*, 2 Apr 1943, box 3819, folder 3, Selznick Archives. Letter, 29 Jun 1943, carbon copy, OF 150: China: 1943–45, FDR Papers.

100. Stanley K. Hornbeck, untitled and undated note, box 49: Chiang Kai-shek (and Madame Chiang), Hornbeck Collection.

101. This summary is based on my own research. Lorraine Dong and Jespersen also have provided insightful studies of MCKS's 1943 tour. See Lorraine Dong, "Song Meiling in America 1943," in *The Repeal and Its Legacy: Proceedings of the Conference on the 50th Anniversary of the Repeal of the Exclusion Acts* (Brisbane, CA: Chinese Historical Society of America, 1994), 39–46; and Jespersen, *American Images of China*. This Hollywood Bowl event raised over $31,000 for United China Relief. David Thomson suggests that Selznick had been suffering a letdown from the success of *Gone with the Wind* (1939) and found new inspiration in the China relief activities of his good friend Henry Luce's brainchild, United China Relief, formed in 1941. David Thomson, *Showman: The Life of David O. Selznick* (New York: Knopf, 1992), 186–191.

102. " 'China'—a Tribute to Madame Chiang Kai-shek," Hollywood Bowl recording from KHJ, 5 Apr 1943, audiotape, Harry Kronman Collection, USC Cinema-Television Library; "Armed Services to Join in Guarding Mme. Chiang," *Los Angeles Times*, 27 Mar 1943, and "Musical Dramatic Salute to Mme. Chiang in Hollywood Bowl," *Los Angeles Daily Variety*, 26 Mar 1943. And Selznick hoped Stothart's score "would . . . become an enormously valuable and continuing piece of propaganda for Chinese-American relations." David O. Selznick to Henry R. Luce, Draft, n.d., 1, box 309, folder 6: Henry Luce, Harry Ransom Humanities Center, University of Texas, Austin, Selznick Archives.

103. "Mme. Chiang Stirs Throng at Bowl," *Los Angeles Daily News*, 5 Apr 1943, 2, 5, 7.

104. The audiotape, "China."

105. In addition to MCKS's New Life Movement, which sought to institute conservative moral reform, Chiang Kai-shek's government was rife with abuses and corruption. One example is that conscription of Chinese into the army quickly became involuntary and forced. See Spence, *Search for Modern China*.

106. Selznick and his team implicitly acknowledged in their production Pearl Buck's significant influence in presenting China and the Chinese to American readers in her novel *The Good Earth* in 1931, combining the novel's images that had been further circulated in 1937 with MGM's film based on the novel, with current wartime propaganda.

107. Louella Parsons, "Hollywood Plans Spectacle for Mme. Chiang Kai-Shek," *Los Angeles Times*, 26 Mar 1943, 11.

108. David O. Selznick to Henry Luce, 19 Dec 1944, box 309, folder 6: Henry Luce, Selznick Archives.

109. Reference to this inquiry is found in the central decimal file 1940–44, box 3164, RG 59, Department of State, National Archives and Records Administration, Washington DC. The inquiry was made on 13 Feb 1943, four days before Martin J. Kennedy introduced a bill in Congress to repeal Chinese exclusion. A complete record of this inquiry was not found.

110. Wen-hsin Yeh maps the hierarchy of the Chinese elite by their location of education. The most affluent went abroad for schooling, the less affluent attended foreign-run private schools, and the least affluent attended Chinese-run institutions. Wen-hsin Yeh, *The Alienated Academy: Culture and Politics in Republican China, 1919–1937* (Cambridge, MA: Council on East Asian Studies, Harvard University, 1990).

111. ER to Roosevelt Boetiger, 28 Feb [1943], 1. In another letter ER writes of going out to dinner and suggesting that FDR dine with MCKS alone; he firmly refused.

112. Jack Stinnett, "Mme. Chiang Gives Guards Difficult Job," Oklahoma City, clipping, box 19: 150–7 MCKS, Secret Service records, FDR Presidential Library. Some China sympathizers believed that Great Britain had begun a campaign in the press to discredit MCKS out of fears that her popularity would indeed sway the U.S. war strategy.

113. Wellington Koo, May 19 Wednesday and May 18 Tuesday, *Diary no. 11*. After her Madison Square Garden appearance, an internal shakeup occurred within MCKS's entourage. The diplomats were out and her nephews L. K. and L. C. Kung took over the running of her tour. Because their idea of proper treatment for MCKS and their view of China's relationship to the United States took little account of the American public and public relations, the tour ended badly.

114. Wellington Koo, 4:30, Nov 3 Tuesday, *Diary no. 8, Sept 21–Dec 6, 1942,* box 215.

115. Sues, *Shark Fins and Millet,* 158, 163. Off the record Tuell, her Wellesley professor, echoed the assessment: Mills's description of MCKS in China had given her the impression of a "flaming, impassioned sort, built for fanaticism." Transcript from Tuell and Mills, 2.

116. Les W., "Sidelights on a Happy Visit," *Rob Wagner's Script,* 17 Apr 1943, 4, box 3819, folder 4, Selznick Archives.

117. "Mme. Chiang Calls for Higher Output," *Los Angeles Examiner,* 30 Mar 1943, box 3819, folder 3, Selznick Archives.

118. Wellington Koo, April 1, 1943, Thursday, *Diary no.10, March 6-May 14, 1943,* box 215, Koo Papers.

119. Owen Lattimore, *China Memoirs: Chiang Kai-shek and the War against Japan,* comp. Fujiko Isuno (Tokyo: University of Tokyo Press, 1990), 141.

120. Mme. Chiang Kai-shek, "The 'Rule of Law': Democracy vs. Olchlocracy," *Vital Speeches of the Day* 9 (1 Jun 1943): 548.

121. Martin J. Kennedy to MCKS, reprint from debate on repeal of the Chinese Exclusion Acts, 78th Congress, 1st sess., *Congressional Record,* vol. 89 (17 Feb 1943): A668.

122. Wellington Koo, April 14 Wednesday [Bear Mountain, NY], *Diary no. 10.*

123. Joshua Gamson, *Claims to Fame: Celebrity in Contemporary America* (Berkeley: University of California Press, 1994), 34.

124. Walter H. Judd to Ida Pruitt, 9 Apr 1943, box 92: Walter H. Judd, 1943–, INDUSCO Archives.

125. Church committee for China Relief, Appendix B: annual report of the director for the fiscal year June 1, 1942–May 31, 1943, 2, box 34, folder 4, USC Archives.

126. Geraldine Fitch to MCKS, 16 Oct 1942, New York, Fitch Papers.

127. Joshua Gamson, *Claims to Fame,* 39.

128. These are in Department of State telegrams, found in LM65–11, Roll 11. Drew Pearson, known to be pro-British, also contributed to these attacks on MCKS.

129. Christopher Emmet, memorandum on the cause and cure of propaganda against the Chinese government in America, n.d., 13, congressional file, box 595, folder 10, subject file: China: Reports: Miscellaneous, Luce Papers. Outraged China supporters claimed that British propaganda had planted these rumors because of MCKS's strong attack on the Hitler-first strategy.

130. Sues, *Shark Fins and Millet,* 327. According to Sues, after W. H. Donald mysteriously disappeared in the Pacific in 1941, the military gained sway over the general. But after the United States signed Lend-Lease (in part fearing a loss of China's support), the general summoned his wife from Hong Kong to visit with the president's special aide, Lauchlin Currie. After this visit, Currie suggested her U.S. visit with the Roosevelts.

131. Harry L. Hopkins, memorandum for files, dictated 27 Feb 1943, 1, box 331, Harry L. Hopkins Papers, Robert Sherwood Collection, China Affairs (1943–44), FDR Presidential Library.

5. TRANSFORMING AMERICAN NATIONAL IDENTITY —
THE CHINA MYSTIQUE

1. Discussing women's integral part in consuming popular culture, Ruiz and Matsumoto have examined the ways in which adolescent nonwhite daughters of immigrants negotiated their Americanization through consuming popular magazines, movies, and fashion. In addition, Jennifer Scanlon has noted how college-educated women in the 1920s and 1930s found careers in advertising because of their presumed ability to appeal to female consumers. American women's increased economic independence during the 1920s and 1930s tended to increase their consumer rather than political power, where more was at stake. Vicki L. Ruiz, " 'Star Struck': Acculturation, Adolescence, and Mexican American Women, 1920–1950," in *Unequal Sisters,* 3rd ed. (2000), 346–61 (see chapter 2 note 2); Valerie J. Matsumoto, "Japanese American Women and the Creation of Urban Nisei Culture in the 1930s," in *Over the Edge: Remapping the American West,* ed. Blake Allmendinger and Valerie J. Matsumoto (Berkeley: University of California Press, 1999), 291–306; Jennifer Scanlon, *Inarticulate Longings: The Ladies' Home Journal, Gender, and the Promises of Consumer Culture* (New York: Routledge, 1995).

2. Conn, *Pearl S. Buck.*

3. Ruiz, "Star Struck."

4. Patricia Hill Collins discusses "the power of self-definition," in which

African American women expressed themselves through art, writing, and music. *Black Feminist Thought.*

5. Harold Isaacs was the first to analyze in historical context the impact of Buck's writings and Soong's U.S. appearance on the American public's perceptions of China. See Isaacs, *Images of Asia.*

6. Summaries of attitudes toward countries considered as postwar problems, n.d., 1, National Stereotypes Research, Margaret Mead Collection, Manuscript Division, Library of Congress (hereafter cited as Margaret Mead Collection).

7. Suellen Chan, summary of Bessie Loo's interview by Beverly Chan, 10 Jan 1980, vol. 2, 38–8, Chinese Historical Society of Southern California Joint Oral History Project, Special Collections, UCLA. Loo was active in the Chinese Screen Actors Guild and gained prominence as a liaison between Chinese American extras/actors and film studios; she translated directions to Chinese-speaking extras and recruited extras from Chinatown.

8. Lyle H. Lanier, "Race and Nationality Attitudes: Exploratory Studies" [1944], 10, Margaret Mead Collection. In a socioeconomic index, pro-New Dealers exhibited less prejudice. The study drew on surveys given to 309 adults throughout the U.S. and 109 high school students in Columbus, Ohio during the winter of 1942–43, as well as altered surveys given to 273 students in introductory psychology classes at Vassar shortly later.

9. Carolyn G. Heilbrun, *Writing a Woman's Life* (New York: Ballantine Books, 1989), 18. Gayatri Spivak, *The Postcolonial Critic: Interviews, Strategies, Dialogues,* ed. Sarah Harasym (New York: Routledge, 1990). The particularly illuminating work of feminist theorists of color on self-identity includes but is not limited to Audre Lorde, *Sister Outsider: Essays and Speeches* (Trumansburg, NY: Crossing Press, 1984); Cherríe Moraga, *Loving in the War Years: lo que nunca pasó por sus labios* (Boston: South End Press, 1983); and Sandoval, "U.S. Third World Feminism."

# Bibliography

ARCHIVAL AND MANUSCRIPT COLLECTIONS

Philip Ahn Collection. East Asia Library. University of Southern California, Los Angeles

Arts Special Collections. University of California at Los Angeles (UCLA)
    MGM Ideas for Motion Pictures
    Twentieth Century Fox Archive

Margaret Bourke-White Collection. Department of Special Collections. Syracuse University Library, Syracuse, NY

British Library Newspaper Library. British Library, London

Clark Library Special Collections. University of California at Los Angeles
    Chinese Historical Society of Southern California Joint Oral History Project
    Kenneth Gamet Collection
    Papers of Paul Jordan Smith
    Victor M. Shapiro Collection
    Robert L. Wagner Collection

Columbia University Oral History Project. Columbia University, New York

Cinema-Television Archives. University of Southern California, Los Angeles
    Warner Brothers Corporate Archives
    MGM Studio Collection
    Herbert Stothart Collection

Film and Television Archive. University of California at Los Angeles

George and Geraldine Fitch Papers. Harvard-Yenching Library. Harvard University, Cambridge, MA

Margaret Herrick Library. Academy of Motion Pictures Arts and Sciences, Beverly Hills, CA
    Anna May Wong biographical file

Anna May Wong clippings file
Film production files
Hedda Hopper Papers
Motion Picture Association of America (MPAA) production code
administrative files
Paramount Pictures Collection
Sidney Skolsky Collection
Turner/MGM Script Collection
Hoover Institution Archives. Hoover Institution on War, Revolution, and Peace,
Stanford
Lauchlin Currie Papers
Victor Hoo Collection
Stanley K. Hornbeck Papers
Walter Henry Judd Papers
Freda Utley Papers
William Richard Johnson Papers. Special Collections. Yale Divinity School
Library, New Haven
Richard Loo Papers. Special Collections. American Heritage Center. University
of Wyoming, Laramie
Alma Lutz Papers. Schlesinger Library. Radcliffe College, Cambridge, MA
Manuscript Division. Library of Congress, Washington DC
Papers of Bess Furman
Edith Beham Helm Papers
Owen Lattimore Papers
Clare Boothe Luce Papers
Ken McCormick Collection of Doubleday and Company
Margaret Mead Collection
National Association for the Advancement of Colored People (NAACP)
Papers
Henry L. Stimson Diaries (microfilm)
Department of Manuscripts. Houghton Library. Harvard University,
Cambridge, MA
Lewis Stiles Gannett Papers
Roger Sherman Greene Papers
Manuscripts Department. Lilly Library. Indiana University, Bloomington
Emily Hahn Collection
Wendell Willkie Papers
Motion Picture, Broadcasting, and Recorded Sound Division. Library of
Congress, Washington DC
Motion Pictures Copyright Registration files
Office of War Information Evaluation files
Anna May Wong subject file
National Archives and Records Administration. Washington DC and branch
depositories
Records of the Department of State. RG 59
Records of the U.S. Army Intelligence

Records of the Immigration and Naturalization Service
  Laguna Niguel, CA. RG 85
  Seattle, WA
Records of the Office of War Information, College Park, MD. RG 208
San Francisco Customs House. Collector's Office, San Bruno, CA
Overbury Collection. Barnard College. Columbia University, New York
Za Phelps Collection. Yale Collection of American Literature. Beinecke Rare
  Book and Manuscript Library. Yale University, New Haven
Rare Book and Manuscript Library. Columbia University, New York
  American Bureau of Medical Aid for China (ABMAC) Records
  Helen Hull Papers
  INDUSCO Archives
  Institute of Pacific Relations Archives
  Wellington Koo Papers and Diaries
Department of Rare Books and Special Collections. Princeton University
  Library, Princeton
  Manuscripts Division
    David Lloyd Agency Files
    John Day Archives
  Public Policy Papers
    United Service to China (USC) Archives
Franklin D. Roosevelt Presidential Library, Hyde Park, NY
  Adolf A. Berle Papers
  George Bye Papers
  Stephen T. Early Papers
  Anna Roosevelt Halsted Papers
  Papers of Harry L. Hopkins, special assistant to the president
  Joseph P. Lash Papers
  Henry Morgenthau Diary (microfilm)
  Eleanor Roosevelt Papers
  Franklin D. Roosevelt Presidential Papers
  Office of the Chief of Social Correspondence, White House
  Secret Service Records
  Robert Sherwood Collection
David O. Selznick Archives. Harry Ransom Humanities Research Center.
  University of Texas at Austin
Special Collections. Beinecke Rare Book and Manuscript Library. Yale
  University, New Haven
Special Collections. Lipscomb Library. Randolph-Macon Woman's College,
  Lynchburg, VA
  Emma Edmunds White Collection
  Student Archives and clippings files
  Nora B. Stirling Collection
Special Collections and Archives. British Film Institute, London
  Microjacket collection (clippings files)
  Stills and Photograph Collection

Special Collections
James Anderson Collection
British Board of Film Censors Scenario Reports
Cinema ephemera, London (Queens Theatre)
Basil Dean Collection
Nasreen Kabir Collection
Personality ephemera
Pressbook Collection
Theatre Arts Collection. New York Public Library (NYPL), New York
Anna May Wong Gift
Anna May Wong clippings file
United Artists (UA) Collection. Division of Archives and Manuscripts. State
Historical Society of Wisconsin, Madison
Wellesley College Archives. Wellesley College, Wellesley
Class of 1917 Collection
Papers of Madame Chiang Kai-shek
Wellesley College Alumnae file
YMCA of USA Archives. University of Minnesota, St. Paul

PRIMARY SOURCES

*Newspapers and Periodicals*

*Birmingham New-Age Herald,* 1939
*Chicago Defender,* 1941–43
*(San Francisco) Chinese Press,* 1936–43
*Era,* 1929–34
*Film Daily,* 1922–46
*Film Pictorial,* 1929–38
*Film Weekly,* 1928–39
*Hollywood Reporter,* 1931–43
*Life Magazine,* 1936–45
*London Magazine,* 1929
*Looker-On,* 1929
*Los Angeles Times,* 1922–43
*Motion Pictures Magazine,* 1924–43
*New York Herald-Tribune,* 1936–43
*New York Post,* 1943
*New York Times,* 1924–45
*Photoplay Magazine,* 1924–29; 1930–45
*Picturegoer/Picturegoer Weekly,* 1928–39
*Pictureland,* 1924–39
*Redbook,* 1938
*Rob Wagner's Script* (or *Rob Wagner's Beverly Hills Script Weekly),* 1932–43
*Time Magazine,* 1931–43
*Variety Film Reviews,* 1926–29/*Variety,* 1921–43
*Vital Speeches of the Day,* 1932–43

*Weldon's Ladies Journal,* 1929–37
*Woman's Journal,* 1929, 1933–34, 1937


*Books and Articles*

Ayscough, Florence. *Chinese Women Yesterday and Today.* Boston: Houghton Mifflin, 1937.
Buck, Pearl S. *American Argument with Eslanda Goode Robeson.* New York: John Day, 1949.
———. *American Unity and Asia.* New York: John Day, 1942. Its retitled British edition is *Asia and Democracy* (London: Macmillan, 1943).
———. *Dragon Seed.* New York: John Day, 1942.
———. *The Exile.* New York: John Day, 1936.
———. *Fighting Angel.* New York: John Day, 1936.
———. *The Good Earth.* New York: John Day, 1931.
———. "Is There a Case for Foreign Missions?" John Day Pamphlet Series, 18. New York, 1932.
———. "John-John Chinaman." In *The Woman Who Was Changed and Other Stories.* New York: John Day, 1979.
———. "On Discovering America." *Survey Graphic* 26, no. 6 (Jun 1937): 313–15, 353, 355.
———. *My Several Worlds.* New York: John Day, 1954.
———. *Of Men and Women.* New York: John Day, 1941.
———. "Race Relations and Race Pride." *Opportunity, Journal of Negro Life,* Jan 1933, 2.
———. *The Story of Dragon Seed.* New York: John Day, 1944.
———. *What America Means to Me.* New York: John Day, 1943.
———. *The Woman Who Was Changed and Other Stories.* New York: John Day, 1979.
Buck, Pearl S., and Carlos P. Romulo. *Friend to Friend: A Candid Exchange Between Pearl S. Buck and Carlos P. Romulo.* New York: John Day, 1958.
Chiang, Mayling Soong (Madame Chiang Kai-shek). *China Shall Rise Again: Including Ten Official Statements of China's Present Progress.* New York: Harper, 1941.
———. *A Letter from Madame Chiang Kai-shek to Boys and Girls Across the Ocean.* Chungking: China Information Publishing, 1940.
———. *My Religion.* Toronto, Ontario: World Service Department of the Canadian National Council of YMCA, n.d.
———. *Sian: A Coup d'État, by Mayling Soong Chiang (Madame Chiang Kai-shek) / A Fortnight in Sian: Extracts from a Diary by Chiang Kei-shek.* Shanghai: China Publishing, 1937.
———. *This Is Our China.* New York: Harper and Brothers, 1940.
———. *War Messages and Other Selections by May-ling Soong Chiang (Madame Chiang Kai-shek).* Hankow: China Information Committee, 1938.
———. *We Chinese Women, Speeches and Writings during the First United Nations Year [by] Mayling Soong Chiang (Madame Chiang Kai-shek) Feb-*

*ruary 6, 1942–November 16, 1942.* New York: China News Service, [1943].

Chiang Kai-shek (generalissimo). *The Collected Wartime Messages of Generalissimo Chiang Kai-shek, 1937–1945, compiled by Chinese Ministry of Information.* New York: John Day, 1946.

———. *A Fortnight in Sian: Extracts from a Diary by Chiang Kai-shek / Sian: A Coup d'État, by Mayling Soong Chiang (Madame Chiang Kai-shek).* Shanghai: China Publishing, 1937.

Chiang Kai-shek, Generalissimo, and Madame Chiang Kai-shek. *We Believe.* New York: International Committee of Young Men's Christian Association, 1943.

Clark, Elmer T. *The Chiangs of China.* New York: Abingdon-Cokesbury Press, 1943.

Kazin, Alfred. *On Native Grounds, an Interpretation of Modern American Prose Literature.* New York: Reynal and Hitchcock, 1942.

Mead, Margaret. *And Keep Your Powder Dry: An Anthropologist Looks at America.* New York: William Morrow, 1942.

Morgan, Barbara. *Martha Graham: Sixteen Dances in Photographs.* New York: Duell, Sloan and Pearce, 1941.

Smith, William C. *Americans in Process: A Study of Our Citizens of Oriental Ancestry.* Ann Arbor: Edwards Brothers, 1937.

Sues, Ilona Ralf. *Shark Fins and Millet.* New York: Little, Brown, 1944.

Thomas, Harry J. *The First Lady of China; the Historic Wartime Visit of Mme. Chiang Kai-shek to the United States in 1943.* New York: International Business Machines, 1943.

*Films and Additional Archival Material*

*Across to Singapore* (1928)
*The Alaskan* (1924)
*The Battle of China* (1944)
*Bits of Life* (1921)
*The Bitter Tea of General Yen* (1933)
*Bombs over Burma* (1942)
*China* (Paramount, 1943)
*China: The Beautiful and Mysterious* (1936)
*China Girl* (1942)
*China Sky* (1945)
*Chinatown, My Chinatown* (1929)
*Chinatown Charlie* (1928)
*The Chinese Parrot* (1927)
*Chu Chin Chow* (1934)
*The Crimson City* (1928)
*Dangerous to Know* (1938)
*Daughter of Shanghai* (1937)
*The Desert's Toll* (1926)
*The Devil Dancer* (1927)

*Dinty* (1920)
*Dragon Seed* (1942)
*Ellery Queen's Penthouse Mysteries* (1941)
*The Fortieth Door* (1924)
*Forty Winks* (1925)
*The General Died at Dawn* (1936)
*The Good Earth* (1937)
*Hai Tang* (1930)
*His Supreme Moment* (1925)
*Hollywood on Parade* (1932)
*Island of Lost Men* (1939)
*Java Head* (1934)
*King of Chinatown* (1939)
*Lady from Chungking* (1943)
*Limehouse Blues* (1934)
*Little Tokyo, USA* (1942)
*Old San Francisco* (1927)
*Peter Pan* (1924)
*Piccadilly* (1929)
*The Red Lantern* (1919)
*Shame* (1921)
*Shanghai Express* (1932)
*Shanghai Gesture* (1941)
*Streets of Shanghai* (1927)
*A Study in Scarlet* (1933)
*The Thief of Baghdad* (1924)
*Tiger Bay* (1933)
*Toll of the Sea* (1922)
*A Trip to Chinatown* (1926)
*When Were You Born?* (1938)

SECONDARY SOURCES

Alexander, David. *Imperialism and Idealism: American Diplomats in China, 1861–1898*. Bloomington: Indiana University Press, 1985.

Anderson, Benedict. *Imagined Communities: Reflections on the Origin and Spread of Nationalism*. Rev. ed. New York: Verso, 1991.

Anderson, Karen. *Wartime Women: Sex Roles, Family Relations, and the Status of Women during World War II*. Westport, CT: Greenwood Press, 1981.

Anzaldúa, Gloria. *Borderlands = La Frontera: The New Mestiza*. Introduction by Sonia Saldívar-Hull. San Francisco: Aunt Lute Books, 1999.

Balio, Tino, ed. *The American Film Industry*. Madison: University of Wisconsin Press, 1976.

Barnard, Rita. *The Great Depression and the Culture of Abundance*. New York: Cambridge University Press, 1995.

Baughman, James L. *Henry R. Luce and the Rise of the American News Media*. Boston: Twayne, 1987.

————. *The Republic of Mass Culture: Journalism, Filmmaking, and Broadcasting in America since 1941*. Baltimore, MD: Johns Hopkins University Press, 1992.

Belton, John, ed. *Movies and Mass Culture*. New Brunswick, NJ: Rutgers University Press, 1996.

Bennett, Tony, ed. *Popular Fiction: Technology, Ideology, Production, Reading*. New York: Routledge, 1990.

Bergfelder, Tim. "Negotiating Exoticism: Hollywood, Film Europe and the Cultural Reception of Anna May Wong." In *"Film Europe" and "Film America": Cinema, Commerce and Cultural Exchange 1920–1939*, edited by Andrew Higson and Richard Maltby, 302–23. Exeter Studies in Film History. Exeter, UK: University of Exeter Press, 1999.

Berle, Beatrice Bishop, and Travis Beal Jacobs, eds. *Navigating the Rapids, 1918–1971; from the Papers of Adolf A. Berle*. Introduction by Max Ascoli. New York: Harcourt Brace Jovanavich, 1973.

Best, Gary Dean. *The Nickel and Dime Decade*. Westport, CT: Praeger, 1993.

Bhaba, Homi K. *The Location of Culture*. New York: Routledge, 1994.

Biel, Steven. *Independent Intellectuals in the United States, 1910–1945*. New York: New York University Press, 1992.

Black, Gregory D. *Hollywood Censored: Morality Codes, Catholics, and the Movies*. Cambridge: Cambridge University Press, 1994.

Blackwelder, Julia Kirk. *Women of the Depression: Caste and Culture in San Antonio, 1929–1939*. College Station: Texas A and M University Press, 1984.

Blair, Karen J. *The Clubswoman as Feminist: True Womanhood Redefined, 1868–1914*. Preface by Annette K. Baxter. New York: Holmes and Meier, 1980.

Blum, John Morton. *V Was for Victory: Politics and Culture during World War II*. New York: Harcourt Brace Jovanovich, 1976.

Bobo, Jacqueline. *Black Women as Cultural Readers*. New York: Columbia University Press, 1995.

Bogle, Donald. *Toms, Coons, Mulattoes, Mammies, and Bucks: An Interpretive History of Blacks in American Films*. New York: Continuum, 1994.

Brewer, John C., and Patricia Neils, eds. *United States Attitudes and Policies Toward China: The Impact of American Missionaries*. New York: M. E. Sharpe, 1990.

Brookeman, Christopher. *American Culture and Society since the 1930s*. London: Macmillan, 1984.

Buck, David. D. "In Search of America." In *The Several Worlds of Pearl S. Buck*, 29–43.

Callaway, Helen. *Gender, Culture, and Empire: European Women in Colonial Nigeria*. Oxford: Macmillan, 1987.

Chan, Sucheng. *Asian Americans: An Interpretive History*. New York: Twayne, 1991.

————. "European and Asian Immigration into the United States in Comparative Perspective, 1820s to 1920s." In *Immigration Reconsidered: History, Sociology, and Politics*, edited by Virginia Yans-McLaughlin, 37–75. New York: Oxford University Press, 1990.

————. "The Exclusion of Chinese Women, 1870–1943." In *Entry Denied: Exclusion and the Chinese Community in America, 1882–1943*, edited by

Sucheng Chan, 94–146. Asian American History and Culture. Philadelphia: Temple University Press, 1989.

———. "Race, Ethnic Culture, and Gender." In *Claiming America*, 127–64.

Carroll, Berenice A. "The Politics of 'Originality.' Women and the Class System of the Intellect." *Journal of Women's History* 2, no. 2 (Fall 1990): 136–63.

Charney, Leo, and Vanessa R. Schwartz, eds. *Cinema and the Invention of Modern Life*. Berkeley: University of California Press, 1995.

Chauncey, George. *Gay New York*. New York: Basic Books, 1994.

Chen, Yong. *Chinese San Francisco, 1850–1943: A Trans-Pacific Community*. Stanford: Stanford University Press, 2000.

Cheng, Lucie, and Suellen Cheng. "Chinese Women of Los Angeles, a Social Historical Survey." In *Linking Our Lives*, 17–28.

Cheng, Lucie, Suellen Cheng, Judy Chu, Feelie Lee, Lee Majorie, and Susie Ling. *Linking Our Lives: Chinese American Women of Los Angeles*. Los Angeles: Chinese Historical Society of Southern California, 1984.

Chu, Judy, and Susie Ling, "Chinese Women at Work." In *Linking Our Lives*, 65–90.

Chun, Gloria H. "Go West . . . to China: Chinese American Identity in the 1930s." In *Claiming America*, 165–90.

———. *Of Orphans and Warriors: Inventing Chinese American Culture and Identity*. New Brunswick, NJ: Rutgers University Press, 2000.

Chung, Sue Fawn. "Fighting for Their American Rights: A History of the Chinese American Citizens Alliance." In *Claiming America*, 95–126.

Chung Simpson, Caroline. *An Absent Presence: Japanese Americans in Postwar American Culture, 1945–1960*. Durham, NC: Duke University Press, 2001.

Clark, Elmer T. *The Chiangs of China*. New York: Abingdon-Cokesbury Press, 1943

Clifford, Nicholas R. *Spoilt Children of Empire: Westerners in Shanghai and the Chinese Revolution of the 1920s*. Hanover, CT: Middlebury College Press, 1991.

Cohen, Lizabeth. *Making a New Deal: Industrial Workers in Chicago, 1919–1939*. New York: Cambridge University Press, 1990.

Collins, Patricia Hill. *Black Feminist Thought: Knowledge, Consciousness, and the Politics of Empowerment*. Boston: Unwin Hyman, 1990.

Conn, Peter. *Pearl S. Buck: A Cultural Biography*. New York: Cambridge University Press, 1996.

Cook, Blanche Wiesen. *Eleanor Roosevelt*. Vol. 1. New York: Viking, 1992.

Cott, Nancy F. *The Grounding of Modern Feminism*. New Haven: Yale University Press, 1987.

Couvares, Frances G., ed. *Movie Censorship and American Culture*. Washington DC: Smithsonian Institution Press, 1996.

Dallek, Robert. *Franklin D. Roosevelt and Foreign Policy, 1932–1945*. New York: Oxford University Press, 1979.

Daniels, Roger. *Asian America: Chinese and Japanese in the United States since 1850*. Seattle: University of Washington Press, 1988.

Darilek, Richard E. *A Loyal Opposition in Time of War: The Republican Party and the Politics of Foreign Policy from Pearl Harbor to Yalta*. Westport, CT: Greenwood Press, 1976.

de Conde, Alexander. *Ethnicity, Race, and American Foreign Policy*. Boston: Northeastern University Press, 1992.

de Cordova, Richard. *Picture Personalities: The Emergence of the Star System in America*. Chicago: University of Illinois Press, 1990.

Divine, Robert A. *Roosevelt and World War II*. Baltimore, MD: Johns Hopkins University Press, 1969.

Dixon, Wheeler, ed. *Producers Releasing Corporation: A Comprehensive Filmography and History*. Jefferson, NC: McFarland, 1986.

Doane, Mary Ann. "The Economy of Desire." In *Movies and Mass Culture*, edited by John Bennet, 119–34. New Brunswick, NJ: Rutgers University Press, 1996.

Dong, Lorraine. "Song Meiling in America 1943." In *The Repeal and Its Legacy: Proceedings of the Conference on the 50th Anniversary of the Repeal of the Exclusion Acts*. Brisbane, CA: Chinese Historical Society of America, 1994.

Dower, John W. *War Without Mercy: Race and Power in the Pacific War*. New York: Pantheon Books, 1986.

Duberman, Martin Bauml. *Paul Robeson*. New York: Knopf, 1989.

DuBois, Ellen Carol, and Vicki L. Ruiz, eds. *Unequal Sisters: A Multicultural Reader in U.S. Women's History*. 2nd and 3rd eds. New York: Routledge, 1990, 2000.

Eastman, Lloyd E. *The Abortive Revolution: China under Nationalist Rule, 1927–1937*. Cambridge, MA: Harvard University Press, 1974.

Edmunds, Robin. *The Big Three: Churchill, Roosevelt, and Stalin in Peace and War*. London: Hamish Hamilton, 1991.

Enloe, Cynthia. *Bananas, Beaches, and Bases: Making Feminist Sense of International Politics*. Berkeley: University of California Press, 1990.

Fairbank, John K. *China: The People's Middle Kingdom and the U.S.A.* Cambridge, MA: Belknap Press of Harvard University Press, 1967.

———. *Chinabound: A Fifty-year Memoir*. New York: Harper and Row, 1982.

———. *China Perceived: Images and Policies in Chinese-American Relations*. New York: 1974.

———. *China Watch*. Cambridge, MA: Harvard University Press, 1987.

———. Introduction to *The Missionary Enterprise in China and America*. Edited by John K. Fairbank. Cambridge, MA: Harvard University Press, 1974.

Fitzgerald, John. *Awakening China: Politics, Culture, and Class in the Nationalist Revolution*. Stanford: Stanford University Press, 1996.

Fitzgerald, Keith. *The Face of a Nation: Immigration, the State, and the National Identity*. Stanford: Stanford University Press, 1996.

Fuller, Kathryn H. *At the Picture Show: Small-town Audiences and the Creation of Movie Fan Culture*. Washington DC: Smithsonian Institution Press, 1996.

Furuya, Keiji, ed. *Chiang Kai-shek, His Life and Times*. New York: St. John's University Press, 1981.

Fyne, Robert. *The Hollywood Propaganda of World War II*. Metuchen, NJ: Scarecrow Press, 1994.

Gamson, Joshua. *Claims to Fame: Celebrity in Contemporary America*. Berkeley: University of California Press, 1994.

Garrett, Shirley Stone. "Why They Stayed: American Church Politics and Chinese Nationalism in the Twenties." In *The Missionary Enterprise in China and America*, 283–310.

Gleason, Philip. *Speaking of Diversity: Language and Ethnicity in Twentieth-Century America.* Baltimore, MD: Johns Hopkins University Press, 1992.

Gledhill, Christine, ed. *Stardom: Industry of Desire.* New York, Routledge, 1991.

Goldin, Claudia. *Understanding the Gender Gap: An Economic History of American Women.* New York: Oxford University Press, 1990.

Goldman, Merle, ed. *Modern Chinese Literature in the May Fourth Movement.* Cambridge, MA: Harvard University Press, 1977.

Goodwin, Doris Kearns. *No Ordinary Time: Franklin and Eleanor Roosevelt: The Home Front in World War II.* New York; Simon and Schuster, 1994.

Gordon, Paul Lauren. *Power and Prejudice: The Politics and Diplomacy of Racial Discrimination.* Boulder, CO: Westview Press, 1996.

Gorman, Paul R. *Left Intellectuals and Popular Culture in Twentieth-Century America.* Chapel Hill: University of North Carolina Press, 1996.

Hahn, Emily. *Chiang Kai-shek, an Unauthorized Biography.* Garden City, NY: Doubleday, 1955.

———. *The Soong Sisters.* Garden City, NY: Doubleday, Doran, 1941.

Hamamoto, Darrell. *Monitored Peril: Asian Americans and the Politics of TV Representation.* Minneapolis: University of Minnesota Press, 1994.

Hamamoto, Darrell, and Sandra Liu, eds. *Countervisions: Asian American Film Criticism.* Philadelphia: Temple University Press, 2000.

Handel, Leo. *Hollywood Looks at Its Audience: A Report of Film Audience Research.* Urbana: University of Illinois Press, 1950.

Harley, John Eugene. *World-wide Influences of the Cinema: A Study of Official Censorship and the International Cultural Aspects of Motion Pictures.* Los Angeles: University of Southern California Press, 1940.

Harris, Theodore E. *Pearl S. Buck: A Biography by Theodore E. Harris in Consultation with Pearl S. Buck.* New York: John Day, 1969.

Hayford, Charles W. "The Revolution and the American Raj in China." In *The Several Worlds of Pearl S. Buck,* 19–27.

Heilbrun, Carolyn G. *Writing a Woman's Life.* New York: Ballantine Books, 1989.

Higham, John. *Strangers in the Land: Patterns of American Nativism, 1860–1925.* Corrected and with a new preface. New York: Atheneum, 1975.

Hill, Patricia. *The World Their Household: The American Woman's Foreign Movement and Cultural Transformation, 1870–1920.* Ann Arbor: University of Michigan Press, 1985.

Hoff-Wilson, Joan, and Marjorie Lightman, eds. *Without Precedent: The Life and Career of Eleanor Roosevelt.* Bloomington: Indiana University Press, 1984.

Hofstadter, Richard. *Anti-Intellectualism in American Life.* New York: Vintage Press, 1963.

Hollinger, David A. *In the American Province.* Bloomington: Indiana University Press, 1985.

hooks, bell. *Black Looks: Race and Representation.* Boston: South End Press, 1994.

hooks, bell. *Yearning: Race, Gender, and Cultural Politics.* Boston: South End Press, 1990.

Hsu, Immanuel Y. *The Rise of Modern China.* New York: Oxford University Press, 1970.

Hung, Chang-tai. "Female Symbols of Resistance in Chinese Wartime Spoken Drama." *Modern China* 15, no. 2 (Apr 1989): 149–77.

Hunt, Michael H. *Ideology and Foreign Policy.* New Haven: Yale University Press, 1987.

———. *The Making of a Special Relationship: The United States and China to 1914.* New York: Columbia University Press, 1983.

Hunter, Jane. *The Gospel of Gentility: American Women Missionaries in Turn-of-the-Century China.* New Haven: Yale University Press, 1984.

Hutchinson, E. P. *Legislative History of American Immigration Policy 1798–1965.* Philadelphia: University of Pennsylvania Press, 1981.

Hutchinson, George. *The Harlem Renaissance in Black and White.* Cambridge, MA: Belknap Press of Harvard University Press, 1995.

Isaacs, Harold R. *Images of Asia: American Views of China and India.* New York: Capricorn Books, 1962.

Jackson, Walter A. *Gunnar Myrdal and America's Conscience: Social Engineering and Racial Liberalism, 1938–1987.* Chapel Hill: University of North Carolina Press, 1990.

Jeffords, Susan. "Culture and National Identity." *Diplomatic History* 18, no. 1 (Winter 1994): 91–96.

———. *The Remasculinization of America: Gender and the Vietnam War.* Bloomington: Indiana University Press, 1989.

Jespersen, T. Christopher. *American Images of China, 1931–1949.* Stanford: Stanford University Press, 1996.

Jowett, Garth S., Ian C. Jarvit, and Kathryn H. Fuller. *Children and the Movies: Media Influence and the Payne Fund Controversy.* New York: Cambridge University Press, 1996.

Judis, John B. *Grand Illusion.* New York: Farrar, Straus and Giroux, 1992.

Kaplan, Amy. "Left Alone with America." In *The Cultures of United States Imperialism,* edited by Amy Kaplan and Donald Pease, 3–21. Durham, NC: Duke University Press, 1993.

———. "A 'Manifest Domesticity.'" *American Literature* 70 (1998): 581–606.

Kaplan, Caren. *Questions of Travel.* Durham, NC: Duke University Press, 1996.

Kaplan, Caren, and Inderpal Grewal, eds. *Scattered Hegemonies.* Minneapolis: University of Minnesota Press, 1994.

Kimball, Warren. *The Juggler: Franklin Roosevelt as Wartime Statesman.* Princeton: Princeton University Press, 1991.

Kerber, Linda. *Women of the Republic: Intellect and Ideology in Revolutionary America.* Chapel Hill: Published for the Institute of Early American History and Culture by the University of North Carolina Press, 1980.

Kessler-Harris, Alice. *Out to Work: A History of Wage-earning Women in the United States.* New York: Oxford University Press, 1982.

Koppes, Clayton R., and Gregory D. Black. *Hollywood Goes to War: How Politics, Profits, and Propaganda Shaped World War II Movies.* New York: Free Press, 1987.

La Guerre, Michel S. *The Global Ethnopolis: Chinatown, Japantown, and Manila Town in American Society.* New York: Palgrave Macmillan, 1999.

Lai, Him Mark. "China Politics and the U.S. Chinese Communities." In *Coun-*

*terpoint: Perspectives on Asian America,* edited by Emma Gee, 152–59. Los Angeles: Asian American Studies Center, UCLA, 1976.

Larson, Louise Leung. *Sweet Bamboo: A Saga of a Chinese American Family.* Los Angeles: Chinese Historical Society of Southern California, 1989.

Lasch, Christopher. *The New Radicalism in America, 1889–1963: The Intellectual as a Social Type.* New York: Knopf, 1965.

Lash, Joseph P. *Eleanor and Franklin.* New York: W. W. Norton, 1971.

——. *Love, Eleanor: Eleanor Roosevelt and Her Friends.* Garden City, NY: Doubleday, 1982.

Lattimore, Owen. *China Memoirs: Chang Kai-shek and the War against Japan.* Compiled by Fujiko Isuno. Tokyo: University of Tokyo Press, 1990.

Lee, Erika. "At America's Gates." Ph.D. diss., University of California, Berkeley, 1998.

Lee, Josephine. *Performing Asian America.* Philadelphia: Temple University Press, 1998.

Lee, Rachel. *The Americas of Asian American Literature.* Princeton: Princeton University Press, 1999.

Lee, Robert G. *Orientals: Asian Americans in Popular Culture.* Philadelphia: Temple University Press, 1999.

Leff, Leonard J., and Jerold L. Simmons. *The Dame in the Kimono: Hollywood, Censorship and the Production Code from the 1920s to the 1960s.* New York: Grove Weidenfelt, 1980.

Leong, Karen J. "The China Mystique: Mayling Soong Chiang, Pearl S. Buck, and Anna May Wong in the American Imagination." Ph.D. diss., University of California, Berkeley, 1999.

Leuchtenburg, William E., ed. *Franklin D. Roosevelt: A Profile.* New York: Hill and Wang, 1967.

Lewis, David Levering. *When Harlem Was in Vogue.* New York: Knopf, 1981.

Lipscomb, Elizabeth J., Frances E. Webb, and Peter Conn, eds. *The Several Worlds of Pearl S. Buck: Essays Presented at a Centennial Symposium, Randolph-Macon Woman's College, 26–28 March 1992.* Westport, CT: Greenwood Press, 1994.

Liu, Haiping. "Pearl Buck's Reception in China Reconsidered." In *The Several Worlds of Pearl Buck,* 55–67.

Liu, Lydia. "The Female Body and Nationalist Discourse." In *Scattered Hegemonies,* edited by Caren Kaplan and Inderpal Grewal, 37–62. Minneapolis: University of Minnesota Press, 1994.

Lodwick, Kathleen L. "Hainan for the Homefolk. Images of the Island in the Missionary and Secular Presses." In *United States Attitudes and Policies Toward China,* 97–110.

Lorde, Audre. *Sister Outsider: Essays and Speeches.* Trumansburg, NY: Crossing Press, 1984.

Lowe, Lisa. *Critical Terrains: French and British Orientalisms.* Ithaca: Cornell University Press, 1992.

——. *Immigrant Acts: On Asian American Cultural Politics.* Durham: Duke University Press, 1996.

McClintock, Anne. *Imperial Leather: Race, Gender and Sexuality in the Colonial Contest.* New York: Routledge, 1995.

McElvaine, Robert S. *The Great Depression.* New York: Times Books, 1984.

McIntosh, Peggy. "Unpacking the Knapsack of White Privilege." In *Race, Class, and Gender: A Reader,* edited by Margaret Anderson and Patricia Hill Collins, 76–87. 2nd ed. Menlo Park, CA: Wadsworth, 1992.

McKee, Delber L. *Chinese Exclusion versus the Open Door Policy, 1900–1906: Clashes over China Policy in the Roosevelt Era.* Detroit: Wayne State University Press, 1977.

MacKinnon, Stephen R., and Oris Friesen. *China Reporting: An Oral History of American Journalism in the 1930s and 1940s.* Berkeley: University of California Press, 1987.

Marchetti, Gina. *Romance and the "Yellow Peril": Race, Sex, and Discursive Strategies in Hollywood Fiction.* Berkeley: University of California Press, 1993.

Marquis, Alice G. *Hopes and Ashes: The Birth of Modern Times, 1929–1939.* New York: Free Press, 1986.

Martin, Brian G. *The Shanghai Green Gang: Politics and Organized Crime.* Berkeley: University of California Press, 1996.

Martin, Ralph G. *Henry and Clare: An Intimate Portrait of the Luces.* New York: Putnam's, 1991.

May, Lary. *Screening Out the Past: The Birth of Mass Culture and the Motion Picture Industry.* New York: Oxford University Press, 1980.

Mazumdar, Sucheta. "In the Family." In *Linking Our Lives,* 29–48.

Miller, Stuart Creighton. *The Unwelcome Immigrant: The American Image of the Chinese, 1785–1882.* Berkeley: University of California Press, 1969.

Moy, James S. *Marginal Sights: Staging the Chinese in America.* Iowa City: University of Iowa Press, 1993

Neils, Patricia. *China Images in the Life and Times of Henry Luce.* Savage, MD: Rowman and Littlefield, 1990.

———. Introduction to *United States Attitudes and Policies Toward China,* 4–24.

Nesbit, Henrietta. *White House Diary.* Garden City, NY: Doubleday, 1948.

Noble, Dennis L. *The Eagle and the Dragon: The United States Military in China, 1901–1937.* New York: Greenwood Press, 1990.

Oehling, Richard A. "The Yellow Menace: Asian Images in American Film." In *The Kaleidoscope Lens: How Hollywood Views Ethnic Groups,* edited by Randall M. Miller, 182–206. N.p.: Jerome S. Ozer, 1980.

Okihiro, Gary Y. *Margins and Mainstreams: Asians in American History and Culture.* Baltimore, MD: Johns Hopkins University Press, 1994.

Ono, Kazuko. *Chinese Women in a Century of Revolution, 1850–1950.* Edited by Joshua A. Fogel, translated by Kathryn Bernhardt, Timothy Brook, Joshua A. Fogel, Jonathan Lipman, Susan Mann, and Laurel Rhodes. Stanford: Stanford University Press, 1989.

Palmieri, Patricia Ann. *In Adamless Eden: The Community of Women Faculty at Wellesley.* New Haven: Yale University Press, 1995.

Pascoe, Peggy. *Relations of Rescue: The Search for Female Moral Authority in the American West, 1874–1939.* New York: Oxford University Press, 1990.

Payne, Robert. *Chiang Kai-shek.* New York: Weybright and Talley, 1969.

Peffer, George Anthony. "Forbidden Families: Emigration Experiences of Chinese Women under the Page Law." *Journal of American Ethnic History* 6 (1986): 28–46.

———. *If They Don't Bring Their Women Here: Chinese Female Immigration before Exclusion*. Urbana: University of Illinois Press, 1999.

Peiss, Kathy. *Hope in a Jar: The Making of America's Beauty Culture*. New York: Owl Books, 1999.

Radway, Janice A. *A Feeling for Books: The Book-of-the-Month Club, Literary Taste, and Middle-class Desire*. Chapel Hill: University of North Carolina Press, 1997.

Raub, Patricia. *Yesterday's Stories: Popular Women's Novels of the Twenties and Thirties*. Westport, CT: Greenwood Press, 1994.

Riggs, Fred. *Pressures on Congress*. New York: King's Crown Press, 1950.

Roberts, Barrie. "Anna May Wong: Daughter of the Orient." *Classic Images*, no. 270 (Dec 1997): 20–24.

Rogin, Michael. *Blackface, White Noise: Jewish Immigrants in the Hollywood Melting Pot*. Berkeley: University of California Press, 1996.

Roosevelt, Eleanor. *The White House Press Conferences of Eleanor Roosevelt*. Edited with introduction by Maurine Beasley. New York: Garland, 1983.

Roosevelt, Elliott, and James Brough. *A Rendezvous with Destiny: The Roosevelts of the White House*. New York: Putnam, 1975.

Rosaldo, Renato. *Culture and Truth: The Remaking of Social Analysis*. Boston: Beacon, 1989.

Rosenburg, Emily. "Gender." *Journal of American History* 77, no.1 (Jun 1990): 116–24.

Rosenman, Samuel I. *Working with Roosevelt*. New York: Harper, 1952.

Rubin, Joan Shelley. *The Making of Middlebrow Culture*. Chapel Hill: University of North Carolina Press, 1992.

Ruiz, Vicki L. " 'Star Struck': Acculturation, Adolescence, and Mexican American Women, 1920–1950." In *Unequal Sisters*, 346–61.

Rupp, Leila. *Mobilizing Women for War: German and American Propaganda, 1949–1945*. Princeton: Princeton University Press, 1978.

Ryan, Mary P. *Womanhood in America: From Colonial Times to the Present*. New York: Franklin Watts, 1983.

———. *Women in Public: Between Banners to Ballots, 1825–1880*. Baltimore, MD: Johns Hopkins University Press, 1990.

Said, Edward. *Orientalism*. New York: Random House, 1978.

Sainsbury, Keith. *Churchill and Roosevelt at War: The War They Fought and the Peace They Hoped to Make*. New York: New York University Press, 1994.

Salyer, Lucy J. *Laws as Harsh as Tigers: Chinese Immigrants and the Shaping of Modern Immigration Laws*. Chapel Hill: University of North Carolina, 1995.

Sanchez, George. " 'Go After the Women': Americanization and the Mexican Immigrant Woman, 1915–1929." In *Unequal Sisters*, 250–63.

Sandoval, Chela. "U.S. Third World Feminism: The Theory and Method of Oppositional Consciousness in the Postmodern World." *Genders* 10 (Spring 1991): 1–24.

Saxton, Alexander. *The Indispensable Enemy: Labor and the anti-Chinese Movement in California*. Berkeley: University of California Press, 1971.

Scanlon, Jennifer. *Inarticulate Longings: The Ladies' Home Journal, Gender, and the Promises of Consumer Culture*. New York: Routledge, 1995.

Schaller, Michael. *The U.S. Crusade in China, 1938–1945*. New York: Columbia University Press, 1979.

Schickel, Richard. *Intimate Strangers: The Culture of Celebrity*. New York: Doubleday, 1985.

Schlesinger, Arthur M., Jr. "The Missionary Enterprise and Theories of Imperialism." In *The Missionary Enterprise in China and America*, 326–73.

———. *The Age of Roosevelt*. Vols. 2 and 3. Boston: Houghton Mifflin, 1957.

Sherwood, Robert E. *Roosevelt and Hopkins, an Intimate History*. New York: Harper, 1950.

Shohat, Ella, and Robert Stam. *Unthinking Eurocentrism: Multiculturalism and the Media*. New York: Routledge, 1994.

Siu, Paul C. P. *The Chinese Laundryman: A Study of Social Isolation*. Edited by John Kuo-Wei Tchen. New York: New York University Press, 1987.

Smith, Valerie. *Not Just Race, Not Just Gender: Black feminist Readings*. New York: Routledge, 1998.

Sollors, Werner. *Beyond Ethnicity: Consent and Descent in American Culture*. New York: Oxford University Press, 1986.

Spence, Jonathan D. *The Chan's Great Continent: China in Western Minds*. New York: W. W. Norton, 1998.

———. *The Search for Modern China*. New York: W. W. Norton., 1990.

Spencer, Cornelia. *The Exile's Daughter*. New York: Coward-McCann, 1944.

Spivak, Gayatri. *The Postcolonial Critic: Interviews, Strategies, Dialogues*. Edited by Sarah Harasym. New York: Routledge, 1990.

Stirling, Nora B. *Pearl Buck, a Woman in Conflict*. Piscatawny, NJ: New Century, 1983.

Stodelle, Ernestine. *Deep Song: The Dance Story of Martha Graham*. New York: Schirmer Books, 1984.

Stott, William. *Documentary Expression and Thirties America*. New York: Oxford University Press, 1973.

Strong, Anna Louise. *My Native Land*. New York: Viking Press, 1940.

Sues, Ilona Ralf. *Shark Fins and Millet*. New York: Little, Brown, 1944.

Susman, Warren I. *Culture as History*. New York: Pantheon Books, 1973.

Swanberg, W. A. *Luce and His Empire*. New York: Scribner, 1972.

Takaki, Ronald. *A Different Mirror: A History of Multicultural America*. Boston: Little, Brown, 1993.

Tchen, John Kuo-Wei. *New York before Chinatown: Orientalism and the Shaping of American Culture 1776–1882*. Baltimore, MD: Johns Hopkins University Press, 1999.

Thomson, David. *Showman: The Life of David O. Selznick*. New York: Knopf, 1992.

Thomson, James C., Jr. *While China Faced West; American Reformers in Nationalist China, 1928–1937*. Cambridge, MA: Harvard University Press, 1969.

Thomson, James C., Jr., Peter W. Stanley, and John Curtis Perry. *Sentimental Imperialists*. San Francisco: Harper and Row, 1981.

Thorne, Christopher. *Allies of a Kind: The United States, Britain, and the War against Japan, 1941–1945*. New York: Oxford University Press, 1978.

Tsai, Shih-shan Henry. *The Chinese Experience in America*. Bloomington: Indiana University Press, 1986.

Tuchman, Barbara W. *Stilwell and the American Experience in China, 1911–45*. New York: Macmillan, 1970.

Varg, Paul A. *Missionaries, Chinese, and Diplomats: The American Protestant Missionary Movement in China, 1840–1952*. Princeton: Princeton University Press, 1958.

———. "The Missionary Response to the Nationalist Revolution." In *The Missionary Enterprise in China and America*, 311–35.

Vasey, Ruth. *The World According to Hollywood, 1918–1939*. Madison: University of Wisconsin Press, 1997.

Wakeman, Frederic, Jr., and Wen-hsin Yeh. *Shanghai Sojourners*. Berkeley: University of California Press, 1992.

Wang, L. Ling-chi. "Politics of the Repeal of the Chinese Exclusion Laws." In *The Repeal and Its Legacy: Proceedings of the Conference on the 50th Anniversary of the Repeal of the Exclusion Acts*, 65–80. Brisbane, CA: Chinese Historical Society of America, 1994.

Webster, James B. *Christian Education and the National Consciousness in China*. New York: E. P. Dutton, 1920.

Westbrook, Robert B. *John Dewey and American Democracy*. Ithaca: Cornell University Press, 1991.

Williamson, Judith. *Consuming Passions: The Dynamics of Popular Culture*. New York: Marion Boyers, 1986.

Wong, Charles Choy. "Los Angeles Chinatown: A Public and Home Territory." In *The Chinese American Experience: Papers from the Second National Conference on Chinese American Studies (1980)*, edited by Genny Lim, Him Mark Lai, Daniel Chu, and Ted Wong, 142–69. San Francisco: Chinese Historical Society, 1984.

Wong, Eugene Franklin. *On Visual Racism: Asians in American Motion Pictures*. New York: Arno Press, 1978.

Wong, Jade Snow. *Fifth Chinese Daughter*. New York: Harper and Brothers, 1950.

Wong, K. Scott. "War Comes to Chinatown: Social Transformation and the Chinese of California." In *The Way We Really Were: The Golden State in the Second Great War*, edited by Roger W. Lotchin, 164–86. Urbana: University of Illinois Press, 2000.

Wong, K. Scott, and Sucheng Chan, eds. *Claiming America: Constructing Chinese American Identities during the Exclusion Era*. Asian American History and Culture. Philadelphia: Temple University Press, 1998.

Wu, Judy Tzu-Chun. *Doctor Mom Chung of the Fair-haired Bastards*. Berkeley: University of California Press, 2005.

Yamamoto, Traise. *Masking Selves, Making Subjects: Japanese American Women, Identity, and the Body*. Berkeley: University of California Press, 1999.

Yeh, Wen-hsin. *The Alienated Academy: Culture and Politics in Republican China, 1919–1937*. Cambridge, MA: Council on East Asian Studies, Harvard University, 1990.

Yoshihara, Mari. *Embracing the East: White Women and American Orientalism*. New York: Oxford University Press, 2003.

Yu, Renqiu. " 'Exercise Your Sacred Rights': The Experience of New York's Chinese Laundrymen in Practicing Democracy." In *Claiming America*, 41–64.

———. *To Save China, to Save Ourselves: The Chinese Hand Alliance of New York*. Philadelphia: Temple University Press, 1996.

Yung, Judy. *Chinese Women of America: A Pictorial History*. Seattle: University of Washington Press for the Chinese Culture Foundation of San Francisco, 1986.

———. *Unbound Feet: A Social History of Chinese Women in San Francisco*. Berkeley: University of California Press, 1995.

Zhao, Xiaojian. *Remaking Chinese America: Immigration, Family, and Community, 1940–1965*. New Brunswick, NJ: Rutgers University Press, 2002.

# Acknowledgments

This project began over a decade ago, when with no small amount of whimsy I became acquainted with the three women whose lives have shaped this book. I thank Mary P. Ryan, who has been a guide, mentor, and friend throughout the course of this project as well as my transition from graduate student to faculty member. I thank Waldo E. Martin, Jr., and Caren Kaplan, whose seminars contributed to the development of this project, and who with Mary allowed me the leeway to explore the possibilities of this project. I thank Jon Gjerde, who has been a model of multicultural teaching and thinking, for his consistent encouragement and interest in my work. I thank the late James E. Kettner for his kindness and support.

For the research that informed the dissertation, and the subsequent research that has shaped the book, I relied on the good graces and helpfulness of many archivists and staffs at the archives and institutions I utilized for this project. I greatly appreciate the knowledge of the archivists and staff, and their willingness to search out documents on my behalf. I thank Karen Anson, Jean Ashton, Charles Bell, Jean Berry, Suellen Chang, Ellen Cordes, Ned Comstock, Jill Dixon, Daniel Glassman, Bill Greene, Charles Greene, Barbara Hall, Susan Karren, Carol Leadenham, Raymond Lum, Leslie A. Morris, Martha Lund Smalley, Dianne Nilsen, Aaron Prah, Margaret Sherry Rich, Nancy Shader, Ellen M. Shea, Wilma R. Slaight, Carolyn Stallings, Neil Thomsen, Frances E. Webb, Bruce C. Williams, Steve Wilson, and Paul Wormser, as well as others I do not name here who assisted me with my research. I thank Philip Leibfried and Vincent Sneed for their encouragement and suggestions when I first began researching Anna May Wong. I especially thank Jennie Lew and Chi-hui Yang for assistance in locating Wong's certificate of identity, and Vincent Chin for use of the scan from his personal collection.

The research and writing of this manuscript has been generously supported by the University of California Graduate Opportunity Program for ethnic minority students, the History Department at UC Berkeley, a University of California mentored research award, the Franklin and Eleanor Roosevelt Research Institute Summer Research Grant, and a Five-College Minority Fellowship at Mount Holyoke. The book manuscript was revised, written, and researched with the support of an Arizona State University College of Liberal Arts and Sciences faculty grant-in-aid and conference travel grants, an NEH summer stipend, and two summer research grants from the ASU Women's Studies Program. Without these sources of support, I would have completed neither my doctorate in history nor this manuscript.

I thank my friends and colleagues who read chapters at various stages and provided critical feedback: Margaret Pagaduan and Kimie Arguello, who have contributed so much to my intellectual development and to the manuscript; Judy T. Z. Wu and Ann Hibner Koblitz for so generously reading the manuscript and providing suggestions; Karen Kuo for her insights and suggestions for the introductory chapter; the members of the ASU women's studies reading group—including Melinda de Jesús, Hyaeweol Choi, Jacqueline Martinez, Ellen Rees, Madelaine Adelman, Stephanie Woodson, Jennifer Parchesky, Gitta Honegger, and Amy Lind—for their wonderfully spirited critique and support as I have adjusted to Arizona. I thank my friend Edith Kaneshiro who first told me about Wong. Through conferences, presentations, and conversation I have benefited from the insights, scholarship, input, and feedback of John Cheng, K. Scott Wong, Vicki L. Ruiz, Judy Yung, George Anthony Peffer, Wei Li, Stephen West, Shirley Jennifer Lim, Timothy Wong, Alice Yang-Murray, Anne S. Choi, Elaine Mae Woo, Floyd Cheung, and Beth Notar. In addition, my thanks to Gus and Barbara Arguello, Gabrielle Lawrence, Mabel Lee, and Louise Avila. My manuscript has benefited from the insightful, challenging, and supportive comments provided by Xiaojian Zhao and two other readers with UC Press, and I thank them for their careful reading. My thanks to Monica McCormick, Randy Heyman, and Dore Brown for their guidance and support through the publication process, and to Edith Gladstone, whose editing has made this a better book.

I am fortunate to work with generous and supportive colleagues in the Women's Studies Program at Arizona State University. Mary Logan Rothschild and Kathleen Ferraro, directors of the program, tried to protect my time so that I could write and ensured that I had the equipment and support I needed to complete this manuscript. Additionally, I thank Georganne Scheiner, Michelle McGibbney, Terrie Hurt, Jane Little, Lisa Schulze, Isabel Meza, Debra Tisdale, Chrys Soto, and Serena Turley for being wonderful colleagues to work with. I especially thank Ann Hibner Koblitz and Lisa M. Anderson for allowing me to drop in to their offices throughout the week to discuss theory, scholarship, pedagogy, and Monday night football. I am equally grateful to Rose Weitz who joined us this year and has already contributed greatly to our program. Thank you, Rose, for seeing the book in my manuscript and helping me see it too. I also thank Mary Margaret Fonow, Duane Roen, Marjorie Zatz, Delia Saenz, Montye Fuse, Melinda de Jesús, Thomas Nakayama, Myla Vicenti Carpio, Tina M. Lee, Shelley Ruelas, Sherril Tomita, Carol Takao, Magdalene Huang, and many others for providing a community of provocative and creative thinkers and doers.

Special thanks to Leonora Tsuchida Jensen, Amy Lonetree, Lisa Fernandez, Helen Fong, and Harry Lew for their support in significant ways, and to the Fongs, Lews, Stevens, and Leongs for their love and encouragement. I thank my father and Dana, Cheryl and Peter, Mark and Sharon, Kim and Geoff, Andrew, Noah, Aaron, Odessa, Boris, and Oscar for their faith, hope, and love. Kim and Cheryl, you are my heroes—thanks for everything. I thank Myla and Maitlyn for the joy they bring to my life. And finally, as before and always, my deepest gratitude goes to my father, Ray Leong, for his constant support and love; and my mother, May Y. F. Fong Leong, for the strength of her example and her love that is always with me.

# Index

Acculturation, 78, 80

Advertising industry, 24, 70, 99, 165

Africa, 147

African Americans, 162, 170, 197n83; and popular culture, 51; and World War II as race war, 45, 46–48

Agee, James, *Let Us Now Praise Famous Men,* 29

Ahn, Philip, 65–66

American Association of University Women, 128

American century. *See* Luce, Henry R.

American Christianity, 20–21, 22–23, 130; and Americanization, 145; impact of liberal theology, 21; and missions, 22–23; and modernization, 120, 138; and Nationalist China, 117–18, 120, 122–23

American Committee in Aid of Chinese Industrial Cooperatives. *See* INDUSCO

American dream, 26, 32, 158

American exceptionalism, 10, 123

American Federation of Labor–Committee for Industrial Organization (AFL-CIO), 148

American Federation of Soroptomist Clubs, 137–38

American Federation of Women's Clubs, 128

American images of China and Chinese, 28–30, 136, 157, 159, 162, 171

Americanization, 159, 161, 200n1

*American Magazine,* 137

American masculinity, 8, 40–41

American missionary enterprise, 3, 109, 122–23, 156; and American orientalism, 7–8, 10–11, 13–15, 18–19; and Boxer Uprising (1900), 15–16; and Burlingame Treaty (1868), 9; changing American attitudes toward, 20–21; in China, 3, 17–23, 106–7, 120, 149, 176n30; and Chinese antiforeigner movements, 15–16, 21–23; and decline in evangelical Christianity, 20–21, 22–23; education of Chinese women, 19; education of U.S. immigrants, 13–14, 61, 183n13; empowerment of Euro-American women, 8, 11, 13–14, 26, 53; gendered division of labor in, 13, 17–20, 159, 163; and gunboat diplomacy, 15, 22; images of Chinese women, 18–19, 75, 176n19; and mission boards, 23, 32, 61, 155, 160, 177n39; and Nationalist (KMT) China, 118, 120–22, 123, 149; patriarchal structure, 19–20, 159; Pearl S. Buck critique of, 31–32, 41; and secularism, 122; and "sentimental imperialists," 10–11, 13; and social gospel, 20–21, 176n33, 183n12; and social status, 13–14, 26; and United States imperialism, 3, 10–11, 15, 155, 156, 160, 175n10

Othering, 51
*Our Daily Bread,* 29

Pacific rim, 7–8, 10
Pageantry, 96; and nationalism, 140,
    141–44
Page Law (1875), 9–10, 13, 174–75n22
Palmer, Mildred, 129
Palmieri, Patricia, 110
Paramount Studios (Los Angeles), 73, 94
Parsons, Louella, 144
"Passing as other," 23, 56, 109
Pearl Harbor (Hawaii), 97
Peck, Willys, 126
*Peter Pan,* 64
*Piccadilly,* 64, 73, 83–84
*Picturegoer Weekly,* 87
Popular culture, 51; and nationalism, 58,
    84, 85
Presbyterian Church and Missions Board,
    20, 32
Privilege, 156, 161
Progressive reform (U.S.), 7–8, 13–14,
    110–11
Propaganda, 101, 141–44, 165
Protocol. *See* Diplomacy
Pruitt, Ida, 50
Publishing industry, 24, 55, 125

Qing (Manchu) government. *See* China:
    Qing (Manchu) government

Race: and American social science, 44,
    50–51; and gender, 160–61, 162,
    167
Racism, in U.S., 9–11, 30–31, 34, 35, 38;
    and African Americans, 41, 46,
    47–48, 162; in American popular
    culture, 56, 64–65, 67, 73, 158, 160;
    and Chinese, 58, 136, 139, 167–68,
    170; and Chinese Americans, 52,
    57–58, 60–61, 63, 67, 90, 149; and
    international politics, 45–46, 50,
    149, 147; and nationality/national
    identity, 10, 85, 146, 165–66; and
    United States law, 78, 81–82, 109
Rainier, Luise, 28, 76
Randolph-Macon Woman's College, 16,
    156
Raub, Patricia, 29
*The Red Lantern,* 63
Revive China Society, 108
Robeson, Eslanda Goode, 182n131
Robeson, Paul, 83
Robinson, Edward G., 141, 142
Rogers, Ginger, 143
Roland, Ruth, 63

Roosevelt, Eleanor, 53, 131, 136, 137,
    139; as First Lady, 137, 197n92; and
    Franklin Roosevelt, 132, 135–36;
    and Mayling Soong, 133–34,
    197n92; *My Day,* 133; role in FDR's
    administration, 134
Roosevelt, Franklin D., 135–36, 142,
    146–47, 153; administration of,
    131–33, 135–36
Rosaldo, Renato, 16
Rossi, Angelo, 148
*The Rotarian,* 137
Ruiz, Vicki L., 200n1
Russell, Rosalind, 143
Russia, 165

Said, Edward, 5
Sandoval, Chela, 182n133
San Francisco (California), 148
*The Saturday Evening Post,* 137
Scanlon, Jennifer, 200n1
Schenk, Joseph, 63
Schlesinger, Arthur M., 175n10
Scudder, Vida, 110–11
Seattle (Washington), 109
Self-definition: power of, 200n4; as resist-
    ance, 55, 170–71; and travel,
    158–59
Selznick, David O., 103, 144,
    198nn101,106
Shanghai, 4, 22, 107, 112–14, 164; fac-
    tory strikes, 113, 115–16; interna-
    tional settlement, 114–17; Municipal
    Council, 114–15
*Shanghai Express,* 64–65, 73–74, 88
*Shanghai Gazette,* 114
Shohat, Ella, 5, 51. *See also* Structuring
    absence
*Sian: A Coup d'Etat/A Fortnight in Sian,*
    124
Social hierarchies of power, 55
Social location, 159
Socioeconomic mobility, 157
Sockman, Rev. Ralph W., 138
*The Son-Daughter,* 73
Soong, Ai-ling (sister of Mayling Soong),
    107, 108, 109, 112, 113, 116, 153
Soong, Charlie Yao-jun (father of
    Mayling Soong), 107–8, 109, 149,
    156, 157
Soong, Chingling (sister of Mayling
    Soong), 109, 112, 116
Soong, Mayling: and African nations,
    147; alienation from Chinese cul-
    ture, 112, 156; American celebrity
    of, 120–23, 124–27, 129, 130–31,
    152; American expectations of, 131,

Sues, Ilona Ralf, 147
Sun Yat-sen, 108, 111–12, 115, 144
Sydenstricker, Absalom and Carie (parents of Pearl Sydenstricker Buck), 3, 12–13, 17, 19–20, 21, 40, 155, 159
Sydenstricker, Grace (sister of Pearl Sydenstricker Buck), 17, 18, 21

Tchen, John Kuo Wei, *New York Before Chinatown*, 5–6
*Thief of Baghdad*, 63, 64, 74
*This Week*, 137
Thompson, Malvina, 136
Thomson, David, 198
Thomson, James, 15
Tierney, Gene, 101, 166
*Tiger Bay*, 64, 83
*Time* magazine, 43, 119, 124, 125, 126, 158
*Toll of the Sea*, 3, 63, 64, 73
Toy, Lee Gon (mother of Anna May Wong), 58, 78–79
Tracy, Spencer, 143
Transnational identity, 35, 49
Travel, 156–57; and self-definition, 158–59; and social mobility, 49, 156; and transnationalism, 11, 159
Treaty of Versailles, 113
Tuell, Annie, 110, 112

United China Relief, 43, 97, 98–101, 152; and education of American public, 132n190; Hollywood chapter, 103; Los Angeles chapter, 95
United Nations, 168
United States: citizenship, 96–97, 145; empire and Manifest Destiny, 5, 7–10, 167; global expansion, 5, 7–8, 164; immigration law and enforcement, 135, 155; isolationism, 120, 164, 165; national ideology and nationalism, 35, 155, 165; National Stereotypes Research Project, 168, 201n8; neutrality, 164; Non-Recognition Doctrine (1932), 73–74; race relations and racism (*see* Racism); relations with Asian nations, 73–74, 167, 164; relations with Japan, 97, 131–32
United States, and World War II, 43, 48, 51, 129–31, 133, 134–36, 165; and alliance with China against Japan, 43, 51, 54, 97, 131, 135, 154, 164–65; and Allied strategy, 135, 146, 163, 165; and American nationalism, 165, 166; and China mystique, 1, 164, 165–66; cross-cultural

education efforts, 44, 48–49, 131; and cultural pluralism, 2, 44–46, 48, 97, 125, 154; homefront mobilization, 97, 127, 140–41, 148, 166; and ideological race war, 43–48, 49–50, 132, 138–39; and international role of United States, 43, 49–50, 54, 123, 166–67; mobilization of American women, 137–38, 165; race relations (U.S.), 52, 131–32, 138–39, 165, 169–70; rhetoric, 46, 166. *See also* World War II
United States Congress, 134, 145, 152; Committee on Foreign Affairs, 152; House of Representatives, 134; Senate, 131
United States Department of State, 128; Far Eastern Affairs Division, 117, 140
United States Immigration and Naturalization Service, 145, 170
United States relations with China, 73–74, 97, 106–7, 155, 157, 167; American views of, 141, 162, 164, 165–66, 168; and immigration policy, 96–97, 145, 157; paternalism of, 55, 167–8; treaties, 9, 155; during World War II, 54, 131–33, 136–38, 140–41, 164–68, 169–70
Utley, Freda, 38

Vanderbilt University, Tennessee, 107
Varg, Paul A., 183n12
*Variety* magazine, 101
Vassar College for Women, 169–70
Versailles, Treaty of (1919), 113
Vidor, King, 29
Visibility, 158
*Vogue* magazine, 137
Vollmoller, Karl, 83
von Sternberg, Josef, 65, 73. See also *Shanghai Express*

Wagner, Florence, 103
Wagner, Robert Leicester (Rob), 60, 87, 103
Walsh, Richard J., 24, 31, 32, 49, 139, 158, 170; and John Day Company, 24–26
*We Believe*, 130
*We Chinese Women*, 138
Wellesley College for Women (Massachussetts), 4, 109–12, 119, 152, 156, 162, 165
Wesleyan College for Women (Georgia), 4, 109
"What My Religion Means to Me," 121–23, 138

25